THE INVISIBLE LIFE OF US

About the authors

Kate Jones is a stylist who runs her own home staging business called Instant Impression. She has five children, including identical twin boys, who were her inspiration for starting *Too Peas in a Podcast*. Kate lives in Melbourne.

Mandy Hose is a sleep, settling and behavioural consultant for children up to five years of age. Her business is called Mandy Hose She Knows. She has three daughters, who are her pride and joy, and one mischievous cavoodle called Rosie. Mandy lives in Melbourne.

THE
INVISIBLE
LIFE
OF US

Kate Jones & Mandy Hose

toopeas
IN A PODCAST

LIFE

PENGUIN LIFE

UK | USA | Canada | Ireland | Australia
India | New Zealand | South Africa | China

Penguin Life is part of the Penguin Random House group of companies
whose addresses can be found at global.penguinrandomhouse.com

Penguin
Random House
Australia

First published by Penguin Life in 2021
Copyright © Kate Jones and Mandy Hose 2021
The moral right of the authors has been asserted.

Cover illustration by Kellie Liddell
Cover design by Alex Ross © Penguin Random House Australia Pty Ltd
Typeset in 12.5/17pt Bembo by Midland Typesetters, Australia
Printed and bound in Australia by Griffin Press, part of Ovato, an accredited
ISO AS/NZS 14001 Environmental Management Systems printer

A catalogue record for this
book is available from the
National Library of Australia

ISBN 978 1 76104 025 2

penguin.com.au

To the five children I 'borned' – J, E-K, M, R and W. You are exquisite human beings. I am honoured that you call me Mum. I think I am going to keep you. xx

—Kate

To my three precious daughters – my love for you will never end. You are the bestest chips.

'Life is worth living as long as there's a laugh in it.'
L. M. Montgomery, Anne of Green Gables

—Mandy

Contents

Part Three: Precious pea shoots

Preface

Too peas on a page

This is the story of a unique friendship. It's not a parenting book, a self-help book, a book about twins or a book about children with disabilities and additional needs. It is a book about us: Mandy and Kate (self-absorbed, we know). It is a story about two women whose views about life changed after having twins. It is a story about how they became different people as they parented their twins, about how they became aware of an education system in need of reform, how they became passionate about embracing mothering diverse families and about creating a space for those families to feel like they belong. It's the story of how two friends chatting in a driveway went on to make a little podcast they thought no one would listen to.

When we started *Too Peas in a Podcast* in June 2019, we wanted to share our experiences as the mothers of twins, and of twins with additional needs, and create a space full of honesty, support and laughter – somewhere to make anyone feel a little less alone. We were two mums with a microphone, an intentionally misspelt podcast title, eight beautiful kids between us and about eight million stories to tell.

What we didn't expect was how quickly and fully such a beautiful community would spring up around us, and how magical it would be to not only be creating the podcast and sharing stories of our days and lives, but amplifying the voices of the women and families in our pea community.

We feel mildly outraged that the majority of media coverage about kids today focuses on celebrity or influencer parents with 'perfect' families. We say all families are perfect and this book is a celebration of the different meanings that that word can and should represent when it comes to kids and families. The book is called *The Invisible Life of Us*, which was a name suggested for the podcast by beautiful pea mum Kylie. This title really resonated with us: the invisible part of our lives is actually the most profound part of our lives! When we started the podcast we wanted to create a space where women in similar positions to us could come to feel seen and heard and acknowledged, so we could all then go on to do a better job. When women (and men) living diverse parenting experiences feel supported and seen and understood, they are better able to understand their children's needs and do the best job they possibly can. Our kids need us to 'do better' than the average parent. As pea parents will know (and as you will see as you read our story), it can be so hard out there being a pea in a rectum world (and if that sentence made no sense to you, please see our terminolopea on p. xii). It can be exhausting and alienating and cruel. In this book we share some of those experiences.

And a quick disclaimer: while Kate has three children over the age of eighteen who can give permission for their stories and memories to be shared, she also has awesome twins who are not eighteen. Mandy's three children are also under eighteen. We use pseudonyms for all of our kids – Kate's twins are Buzz and Woody, and her three older children are Sound Engineer, Number One Daughter and Scholarship, while we call Mandy's twin daughters Milly and Molly, and her youngest daughter Miss Ten – and there are no photos of them in here or on social media. Sorry, but you will have to put up with middle-aged women instead.

Out of respect for our children, who have the rest of their lives to share their stories, we won't discuss all of our twins' diagnoses or anything much beyond their primary school years (to be honest, we are still pretty stoked we survived the toddler and primary school years mothering twins!). It might seem strange but this is our story, not theirs!

Maybe you're a long-time listener to *Too Peas*, in which case, welcome home. Maybe you've never listened to our podcast, but are the parent of a little pea shoot who is looking to feel less alone. Maybe you're an outer rectum who cannot get enough of our comedy (we don't blame you). Maybe you found this book in a street library and have no idea who we are or why you have just read the words 'outer rectum'. Whatever the case, we're so pleased you're here. Let's get started, shall we?

Terminolopea

Just so we're all on the same page, here is a brief glossary of words and phrases we use on the podcast and throughout this book.

ankle-foot orthosis (AFO)	Leg brace for children with cerebral palsy
Buzz and Woody	Kate's twin boys
chickpea	An extended family member of peas
CPAP	(pronounced 'see-pap') When prongs or a mask is positioned by the nostril or nose, and air or oxygen is blown in at a constant pressure. The baby does their own breathing, but the machine helps keep the lungs open in between breaths
Dr Shane	Mandy and Kate's favourite paediatrician
explicit rating	The warning that had to be added to the start of the podcast after Mandy's mum's horror at all the swearing
grandpeas	The grandparents of pea shoots
Intubation	A process whereby a plastic tube is inserted through the nose or mouth into the windpipe, and air or an air and oxygen mix is blown in and out of the lungs under pressure. The machine does most of the breathing for the baby
live pea	Matt, who organised our live show and book
Mandy Hose She Knows	Mandy's business
Milly and Molly	Mandy's twin girls

Miss Eight (then Nine, now Ten)	Mandy's youngest daughter, as the years go by
National Disability Insurance Scheme (NDIS)	A national government initiative to make sure that pea shoots (and grown-up pea shoots) get better funding and support than they did before it existed
Neonatal intensive care unit (NICU)	NICU (pronounced 'nee-kyoo') is an intensive care unit specialising in the care of sick or premature babies. The word 'neonatal' actually means newborn or the first twenty-eight days of life. Neonatal care has been around since the 1960s
Number One Daughter	Kate's elder daughter
outer rectum	A person who makes thoughtless and inappropriate comments to peas
pea	A parent of a child with a disability or additional need
peacher	A teacher with a heart for pea families
peafessional	A professional with a heart for pea families
pea friends	People with a heart for pea families, and who commit to a friendship with them
pea shoot	A child or adult with a disability or additional need
pharmapeas	Chemists
podbar	Where *Too Peas* is recorded
poofessional	A doctor from the outer rectum
Scholarship	Kate's younger daughter
The Special Care Nursery (SCN)	The SCN takes babies from thirty-two weeks gestation and caters for a range of babies' needs. Babies need extra care from specially trained staff. Babies may need this even if they can breathe on their own and maintain their temperature
singleton	A singleton refers to one baby, as opposed to multiples, which are two or more babies. It's a term you learn and use once you give birth to twins or triplets, etc. Who knew!
Sound Engineer	Kate's eldest son, who produces the podcast
split peas	Pea parents working from home as well as online learning with pea shoots
tea peas	People hurriedly drinking tea in between appointments

terminolopea	Glossary for peas
'Thanks, asshole!'	Our favourite retort to outer rectums, as said by American pea Lana
therapeas	Physios, OTs, speech therapists, dieticians, psychologists, etc.
twin-to-twin transfusion syndrome (TTTS)	A rare, serious condition that can occur in pregnancies when identical twins share a placenta – abnormal blood vessel connections form in the placenta and allow blood to flow unevenly between the babies

Introduction

Beginnings

Before we get any further into *The Invisible Life of Us*, we want to take you backwards – to a time before we were *Too Peas*, to a world before podcasts, even. That's right. We're taking you right back to the start, to give you a little more information about who we are, where we came from, how we met and why you can't get us out of the podbar.

Kate

If you have never listened to the podcast ... hi, I am Kate, one half of *Too Peas*. The thing is, I am remarkably ordinary. I haven't made any amazing discoveries, trekked the Himalayas or even backpacked through Europe, but one thing I'm very aware of is that every human has a remarkable story somewhere in their life. Or lots of little *almost-remarkable* stories that make us who we are. When we re-tell those stories over coffee or wine or, say, in a book and let them intersect with other people's stories it unites us, brings strangers together and changes lives. Here are mine.

My almost-remarkable childhood

The most interesting thing about my cultural background is that my dad was Irish. This may not seem all that exciting but, growing up in very white suburban Melbourne in the 1980s, our Irish heritage did add a little spice to my childhood. Well, maybe not spice but certainly potato. Dad was brilliant and loud and full of fun. He was passionate about what was right and wrong, and no one could silence him when he got going. The apple didn't fall far from the tree in that respect and that is a gift I am forever grateful for, especially now that I often act as an advocate. All parents can relate to advocating at school or at the local sports club, but when your child has additional needs you advocate on steroids; it becomes a part of who you are. I was lucky to have a role model who wasn't scared to speak up when something was unjust or unfair. Now, aside from my parent advocate role, I also have the privilege of speaking to thousands of people each week on our podcast – advocate by podcast you could say!

Back to Dad. He loved me fiercely, which was beautifully empowering. That Irish rascal passed away in 2016 and left a gaping hole in my life. I lost his amazing wit, lilting accent and stories from a childhood so different from mine. But even though I still ache with loss, his unwavering love has made me who I am.

My lovely mum is quiet and competent and clever, but if a teacher ever did me wrong, boy did they know about it! That quiet woman would not see her kids mistreated. She can grow anything; the garden is her easel, and our childhood (and even my adult life) was filled with fresh produce she grew in the Yarra Valley. She was the calm to my dad's boisterousness, and is passionate about her kids, grandkids and her faith. What that meant for me was that I had both parents on my team! You don't get much luckier in life than that.

Dad was, of course, Irish Catholic, while Mum was a basic Protestant, but religion wasn't a big part of their lives till I was about five, when we (not just my immediate family, Mum's entire side of the family) joined the Seventh-day Adventist (SDA) Church.

In that way, my childhood might have been a little different from yours. Being in a minority religion changes the way most people see you — and probably changes the way you see other people. We attended church schools, our weekends were dominated by church activities, we made friends with church people and truly lived the lifestyle of the SDA Church. The church was a huge part of my life right up until the year Buzz and Woody were born (and if you want to know more about how I feel about faith, please see Chapter 4). It's fair to say it formed a huge part of who I am today, but definitely not *all* of who I am today.

My ~~almost-remarkable~~ kids
extraordinary, life-changing

I attended high school in the outer eastern suburbs of Melbourne, where it was cold and foggy in winter and your school dress stuck to the plastic chairs in February with sweat. During school I had no idea what I wanted 'to be' but I really loved being with people, and I had a beautiful best friend at church called Shannon. Shannon lived with trisomy 21 (Down syndrome); he passed away a few years ago from melanoma. He was such a great friend and we had such fun together that after I completed the HSC (fun fact: the last year before Victoria introduced the VCE) and went to uni, I chose to study a double degree in nursing and intellectual disabilities.

I didn't finish my double degree in nursing and intellectual disabilities, but I *did* give birth to a baby and you do get a certificate for that! I should mention here that the baby was not the result of an immaculate conception (despite being a church girl I didn't manage that!). When I was still at school I met my now-husband, David; he was eight years older than me, so, although I married young, he didn't. We married when I was twenty (remember: early '90s and involved in a church; it was, as they say, 'a different time'). Together we were involved in a lot of music at church. He used to play the piano and I led out in the singing. The love of music remains to this day, but it's the kids who have to hear me sing now! They love it, I can assure you.

Having a baby was the most miraculous thing that ever happened to me. I will never forget staring down at tiny Sound Engineer and knowing that my life had changed. I had spent my entire life around children and loved them. When you grow up in a big family and attend a growing church, there are a lot of babies around. I have three little brothers and was ten when my youngest brother was born. I heard him wake at night and went and rocked his cot or gave him a bottle. I loved being his sister. We have a strong bond to this day, and, believe it or not, he is even more outspoken and bossy than me! Motherhood, though – this was something completely different. Being a mum is so remark-able in so many ways, but the moment my first child was born I truly felt myself becoming something new.

I went on to have four more babies (it's a bit addictive, to be honest). If gender matters to you, we had boy, girl, girl, boy, boy, although in my opinion gender has very little to do with anything – certainly not the amount of washing you do or how often you cook dinner. During my fourth pregnancy, the tiny egg split and we got two for the price of . . . well, two. Five kids is a lot more than three, I will tell you that.

Having Buzz and Woody was one of those life-defining moments. It completely changed me as a person, mother, friend and worker. It was pretty much *Extreme Makeover: The Kate Edition*. The Kate writing this book is different, so different, from the Kate pre-twins, that I almost feel a disconnect thinking about that time in my life. This new me is less carefree but enjoys carefree moments much more. I have learnt to really value friendship and belonging to my little tribe. I love live music, rooftop bars and watching my kids ski. Having lived half my life (probably more, let's be honest here, definitely more than half!), I have the peace that comes from not giving a shit about much, but when I do give a shit, it's worth it! I back myself now, and that is an awesome time in your life, believe me! But mostly I love hanging on the couch with all five of my kids. I am in awe of my body – I mean, they came out of me!

My almost-remarkable career

I worked sporadically while the kids were very small, doing lots of volunteer work and working as a freelance writer. I wrote wedding speeches, twenty-first birthday speeches and eulogies for people. It was a great job to have at home with the offspring around. I also wrote articles for Christian newsletters and magazines. After we left the church, a lot of that work dried up; once the twins were at kinder and I had managed to have a cup of tea in peace (an actual entire cup of tea!), I decided to get back to work. But how do you work when you have twins with additional needs? (And three other kids thrown in for good measure!) I had heard of flexible workplaces, but I had also heard of leprechauns. So I took matters into my own hands and slowly started up a home staging business.

Now I hear you ask the question that everyone asks: how did you do home staging after studying nursing? More to the point, what even is home staging? Well, I have always loved interior styling. I consumed interior magazines, moved my furniture around constantly (even my bedroom as a child) and loved decorating my home. Which in a roundabout way led me to staging. Staging is a sort-of interior styling. When someone is selling their house, I come in and bring furniture, artwork, cushions, lamps. Stage and Style for sale . . . I am still working at this little business today.

I love walking into an empty house and walking out of a fully furnished one. Job done, woohoo! The mere act of completing a task is a rarity at my house. Perhaps your home isn't like this, but I often clean the kitchen, go do a wee and come back to find a toaster, a knife with Nutella on it, three tea mugs, twenty-five glasses and an empty packet of biscuits have all mysteriously materialised on the bench. As I look around me now there are pieces of Lego, two pencil cases and a heap of folded washing sitting on the dining table, plus twin boys being 'remotely' schooled (or 'not even remotely' schooled . . .), so setting up a house that will remain orderly and beautiful is therapy for me. It is the yin to my home life yang.

My ~~almost~~ *very*-remarkable friend

When I wake in the middle of the night and I am half-awake but somehow not half-asleep, my mind meanders along and I start to think about what really matters to me. I don't want to mislead you and have you believe I am a deep, introspective thinker; I also spend time thinking about a whole lot of insignificant things that definitely don't matter. But the point my mind keeps meandering to is that at the end of the day, what really matters is relationships. When my dad died, I didn't miss his car or his house; I missed his character and personality. I missed all the love he had for me and the love I had for him. It has nowhere to go now. I don't miss going to the cricket with him; I miss him at the cricket. His loss has made me more and more aware about the power of friends. How much they mean to me, how much I need them and that, even when I am awake, relationships are what matter most. I am going somewhere with this, because, you see, this book and the podcast are actually about friendship; it is about a deep and unique relationship and how sharing that friendship somehow changed not just our lives, but a whole lot of other people's lives too. People with stories that had nowhere to be told, with love that no one wanted to hear about. When Mandy and I shook up that Diet Coke and let the lid off, we had no idea how much there was fizzing under the surface just waiting to get out.

Is friendship at first sight a thing? If not, it sure should be because that's what happened when I met Mandy. Lots of people assume we were friends pre-twins but it was those babies who brought Mandy and me together. Through a haze of sleep deprivation, hundreds of nappies, very early mornings and middle-of-the-night ear infections we bonded. Get this: we are so old that we were friends pre-Facebook! We were twenty-first century enough to meet online, though, through the Australian Multiple Birth Association (AMBA) online forum/chat room.

This is kind of a secret, but we're truth tellers, so I will let you in on it: if you have twins and you meet another twin parent you have an immediate bond, or maybe not bond, maybe an affinity. You share something other people don't, because you took parenting up a level, and once you have levelled up, you see things differently. When I went to my first dinner with the AMBA mums, I knew there would be something in common, but I didn't know how much. Then . . . Mandy happened. And she happened to me! And turns out we had a fuck-tonne in common.

I believe more in friendship soulmates than I do 'life partner soulmates'. What a gift a kindred spirit is. Sitting there at the dinner, over a large tandoori pizza, it was like our suburban lives had been weirdly parallel. Here was this woman who had also stood up the front in her local church's worship service, leading the hymns and gospel songs, loved to laugh and sing, had her twins prematurely and was going through a diagnosis with her twins; all this in common and she lived five minutes away? I genuinely can't remember everyone at that dinner but I remember her.

I don't want her to get a big head, but Mandy is one of those people you are drawn to. You want her at your party, coffee morning or book club. She is fun, and man, can she laugh! But the flip side is she wears her heart on her sleeve like no one I know. She shares her sorrows, ups and downs, and gets up and laughs again.

Mandy listens. Not many people listen, but Mandy does. She listened to me, and she in turn talked to me; she told me her truths. We have very different kids with very different lives, but somehow we found a common ground, probably because we didn't really fit in anywhere. I remember sitting in her car talking one night about how no one cared about our stories! Everyone wants the elusive 'perfect' twins story. Well, ours were not really that, but they were amazing stories. Our stories made us feel alone, yet in that car we didn't feel alone, we felt like we could maybe do something with these stories.

Now that I have made a podcast with Mandy, I realise our friendship is not just a precious gift for me. It turns out just being a friend and having this friendship is an extraordinary gift for all the peas who listen to us as well. So many beautiful people (or pea-ple, as we like to call them) were lonely and felt excluded from life because their kids were not neurotypical. I had no idea that Mandy and I sharing our friendship would make other people less lonely too, and that they would feel like they were our friends. It makes me cry, to be honest. This friendship of ours that grew over nachos, late-night tears in a driveway, honest and hilarious discussions about our amazing twins – this thing we maybe took a little for granted, has changed more lives than our own!

All those chats we had over the years have turned into conversations that get downloaded every day. Every day, people who felt alone, judged, excluded and left out, whose kids weren't invited to birthday parties or sleepovers, who themselves felt judged due to no wrongdoing, joined the pea tribe and said 'Fuck off!' to all those people who didn't want us! A simple friendship did all that!

It is no secret how much Mandy and I really love a musical, and since we had both left a church life behind post-twins, we were pretty excited when we heard about *The Book of Mormon*. Imagine our absolute delight when *The Book of Mormon* came to Melbourne and we counted down the days till we could buy tickets. Might I say, due to the fact that neither of us read the dates properly, we bought those tickets eighteen months before the show opened, but hey, we were there in the first week of it opening, along with Melbourne's 'elite'.

We laughed till we cried from the moment the curtain opened till the minute it shut. Later, when we decided to actually sit down in the podbar and press record on our podcast about families and inclusion that would go on to change our lives, on some level I believe we were inspired by the words of Trey Parker, Robert Lorez and Matt Stone, thinking about how we would change the world together. Mandy and Kate . . . and a whole bunch of peas!

Mandy

If you've ever listened to the podcast, you'll know I'm bawling my eyes out right now after reading those beautiful words from Kate about our friendship! Before I get to my thoughts on her, I'll tell you the ordinary stories that make me who I am.

My almost-remarkable childhood

It's a big deal growing up with two names. My parents named me Amanda, which, according to Mum, turned to Mandy when I was about three. I have spent so many years being Mandy that the name Amanda doesn't really seem like it's mine. The only time I ever use it is in doctors' surgeries or at Centrelink, where I put on my formal name and pretend to be a more formal woman. The last memorable time at Centrelink (and there have been a few), I was sitting in the waiting area, just scrolling on my phone when I heard the woman at the counter say, 'Amanda Hosé? Amanda Hosé?' I started laughing hard, and when I got to the counter I said, 'I'm sorry, it's just "Hose".' Then she started laughing too. It was so inappropriate but hilarious and I think we laughed the entire conversation.

I also have had two surnames that are nouns. Ball was my maiden name and Hose is my married name. I have lots of funny memories of when I changed my name, long after I married, and my colleagues started calling me 'Amanda Ball Hose', much to their absolute amusement. Those dear friends still call me that to this day.

Amanda Ball was born at Box Hill Hospital in 1976 to Margaret and Graham Ball. We lived in Ferntree Gully, an outer eastern suburb of Melbourne. Living so far from central Melbourne was a big change for my parents, as they had grown up in the suburbs of Camberwell/Burwood and Carnegie. They had no family around them and then they had me a year after they were married. I remember coming home from one of my first jobs working in Early Childhood and saying to them, 'Imagine growing up knowing you were an accident?', and then them looking at each other and laughing. I remember thinking, 'You have just blown my twenty-year-old mind.' Mum denies laughing now, but I remember and think fondly of this moment.

I was the first grandchild on Dad's side and the seventh on Mum's side. Dad is one of four boys and is an identical twin. I knew my paternal grandparents loved and adored me. My grandpa had deafness from the war, so my first walk into the world of disability was beside him. He had a special wireless with headphones so that he could hear the radio and we always had to talk loudly to him. Time with the Ball family was always funny: jokes, jokes and more jokes and Grandma was so happy when she had all her family around her. She always told me that I would have twins too, and I believed her.

I don't remember Mum's parents, as they died when I was five years old. I don't know how Mum coped with two little children and losing both her parents in a year, and all while she was in her early twenties. Mum's family was big – she was the fifth child – and family Christmas with all my cousins and aunties and uncles was the highlight of our year. There were talent shows, presents and pavlovas, and we all look back fondly on those years. It was an important connection for me and for all the cousins who came after me who never knew our grandparents.

I was the eldest child. My sister, Annelise, came along three years after me and has been by my side ever since, and my brother, Adam, seven years after that. I will never forget when Mum and Dad sat Annelise and me down to tell us that Mum was pregnant. Dad said, 'Okay, do you want a cat or a baby?' We both said, 'A cat, a cat!' and then they had to tell us that in fact we were having a baby. But we loved Adam (even though he wasn't a cat). I was nearly eleven when he was born, and I did as much for him as I could. I made woollen pompoms for his bassinet, and have a great memory of cuddling him in the lounge room while wearing my roller skates – and getting into trouble.

Mum was an expert when it came to babies; she taught me everything I know. She loved babies and little children, and took immense pride in white cloth nappies hanging outside on the line. She loved a clean house and was a proud homemaker. She taught me about home decorating and gave me every tip about cleaning she could; much to her dismay I just never really caught on. Dad took us to all our sport and clubs and always drove us anywhere we wanted. Mum baked fruitloaf for afternoon tea, which we had with lashings of butter when we walked in the door after school.

My almost-remarkable school years

We moved to Wantirna when I was in Year 5, and I changed schools. It was such an excellent time for me, making new friends and having leadership opportunities at a new school. I loved our house with my own bedroom and living so close to Knox City Shopping Centre. I often walked over there with Adam and people looked at me as if they were trying to work out if I was his mum.

Our lives were very busy attending our local church. All our socialising happened around it. After church, I spent my time carrying around babies and toddlers and leading Sunday school for the three-year-olds. I loved it. Once I got to high school, I did my work experience for Years 9 and 10 at the church's kindergarten, and I realised that all I wanted to do was work with children.

I got on in secondary school, but found it challenging. I was distracted if the work was hard and got kicked out of the class-room too many times to count. Every school report began: 'Mandy distracts others.' I loved English and Literature, typing, home economics, drama and PE; I was in two rock eisteddfods, learnt the flute and loved being in concert band. I loved the run of 'bomb' threats at Wantirna Secondary College in the 1990s that meant we got out of double maths. I loved mischief and enjoyed taking up smoking with my friends in Year 9 – but I only smoked in the mornings, walking to school with my friend Amy. It was really the only risk I took. Impulse body sprays were very important so that Mum didn't know I'd been smoking!

As a teen I loved going on church camps. Dad sent me on my first one in Year 7 when I knew no one. He put me on a bus and little did I know I was about to meet some of my best friends – Becky, Ange and Maryann – who are still by my side today. Those camps were a taste of freedom away from home, and I loved being loud, fun and naughty as much as you could be on a Christian camp.

My almost-remarkable career

I knew I wanted to work with children and I loved babies. When I found a two-year diploma in mothercraft nursing at Outer Eastern TAFE, I was sold. I didn't need an ATAR score, which was just as well as I was often the first one to leave exams. Study just wasn't for me.

I loved TAFE. The assignments were easy, the placements were practical and I was good at them. My first placement was in a home with a mum who had a three-year-old, an eighteen-month-old and month-old twins. Twins are my lot in life, to quote *Anne of Green Gables*. I loved my two weeks with Jo and her beautiful kids and we are still friends to this day. I also started working at Educational Childcare in Scoresby. I worked in the babies' room, where there were ten babies under two years old. I remember folding one hundred cloth nappies in ten minutes. I was a master. The centre also was the first in Australia to be open twenty-four hours a day and I happily worked on the weekend with my friend Merryn, looking after children of nurses, pastry chefs and police – the shift workers who needed weekend care.

When I finished TAFE I got my first job as a 'qualified' in the zero to twelve months room at a childcare centre in Wantirna. I took great pride in running the room and being in charge of three educational assistants. I loved the room being organised and having the babies looking clean and tidy when their parents picked them up.

By 1998 I was ready for my next adventure and applied to Camp America to go and live and work in the USA. I was *so* excited and eventually was successful for a camp in Ohio. Swoneky stood for 'South-west Ohio, North-east Kentucky' and it was a Salvation Army camp. I was a shoo-in. I had so much camp experience as well as working with children. My family had never been overseas before, and I had only flown to Sydney once before getting on that plane and heading to America. I met up with a girl called Kristy and we spent the next four months together. She was awesome and we clung to each other when we were homesick.

I got to Ohio and boy, was I put to work. I was far out of my depth in the beginning, but once the children had arrived on the big yellow buses, and had had head lice and tinea checks done, I could welcome them like no other. We held eight week-long camps in the summer. The first six to seven camps I was so welcoming: 'Hi, I'm Mandy. I'm from Australia, come with me.' I'd make their beds and cuddle them if they were scared. By the last week I remember saying, 'There's your cabin over there.' I was exhausted.

Before I went to America I was dating a guy called Darren. He is the total opposite to me – loves details and taking time to think things through, exercising and taking care of his health – but the first thing I noticed about him was that he listened to me. He listened for hours, in fact, and the interesting thing about that is that he has a hearing loss. Being around someone with hearing loss wasn't unusual for me as I had grown up with my grandpa being deaf, and I got used to hearing aids and changing the way we lived to make sure it was safe for him.

After proposing on a bridge, just like in *Anne of Green Gables*, Darren and I got married in 2001 just after September 11 and had the most wonderful wedding surrounded by all our family and friends. We were – and still are – very fortunate to have some of the best friends you could ever ask for.

In the year 2000 I got a job at QEC Early Parenting in Noble Park. It was shift work, so I wasn't used to that, but it felt exciting and so wonderful to be treated like a professional. I will never forget my friend Chris's face on my first day when she asked how I went getting the babies to sleep. I said, 'Easy, I patted them all,' as that was something I knew how to do really well from my child-care days. She was horrified as we were meant to be teaching the babies to self settle, so I quickly worked out that I had to learn what they were teaching. Over my seven years in total at QEC, I met the most amazing colleagues, women with such knowledge and patience and fire in their bellies as often nurses have. Maternal and child health nurses and mothercraft or early childhood workers (as we were called in the 2000s) were the perfect team. The MCHN could handle women after birth and breastfeeding and checking health and development, and we wrangled the toddlers and pre-schoolers. The older mothercraft workers were especially awesome at getting babies to sleep.

I also began working with families in child protection. This was when my world actually started crashing a bit. I never knew such neglect and abuse could occur on this level. I was profoundly changed as a person working with these families. In the centre and in their homes, I learnt a lot about generational abuse and neglect and I also learnt very quickly about judgement and how to not have it. I prided myself in going into any home and treating everyone with respect, as I was the visitor. I went into blocks of flats, and what felt like every housing commission tower in the south-east of Melbourne. I saw babies in every situation possible and, heartbreakingly at times, saw them removed from their parents. I started swearing, something my mum has no time for. I think it was because I was seeing humanity like I never had before.

I returned to work at QEC for a little while when the twins were two, but after having my third daughter, and spending a short time in retail, I knuckled down on full-time mothering. Fast forward to 2014 and I had two nine-year-olds and a three-year-old. I wanted to work, and we needed the income. I knew teaching parents about sleep and settling was something that came easily to me, but I couldn't imagine working for an organisation again while raising my own family, so I decided to try my hand at running my own business.

I was on a mission to come up with a catchy name for my business when one day I had a tradesman come to my home. His business was called 'Dave will do it' and I remember asking him, 'How did you come up with the name?' He said, 'My wife kept saying, "Dave will do it," so we just called it that.' So I chose Mandy Hose She Knows, as I did know about sleep and settling.

What was important to me was working with families of premature babies, multiple births and also families of children with disabilities. I simply had to make sense of what I had been through as a mother, and blend it with my work so that it could feel more meaningful.

I had never used Skype or Facetime before, but I knew I would work this way, as I had no time for home visits. I just started a Facebook page and off I went.

I had one hundred clients in my first year and I was so proud. I worked with families all around the world, and it was so fun to adapt my terminology depending on the nationality of the family, such as nappies/diapers and dummies/pacifiers. I started up doing sleep talks with multiple birth clubs in Melbourne and proudly still do these today, albeit over Zoom now. Too Peas has given my business even more exposure and I am so thankful for that.

My ~~almost-remarkable~~ kids
extraordinary, life-changing

After being married for around four years Darren and I decided it was time to try for a baby. I thought it would take time, but it didn't. We were pregnant first try and I don't think I will ever truly understand that privilege. I can look back and see it now, but at the time I didn't appreciate it. We were very excited and nervous, but in truth I had been preparing for this moment for many years. In fact, when the twins came home from hospital, I found my old book of school memories and started reading my diary. It said:

1990 – Year 8
Things I would like to do when I grow up
Get married, have four kids (twins), be a kindergarten teacher.

1991 – Year 9
My ideas about my adult life
To get married and have twins (girls).

1992 – Year 10
My ideas about my adult life
I would like to be a teacher, then have children, hopefully twins.

1993 – Year 11
My ideas about my adult life
To be married, teach kindergarten children, then hopefully have kids, preferably twins.

1994 – Year 12
My ideas and goals
I would like to pass VCE then go on to become a primary school or kindergarten teacher, hopefully get married and have an average of three children (twins).

Nailed it!

My ~~almost~~-remarkable friend
very

Friendship: it makes me laugh and cry and everything in between.

I am very fortunate to have always had lots of friends. Mum set the tone for how I felt about friendship every day as I left for school. She spat in her ironed hankie, wiped my mouth and said, 'Be a friend to everyone, Mandy.' I tried. Mum also told me, 'Always look out for the shy people. You can make friends easily, so look out for them and include them.' Mum herself had been a shy child and was probably overwhelmed by me as her first-born – loud, brash and full of life. She did her best to channel it for good. I remember at my fortieth birthday party, where I had invited as many people as I could afford, I said in my speech, 'Mum, I hope you are proud of me. I have tried to be a friend to everyone.'

One of the most profound groups of friends I have is my book club. We started off in August 2002. What can I say about these women? Many have stayed in the original group; many have come and gone, but they have all been a stable part of my life in unstable times. When I had the twins, I just didn't have time to read for a few years, so I came and went, and they always welcomed me back with open arms, listening generously when I was traumatised and exhausted. We have shared a lot together and I am grateful to everyone who has belonged in our book club for their friendship.

There have always been rough patches along the way in my friendships and there will be people reading this who will have their own side to our friendship story. I know I have made many mistakes over the years and hurt people and for that I am sorry and wish that I could go back and be a better person, be less jealous, be more forgiving, and show more grace.

Meeting the twin mums was absolutely integral to my starting to thrive in my mothering journey. Firstly, at the premature support group, my first taste of friendship in Yvette and Linda who had also had premature twins. We just wanted to be friends straight away and I will always be grateful for them. Then, after diagnosis time, finding twin mums who were navigating this whole new world. I met Christie and Carly through the internet, and we laugh now about the fact that we never even checked if we weren't serial killers; I just opened the door, rolled the double pram into my house and got on with the new friendship.

My friend Helena and I met while she was living in America. My aunty met her on an overseas trip and immediately told me, 'You won't believe this person has twin girls the same age as yours and one of her twins has cerebral palsy.' We hit it off immediately and have shared schooling and laughter and tears and the realness and rawness of our twin mothering journey and I am so grateful for her friendship. Then there's my friend Nicole, who has also become an integral part of my life. We knew our friendship had changed forever after I told her my babies' diagnoses and she told me hers. We received them in the same week.

Through my friendships I have encountered women who have experienced the loss of one or both of their twins. That isn't my story to tell, yet the imprints of my friends' twins' deaths at birth and then later as children and teenagers have profoundly affected me. I am forever changed from their loss, their friendships with me and the grace they have always shown me when they are living with unspeakable pain. Sitting beside women at this time in their lives is such a privilege. I will never forget their children, or the fact that they are twin mums. Their children's names were Joshua, Annabella and Sunshine.

When my girls were around twelve months old, I met Kate, out for dinner with the twin mums. I couldn't believe my ears when she introduced herself and talked about having her twins as children numbers four and five. I was stunned. Here I was juggling two babies and she was doing that as well as mothering three older children.

What a woman. Immediately I was drawn to her. She spoke the truth, she loved going out for dinners, wearing lovely clothes, dressing her babies in matching and coordinating outfits (something I absolutely loved doing myself). She with her matching identical twin boys and me with my matching fraternal* girls. Don't hate us, reader, for loving to dress our twins the same; from my perspective, it came from pure pride. I was *so* proud to have my twins that I wanted to scream to the world how incredible they were and look, look, look at them; they are so beautiful and I am so very fortunate to have them here in my arms.

Listening to Kate talk about her pregnancy and how traumatic it was was sobering to me. Mostly my pregnancy was okay until about twenty-six weeks; hearing that she had had such a difficult time from so early on was important for me to understand.

One of the things I love and admire about Kate is that when you are her friend, she welcomes you in, she opens her home, she gives thoughtful gifts (I have always said she has the spiritual gift of giving gifts; you should see her gift-wrapping station in her home), she prepares food, she will bust herself to get to dinners, after juggling five children and their needs. She makes the best gingerbread; it's pretty famous in the multiple-birth world. It is, in fact, one of my Molly's favourite Christmas foods; she even closes her eyes when she eats it each December, that is how delicious it is.

When I realised that Kate was also leaving her church, I couldn't believe it. I was so thankful to have someone to talk about this

---

* Fraternal twins develop from separate ova and are therefore genetically distinct and not necessarily of the same sex or more similar than other siblings.

with and we would sit in the car for hours after a dinner sharing the difficulties of this time.

It's a pretty rare thing to be leaving a church and to have premature twins and to have an unfolding diagnosis. We would sit in the car and share and cry and laugh and try to sort out who we were. She understood the things I said, the Christianese language I spoke and the pain of that time. I was so grateful to have a non-judgemental friend who got me.

Kate and I didn't spend that much time together before the podcast but we always had each other's backs. Starting a podcast with her was so much fun. Kate threw herself in, opened her home, took on the social media and helped us get sorted with an accountant and so on; we laughed, we cried and I just love her tender heart, her loud laugh, her incredible cheese platters, her generosity, her love of good times and also the woman she is changing into every day. I am thankful that I can cancel on her, I can muck up dates and times, I can tell her my honest brutal truth and she stays by my side. That is a gift.

Kate is my bosom friend.

Being lonely is debilitating, but having someone to vent to, or someone to give you advice (the two are very different, mind you!) when you need it is a game-changer. And that creates a bond.

One of the main drivers for creating *Too Peas in a Podcast* was because we had felt lonely. We hope that *The Invisible Life of Us* makes you realise you are not alone.

How we started the podcast

We are absolute podcast tragics. Mandy started getting into them first. Since the twins' birth, she hadn't had much free time to dedicate to reading books, but boy, did she yearn for stories. Podcasts were the perfect solution. She spent many an hour in the kitchen with an earphone in one ear (the other ear listening out for any family chaos that might be occurring). She walked the four Aldi aisles every week with *both* earphones in. One of her favourite podcasts, *Terrible, Thanks for Asking,* was a standout. She couldn't believe people were talking about real stories in this format and laughed and cried along with the host, Nora, and her guests. She then peer-pressured Kate to join in, as all good friends do, taking Kate's podginity with *My Dad Wrote a Porno*, which brought constant joy and raucous, tears-down-the-cheeks laughter to us both.

Mandy noticed that the podcasts she listened to were mostly created and hosted by women and centred around women telling their stories. She wondered if one day she too could have a podcast. But, being more of an ideas person and not really the type to go out and buy a microphone, she knew she needed a partner in crime. Someone who also loved stories, loved to laugh and who had an adult son who knew about buying microphones. And suddenly, one idea became too peas.

'Doesn't everyone have a podcast these days?' we hear you ask. Well, that is sort of true, but we wanted to do it because after the many private conversations in each other's cars after a movie or dinner, laughing or crying about our amazing kids, we realised how important it was to share our stories. Until we met each other, we hadn't comprehended how much we *needed* the connection that comes with speaking to someone who under-stands what life mothering twins is like – particularly twins who don't tick the boxes that society wants ticked in a certain order. The multiple-birth world is lovely and very well supported, but there is a small subgroup who don't have much representation (or didn't before we very loudly entered the podbar and turned the microphones on): multiples who have additional needs and disabilities, multiples born prematurely, multiples who were conceived but one or both precious babies didn't get to come home from hospital. Where were those amazing human stories? Mandy had a nagging feeling, a voice in her head, saying, 'You need to do something about families of twins with disabilities, no one ever talks about them.'

Plus, let's face the truth: we have a lot to say. We were the kids at school always getting in trouble for talking, and it turns out we have used that talent to the best of our ability – we don't just have a podcast, now we have a *book*, so take that, Mrs Windsor!

When we first decided we would actually start a podcast, we bought a couple of microphones (well, Kate's eldest son did), and decided that, whatever our podcast looked or sounded like, it would include laughter. And that was that! There was no mucking around, no target-market research – we just had voices we couldn't silence any more. We hoped thirty or so people would listen each week and we could establish a little tribe to ease the crying-on-the-shower-floor loneliness (we have a chapter on that, don't worry!) that can sometimes accompany parenting multiples with additional needs (it can accompany all parenting, really) and give us somewhere to talk about our families. Not the 'typical family' but our beautiful, messy, frustrating, miraculous families.

There was one major stumbling block standing in the way of us and our podcast dreams: we didn't know what to call it.

You think naming a baby is hard? Well, sit right down – naming a podcast is almost *impossible*. We did what we always do when we can't solve a problem: we chatted with friends who had families like ours and asked them, 'What do you think we should call our podcast that you haven't listened to and know very little about?'

And boy, did they deliver. We also realised, as the potential names came thick and fast, how much this podcast was needed, and that we had listeners before we even uploaded the first (pretty ordinary, looking back) episode.

The names we came up with were *Multiple Diagnosis* or *Just a Healthy Baby* (we also have a chapter on that, so put the kettle on), and, to be honest, we still think those names are pretty fab, but we're glad we chose someone else's idea. Here, though, are some of the names our pea friends suggested:

- *Fucking Amazing Mums* (You can see how fabulous these names are going to be, can't you?)
- *We Survived*, or *We Are Surviving*
- *Ten Little Fingers and Ten Little Toes* (Again, something we probably all say without thinking about the fact that having ten little fingers and ten little toes is not an achievement or a choice. And lots of people have hand or foot differences.)
- *I'm So Fucking Over This!* (What parent hasn't uttered this line? We laughed a lot at this one; imagine seeing that in the podcast charts.)
- *Understanding Us* (This actually underscores the podcast, no matter the name.)
- *This Is My Actual Life!*
- *Wait and See!* (This is not a 'wait and see what Santa brings', this is a 'wait and see' when it comes to children's health, milestones and genetic conditions.)
- *This Is Real and Raw*
- *Just Another Family Keeping It Real*
- *Getting the Fuck on with It!* (Amen to all of us, in all walks of life, doing that today!)
- *Stop Staring or I Will Punch You in the Face* (Oh my word, we laughed. But seriously, stop staring!)
- *It Could Happen to You!*
- *This IS Our Normal* (We loved this one, too.)
- *Daily Challenges* (We thought this sounded like *Survivor* and loved it. 'Okay, Mandy, if you survive these five daily

challenges before 7.05 am . . . you get nothing, not even a mum buff. But you might get your kids to school! Winner!')

- *My New Normal* (You get to view the world with a different lens – not good, not bad, just different.)
- *What Is Typical, Anyway?* (This is fab. And yeah, what is typical, apart from the fact that it will rain when you hang the sheets on the line?)
- *These Smiles Have Tears Too*
- *The Invisible Life of Us* (Powerful, right?! See how hard it is to choose? At the time we were like, fuck, that is a good one. We didn't use this for the podcast, but we did end up using it somewhere!)
- *What Happened Next . . .* (Actually, a great name for a podcast.)
- *Bet You Didn't Expect This When You Were Expecting!* (This made us roar with laughter and, come on, can't every parent or caregiver relate?)
- *It's Nothing Like Fucking Holland.* (This is a reference to a poem. Google it, but it's actually called 'Welcome to Holland'. We have an episode on it if you want to listen.)
- *My Only Special Need as a Parent: A Bigger Wine Glass!*
- *You are So Lucky to Have a Disabled Parking Sticker!* (People say this to Mandy. It still takes our breath away – as in, a shocked gasp, not oh-the-view-of-the-city-at-night-takes-our-breath-away!)
- *My Kid Doesn't Fit in the Box*
- *Don't Dis the Ability*
- *The Unexpected Path.*

We obviously didn't go with any of these extremely worthy and amazing names; we went, of course, with *Too Peas in a Podcast*. That was because at the end of one of Buzz and Woody's visits to the paediatrician (who also treats Mandy's daughters), Kate said to the doctor, 'Mandy and I are going to start a podcast.' He looked at her and said, 'Yes, you should. And it should be called *Two Peas in a Podcast*. You both have twins, you are like two peas in a pod, and you share a story.'

What a brilliant idea, but we expect nothing less from Dr Shane. We have both been seeing him since our twins were born. Now, we know it is the kids that actually see him, but if you have a beautiful, supportive paediatrician, you will know: you *all* see the doctor!

Of course, we then discovered that sadly there are already many podcasts called *Two Peas in a Podcast*. One has even been going since 2013! But we realised that actually it wasn't just us in the pod, it was you too (#peatoo). We are in this pod together. So *Too Peas in a Podcast* (which is the spelling nightmare you imagine it to be when people try to find it online) was born. A baby that we birthed together without any drugs. And what a movement it has been! Almost as good as the first bowel movement post-childbirth. We can't imagine our podcast having any other name.

The other question we receive every time we are interviewed – from people wanting to start podcasts themselves, and even from random people on the street – is 'Why do you think your podcast resonates with so many people – people who are not parents, people who don't have twins, people who don't live with or alongside a disability?'

To that we simply say, 'Two reasons, random citizen.'

1   This is a podcast that captures contagious friendship, even when life throws you curve balls – and shit balls, for that matter.

2   It resonates with a diverse audience because we are all humans. We are telling human stories and the fact that some people find it hard to understand why it could be relatable about children with a disability or additional needs

or families living that journey, probably goes to show why we had to make a podcast in the first place.

Did we expect people to listen in the thousands? No, never! While we think the topics are amazing, we are very ordinary people with no media training, so we didn't even know if we had the skill to do this. Now we find it hard to keep an episode under an hour and a half! Turns out, ordinary people are actually bloody interesting. Our podcast is mostly ordinary families, parents and kids talking about how life looks and works for them, and that is not ordinary at all!

We hope that *The Invisible Life of Us* gives you a place to cry (and feel supported), an opportunity for a therapeutic laugh and that hearing our stories and rants and memories gives you comfort and the realisation you are not alone. Everyone is welcome in the pea tribe. We're here to celebrate everyone's stories, everyone's family – no matter how it looks! Parenting wasn't ever meant to be easy, but it is meant to be messy, joyous and inclusive.

PART ONE
FINDING YOUR TRIBE

Loneliness

Let's see what the experts say about loneliness . . .

> While common definitions of loneliness describe it as a state of solitude or being alone, loneliness is actually a state of mind. Loneliness is defined by researchers as feeling lonely more than once a week. Loneliness causes people to feel empty, alone, and unwanted.[1]

Ugh, how does that make you feel? Alone and unwanted? Being lonely is . . . well (and we don't know if this is allowed to be printed on the first page of a chapter), the devil's arsehole.

Even though the peas love to laugh, if you have ever listened to the podcast you will know that the tears regularly come and go. No one goes through life without shedding a few tears, and this is particularly true for parents. There is cheering, though; we all cheer for different reasons and sometimes we cheer and cry at the same time. It's a funny old thing, parenthood. Some parents cry when their kids take their first step; others cheer. Neither response is wrong; we just have different reactions to events because we are all different. No one should be judged for tears or sadness, and *Too Peas* is a judgement-free zone! But when your tears (or cheers!) in your parenting journey make you feel alone, that is not fun.

To this, the peas say 'loneliness is so 2019!' (specifically, so May 2019, which is just before *Too Peas in a Podcast* started).

Like Buzz said so profoundly one day, 'You know why people love the podcast, Mum? It's because you and Mandy don't know anything, but you don't know anything together! No one likes being alone and not knowing things, Mum. It's like at school when you have no idea what's going on and then you find a friend who also has no idea, and you are together, not knowing anything but not knowing it together!'

That perfectly sums up the podcast, and our friendship: we don't know anything, but we are together.

Even the bloody word 'lonely' sounds lonely, don't you think? I think we all know what it is like to feel lonely. Everyone has probably experienced some version of sitting in a room full of people and yet somehow feeling apart. It's different from being alone; often we crave alone time, but you can be lonely and alone, and you can also be lonely while sitting at a table with friends.

According to Beyond Blue, women carry a bigger burden when it comes to depression and anxiety, so right now we want to chat to our fellow gals. Look at these stats, from their website.

While good mental health is essential to the overall health of both men and women, women experience some mental health conditions at higher rates than men. In fact, around 1 in 6 women in Australia will experience depression and 1 in 3 women will experience anxiety during their lifetime. Women also experience post-traumatic stress disorder and eating disorders at higher rates than men. Depression and anxiety can affect women at any time in their life but there is an increased chance during pregnancy and the year following the birth of a baby. Up to 1 in 10 women experience depression while they are pregnant and 1 in 6 women experience depression during the first year after birth. Anxiety conditions are thought to be as common with many women experiencing both conditions at the same time.[2]

There are so many things that can make you feel lonely. Sometimes it's having a belief system that no one around you shares, or speaking a different language, or starting at a workplace or school with a bunch of people who have an established friendship. And sometimes it happens when life throws you a curve ball. When you catch it, you lose your footing and, by the time you get back up, everything has somehow changed around you. That's the kind of loneliness that happened to us, that's what we are talking about.

Peas sometimes get excluded and it's not always intentional (although you can be intentional in your desire to be inclusive!). Maybe you have to walk your pea shoot into their classroom for some reason, and when you get back to the school gate the other parents have gone for coffee without you. Those moments create a little splinter digging into your heart.

The cure for loneliness is something much bigger than we can impart with our very limited knowledge of psychology. We can only talk about our own lived experiences, and for us, we became less lonely when we found people who had similar experiences. Not the same experience, but a somehow relatable experience. There is no 'typical' family. No two-point-three kids and a picket fence. Most of us don't relate to that anyway. We all try to find our people, our kindred spirits, friends with similar values and senses of humour.

If you are feeling lonely and disconnected, well . . . you are not alone in that feeling. Pretty much all of us will experience loneliness at some point or another in our lives, and as we have learnt from Beyond Blue, women in particular can feel it more. When you add in complex parenting, it is sort of a recipe for a very sunken cake. As hard as it is, if you're feeling that way, you need to tell someone, whether it's a spouse, a friend, a relative or your doctor. Whisper it or shout it, over wine, coffee, Messenger – you just need to share it.

We had no idea how much less lonely the podcast would make us feel: this huge blanket of women (and some awesome blanket-carrying men), wrapping around us and themselves, all in the pea pod together, so to speak. And this is the best thing about podcasts (and our audiobook)! You can listen to them in the car, late at night when you can't sleep, when you are folding laundry, commuting to work, almost anywhere! Anyone can listen at any time; everyone, together. Somehow listening to a shared story or a conversation that really grabs you in the feels can make you less lonely; just knowing there is someone else out there in the 'burbs going through something similar is so powerful. We are proud to have achieved this.

Kate says

After I had Sound Engineer at the ripe old age of twenty-one, I was lonely. Like, bone-achingly lonely. None of my friends had babies yet. None of them was even married. I felt this weird joy from being a new mum and having this little baby whom I had such strong feelings for, but also lonely as no one I knew was experiencing anything similar. I got to have the awesome gift of friends in my mums' group, but they were at least ten (and some were twenty) years older than me. They were buying holiday houses while my husband and I were worried about paying the rent. I still had church, so I had a group of people to see, but again, no one my age with a baby. Age doesn't matter for loads of things – I love having friends of all ages – but when you are a young mum, finding other young mums is really important.

I managed to fight back against that lonely shit feeling by starting a playgroup for younger mums. Somehow my loneliness drove me to create a space where I didn't feel so alone. I found out then there were other parents feeling the same way. We sat in a sparse hall, put the kids on the mat and had a cuppa. It worked; I had rolled the dice and found some friends. It doesn't always work but hey, no harm in trying if you can get past the washing and nappy bin to do it! I also found a friend who liked having lunch dates in parks so was able to deal with the baby–no-baby divide. And the other antidote was time. As I had more babies and they started to get older, I made friends at kinder and preschool and school.

I also learnt a really valuable lesson. Now, most of you probably are aware of this, but it bears repeating: your chosen life partner (if you are lucky enough to have one) cannot be your best friend, support crew, soulmate, co-parent and party friend all rolled into one. If you are expecting them to be everything to you all the time, you will also feel lonely in your relationship, which bites! For example, my husband works excruciatingly long hours, which means that I have learnt to parent on my own, to be self-sufficient (although not in the same way as sole or single parents at all). I had to realise that, for me, lots of parenting was going to be solo. Once I had worked out that that was the way it was, I didn't resent it – and hey, it gives me guilt-free time to sneak to the Corner Hotel and see live bands, as I have accrued a lot of time-off-in-lieu.

Being a young mum was isolating in many ways, but I also experienced some revoltingly lonely days after Buzz and Woody were born. I remember thinking it was odd because I was being supported by the most wonderful group of friends. Why did I feel the way I did?

It was probably a combination of the fact that I had just experienced a pregnancy unlike any of the pregnancies that my friends had had, I was exhausted and I was in the process of limping away from church. Happily limping, but it was still painful. I couldn't really see a light at the end of the lonely tunnel.

I will be forever grateful for the fact that my friend Mara incessantly nagged me about the Australian Multiple Birth Association Forum, refusing to drop it until I joined. And it was a game-changer. I found solace in people who understood the pain of not being able to 'properly' soothe two screaming babies and who appreciated the Twisties and Diet Coke lunch diet. Finally, I had found a group of women who understood twin-pram frustration (this is a thing: shops are too narrow for twin prams, and I know wheelchair users share this frustration). Here was a group of people who had all these twin parenting tips, like Cheerios are good for fine motor coordination and lunch, but Froot Loops are for dessert. I made friends who didn't give a shit if I forgot to call them back, because they knew that I was so under the bloody pump you couldn't even see the pump sign! Real friends, friends who will message you when Huggies nappies go on sale, or the baby formula is back in stock. Wow! That old shared experience, so powerful.

Here is a secret, though. I have felt at my loneliest surrounded by beautiful friends. Friends who love me and my children, but who would start talking about all the amazing after-school activities their kids do while ignoring or not asking about our struggles with finding activities. Or the friend we had over for dinner, when Buzz at the age of three stood up, proceeded to hop onto the table (yes, on the table), run the length of it dodging food, drinks, bowls of chips and salad, only to grab a bottle of juice, weave back down the table and sit down with his juice!

My friend turned to her husband and said, 'Oh Greg, we are so blessed with Lucas.'* What, I am not blessed? Did you see how Buzz ran down that table? He didn't even knock anything over!

---

* Names changed to protect my friendships.

And he is independent. He might behave differently from yours, but you don't have to say shit like that. I have never forgotten it.

I have had very similar feelings on lots of occasions, such as at a school morning tea, when everyone was standing around eating Arnott's Family Assorted biscuits and discussing exam results and NAPLAN scores, sporting triumphs and English Extension. I wasn't lonely because people were excluding me; I just knew my life was different. I worried that these parents might judge my stories or, worse still, judge my kids if I shared those stories. You feel lonely listening to chatter that you cannot relate to. It's no one's fault, but it still happens.

I remember after my dad died, and I would go to the shops for bread and the cashier would say, 'Hi, how are you?' I wanted to scream, 'I am bereft actually. I am so sad that it takes effort to breathe right now. Grief has overwhelmed me.' But of course I just said, 'Great, thanks. Lovely day, isn't it?' It was the type of grief I was completely alone in because no one else had the relationship I did with my dad. It had been ours and it was gone forever. Sometimes being lonely as a parent has felt similar. There have been parents all around me, but no one experiencing anything remotely similar to me.

I don't need validation that I am parenting in the right way. I have five kids; I know there is no single right way to parent, but it's the sharing of stories that bonds us with people. I was so lucky to find the Australian Multiple Birth Association group, and the amazing cohort of women within it. But every situation is different, and what if you can't quite find your people as easily as I eventually did?

What if you want to bond with people who celebrate the ordinary? Whose kids have never 'been seen', never 'been chosen', never won stupid awards, whose kids try twice as hard but no one notices. It's bloody lonely without those people in your life. I was lucky; I had Mandy to bitch to and a group of twin mums who were 'just like me' . . . and, well, the rest is pea history. These women have validated all my feelings, shared my frustrations, encouraged my chocolate and wine consumption and allowed me to vent (daily!). They send flowers and hugs, not judgemental advice. They allow tears for tears' sake. They took my loneliness, screwed it up and chucked it in the bin, and I hope with the podcast and this book we can take some of yours too.

Being lonely is sort of like having a piece or two missing from a jigsaw puzzle; you can still see the picture, but it gnaws at you every day you see the piece missing. Mandy and I don't want people to feel like we did. That's why, one cold Melbourne winter's night, we started talking into two microphones, hoping that we might reach someone – even just one person – and make them feel less lonely (and, if we were honest, that we would feel less lonely). We were two middle-aged women (all right, Mandy, you might not quite be middle-aged yet), with no skills in podcasting or interviewing people, but, as Buzz said, even though we weren't experts in anything, we were together and we felt empathy, and we created a safe space for us and for anyone listening.

And you know what? So many peas, rectums, therapeas, peafessionals, chickpeas and pea friends all found a community and a connection. All found a piece of the puzzle they thought they might never find. We didn't know this would happen, and mostly it isn't due to us; it is due to the mighty pea tribe supporting and listening, downloading and connecting.

This pea tribe has been transformative: like before and after photos from a weight-loss advertisement, we are the same Kate and Mandy but oh so different. The friendship we found in each other has grown and grown.

Do you know the story in the Bible of the loaves and fishes? The story goes that Jesus was talking to a few thousand people for several hours, the people got hungry but there was no food. One little child had five little bread loaves and two fishes. Jesus performed a miracle and fed around 5000 people with those few loaves. Don't ask me how; I wasn't there. But I have seen what it is like to share pea stories with thousands of people and we all 'get fed' and feel so much less lonely. People always say, 'It's like you two peas are sitting with me at my kitchen table, chatting.' That is the highest praise we can get!

Mandy says

Most people know the poem 'The Road Not Taken' by Robert Frost. I will never forget the time that my beautiful friend Helena told me that we were on the road less travelled. I immediately knew what she meant. It was a very different road from the one all my friends who were having babies around me were on. I didn't know anyone else who had premature twins, both with a diagnosis. I used to say, 'I don't fit in with the singleton mums, I don't fit in with the twin mums, I don't fit in with anyone, anywhere.' That became my inner voice, but I was determined to keep finding my people, and trying my hardest to make friends regardless.

I am no literary scholar and I am absolutely not a poet. My introduction to poetry was reading *Anne of Green Gables* and being able to recite 'The Lady of Shalott'. These days my repertoire has expanded to Dr Seuss but not much further. But 'The Road Not Taken' really spoke to me.

For me, a twin pregnancy, premature birth and leaving my babies in hospital for two months, and then the subsequent diagnosis meant that my experience as a mother was different from the beginning. I was so proud to be a twin mummy. I felt special, and people treated me with interest wherever I went; for example, the beautiful mum who was a Sudanese refugee whom I worked with while I was at QEC while I was pregnant. She would greet me at her door and say, 'Oh Mandy, two babies,' and kiss my stomach twice. It's one of the most precious memories I have of my pregnancy. Boy, could that mum teach me a thing or two about being lonely. All the women I had worked with who had fled war and torture and trauma remain with me and also give me an inner strength as I remember their eyes and their faces and their hands and the pride they had in their new homes, learning English, loving their children, buying one too many bottles of Fanta and fearing for their families' lives in their home country. What amazing women.

Everywhere I went after I had the twins, I was seeking people who were like me. And everywhere I went, I encountered wonderful people but, at one point or another, their roads had diverged from mine.

- Family: My family loved us all so much and helped whenever we needed it, but no one had experienced a premature birth (let alone two).
- Mothers' group: There were a lot of other first-time mums in the group, and we were all trying to figure out motherhood and where the hell to buy formula and nappies on sale, and talking about expressing, feeding, bottles, food, clothes, crying and laughing together each week – but they were all singletons with term babies. I did manage to find another mum who had twins and she was certainly living in similar chaos, but she hadn't experienced premature births or a diagnosis.
- Premature birth group: The mums here became loyal friends of mine and understood much about having premmie babies, but I was the only mum whose twins had received a diagnosis.

- Twins group: We were all familiar with chaos, that's for sure! Within the twins group there were some premature births, and a whole range of twins with diagnoses, but none quite like my girls.

- Old friends: Most of my old friends who were mothers had had term singletons with no diagnoses. They loved me no matter what, and supported and encouraged me – although I think they were slightly shocked that my approach to parenting involved so much swearing.

- Online friends: This was where I got to meet mums who also had premature twins with diagnoses – but only online, as they lived all over Australia.

- Cerebral palsy friends: This was a valuable community to be part of, and within it we met other twins and singletons, with hemiplegia, diplegia, quadriplegia, and those who were classified at varying gross motor function classification system (GMFCS)* levels.

- Church friends and many acquaintances: They loved me, missed me, encouraged me, and also didn't understand the new me, and were shocked at swearing me.

- Work friends: They missed me at work. Some were mothers and some weren't, but loads of them came and sat with me in hospital. My friend Raylene came to my house and bathed the babies with me; another friend, Jacinta, called me every week for years, listening with only love for me. But despite all this, I still felt so different from them.

- Waiting rooms at hospitals, therapies: twins, singletons, hemiplegia, speech delay, no speech delay, can use two hands, only uses one hand, can walk, can't walk. I would strike up

---

* This is a system of classification that is applied to children with cerebral palsy, and ranges from 1 to 5.

conversations with mums while waiting, ask questions about where they got their AFOs, whether their child was having botox, etc. We had a few random playdates, but everyone was so busy that it was hard to find time for those friendships.

- Kinder and school: singletons, twins, diagnosis, no diagnosis, disabled parents, siblings with disabilities and additional needs, refugee women, single women and solo-parenting women, all on life's differing paths.

Was there something about me that was desperate to fit in? I knew I wasn't the first person in the world to not feel the same as everyone else, but it was the first time for me. Apart from my involvement with the church, and having school and work friends thinking that was weird, I had pretty much been a run-of-the-mill white woman living in suburban Melbourne, married in my mid-twenties with a mortgage and a job.

I started to look around and understand what it must feel like to be seen as 'different' by the majority of people. Here I was desperately trying to find my people and then having my eyes opened wider and wider to the minorities who surrounded me every day. It's a well-known fact that people with disabilities (PWD) are the biggest minority in the world, but what does that make their mothers?

The loneliest I have ever felt is when my girls have been in hospital, suffering and in pain. I can't describe the feeling of walking along the quiet hallways of the Royal Children's Hospital by myself at night, not wanting to talk to anyone, but also desperate to talk to someone. Sitting eating a cheeseburger alone, trying not to cry, but then crying.

So many times I have been on the floor with my daughters, crying together about why their lives have been difficult. The feeling of not being able to help your child is one of the worst

I have ever experienced. Or worrying that their pain, discomfort, stress and trauma is something that you have contributed to by agreeing to having casts put on their legs or to surgeries that doctors have recommended. That's when I feel angry about how unfair it all is. 'Why my precious girls? Why do others not have to go through this?' I would think, even though I knew so many of my new friends from various support groups were indeed going through their own version of this every day.

There have been other times, usually when I was walking home after dropping the twins at school, chasing my singleton down the hill past all the other mums, that I felt a similar sense of alienation. I had trouble joining their conversations because I sensed their pity. They knew they couldn't complain in front of me, but they would do it anyway – and then send me a text message to apologise. I would spend so much time listening to other women because I was the 'poster mum with disabled twins', so teachers sent people my way. I kept going out of my way to do what my mum had told me: 'Be a friend to everyone.' Mostly this was awesome but sometimes I just didn't have it in me to listen to other people's stories at 9.03 am. But that is the time of day that women have to share and dump and let go of the last three hours of wrangling, meltdowns, getting dressed, feeding, teachers saying something mean at drop-off, who has their student support group (SSG)*, who forgot to put undies on their daughters this morning (well, that was really only me) . . . If I didn't listen, who would? And I knew what it felt like to feel lonely. Some of life's greatest talks and reflections happen at the school gate – except, of course, if you are at a specialist school, then all of that happens at the bus drop-off at 7.45 am instead, if you are lucky enough

---

* Meetings between parents, teachers, therapists and support staff in which we would plan goals for the next term.

to have a friend there. So many times I have run down the road with wet hair and sometimes in my PJs to get to the bus on time and told all my woes to my friend Michelle. We shared so much at 7.45 am for many years.

You will hear us talk in the podcast about casting out loneliness a lot, and if this is the legacy of *Too Peas*, I will be stoked. Casting out loneliness was also the reason for the creation of the Too Peas Hangout on Facebook. We started the page so that parents could have a place to talk about the podcast, and seek support from each other. Kate and I are in there every day, but what I am most proud of is our listeners being able to access each other's wisdom, humour and empathy.

2

Empeathy

Let's see what the dictionary says about empathy.

The psychological identification with or vicarious experiencing of the feelings, thoughts, or attitudes of another.

Or this one:

The ability to understand and share the feelings of another.

To be honest, peas, pea friends, pea shoots, rectums and everyone else, we were hesitant to write this chapter, mostly because there are entire books out there on empathy written by people with the most beautiful articulate words, people with degrees in psychology and social work. But, in our hearts, this is actually a topic so dear to us we had to try. If we had a magic wand and a pot of gold we would start the 'enable empathy' initiative and go around to schools (and workplaces, for that matter) and talk about empathy, real life empathy, learning it, really learning it so that you can live it. Because here is the mic drop: empathy has to be taught, and for us it is much more important than Year 10 maths or Year 12 English! The world would be transformed if we all lived empathetic lives.

We won't re-hash the multitude of books and quotes and memes on empathy, but instead we will talk about what it means for us and our families and share what it means to some of our peas. What does it mean to step into the shoes of another person? And how can we learn from that?

Empathy is not sympathy. We *express* sympathy and *share* empathy. We send a sympathy card after someone loses a loved one, but to show empathy we would sit with that person, lean in and let them grieve. We would listen without talking, and we wouldn't try to 'cheer them up'.

Sometimes it's easier to opt for sympathy – it puts us at a bit of a remove from a situation and we can express what we need to and then move on. But we peas want to encourage empathy where we can! We want to embrace it and live empathetic lives.

 I think empathy is such a hard thing to describe and probably means different things to different people. For me, I worked on being a kind and tolerant person to my twins as they grew up and as young adults I look at them, I see how they treat people, and I realise they are kind and tolerant (another example of how you have to teach it). *Pea friend Jenny*

 Empathy to me is walking, journeying with someone, as opposed to sympathy or pity, which is commiserating but not being in the muck with someone. I hate sympathy! But it's easier for people, empathy is harder! *Pea friend Amelia*

This really spoke to us. No one wants pity, it's the mucking in that counts. Imagine this (try to empathise!). You are a parent of a fantastically neurodiverse child who is overstimulated after having spent all day at school enduring loud noises and trying to be 'what school wants them to be', so now they are having a well-deserved 'meltdown'* at the swimming pool while their sibling

---

*   We hate that word, 'meltdown'; that's something you do to chocolate, isn't it? Let's not call it a 'meltdown'; let's call it a 'response behaviour'.

has a lesson. What would you rather your friends do? Ignore you? Or muck in and help? Offer to take the pea shoot outside, or to watch your child swim and take photos of their awesome diving efforts (it is hard to miss out on things as a parent, so always offer to take a photo!) while you allow your child to calm down, or let them sit with you in the car with an iPad?

Or even in a supermarket. What would you rather from people who walk past? Pity? Or would you prefer them to jump in, stop your trolley from rolling away and prevent your other toddler from escaping to the chocolate aisle? Maybe ask you if there is anything you need? Always offer to help and be prepared to do what you offer!

There is nothing in that scenario that deserves pity anyway. When did a 'response behaviour' need pity or judgement? Have you watched *The Bachelor* recently? Those people have massive meltdowns all the time and are rewarded with fame and roses because of it.

 For me true empathy is treating everyone with respect and dignity, and no sign of being patronising or condescending. I'm always most impressed and admiring of the problem-solvers who do their best to remove barriers, especially to disability being a challenge. Like the staff on my son's Year 4 camp, who, without any fuss, organised a bush walking chariot-wheelchairy-thingy which meant he could take part in the bushwalk. *Pea friend Dianne*

This is amazing. And the parent didn't even have to muck in; some wonderful peachers did instead! See how life-changing empathy can be?

 Empathy is not only for our children but for us too, it's being aware of our own pre-conceptions and then showing ourselves compassion when things have been different than expected. Empathy means realising that we have pre-conceived notions about our kids and then when we have had to really meet them where they are, rather than what we think they could/should have been. It's realising that we can create our own goals and achieve them but to truly meet someone else where they are, we have to consider things from their point of view. That's when we are truly able to drop the stereotypes or the judgemental language and just be present for what it is. For example, I never realised how much I valued education and achievement and self-consciously considered everyone successful only if they had achieved those things, until I had my girls. That was a rude awakening for me, to realise my twin daughters' achievements have nothing to do with me. Sounds kinda narcissistic, but when you think of it, we are promised a story and it's not until it changes – drastically, usually – that we have to see things from another person's point of view. And adjust our views! *Pea friend Lisa*

Actually seeing the person and treating them with honour and respect, so that judgement is actively shut down. My daughter has regulation issues, so this comes into play often with my girls watching and learning from what I chose to do and what I chose not to say! *Pea friend Jodie*

Choosing what to say and what not to say can be powerful. You don't have to say everything you think, and remember that judgement is the enemy of nearly everything! (Of course, that is just our opinion, and yes, we do see the irony there.)

Empathy is understanding what is unique about someone else's situation, putting yourself in their shoes, and walking around in them (even if they give you blisters). Everyone's situation is different, even if it may appear the same on the outside. I think that's where respect comes in – respecting the differences, really respecting them, not just paying lip service. *A pea dad!*

 For me, empathy is about letting go of your own and others' egos. People tend to make your situation about them and that seems to be unfortunately a by-product of the self-entitled society we live in. I have come across people who wrap up empathy, but get miffed when I can't return the same due to the different situations I am in. The only people who truly understand are the ones living very similar lives. For example, someone will do something for our family and it seems like showing empathy, but down the track they expect something in return. I feel pressured and the cycle begins, they almost forget our situation is permanent and not temporary. *Pea friend Kelly*

This is another important point for us all: empathy gives without expecting anything back. What it does is change us for the better. That's the gift in return.

 I have found it extremely challenging to teach my boys (eleven and nine with ASD [autism spectrum disorder]) how to show and feel empathy. I try to explain to them how it may feel to be the person whose feelings have been hurt or are struggling with something. I have tried to help them see things from others' per- spectives when it is indeed almost impossible for them, however it works okay when it is me who is the person whose feelings have been hurt or is struggling to overcome something. My boys show me endless love to console me. However, with Master Nine if it was something he said or did that was hurtful or inappropriate, my attempts at trying to teach him empathy most often end in him being incredibly angry. Angry at himself, angry that he upset someone, angry that he is in trouble, angry that he didn't mean it. I guess that is his version of empathy, and it is just different. *A pea friend*

Let's never assume we know what someone else is teaching or experiencing with their child and never assume everyone responds or learns in the same way. Difference is beautiful, and let's not expect that when we give empathy it will always be returned in the way we gave it, or returned at all.

 I always thought I was empathetic – maybe not so much now. I believe putting yourself in someone else's shoes is a good place to start, and I wish I could have applied that more to my son's situation. Particularly when school is telling you how non-compliant he is and how little empathy they show to kids walking a different path. Ten years in and I don't believe there is much empathy. Just people getting on with their lives and people not wanting to hear or help. The only tribe who get it are ones in the same position. *Pea friend Anonymous*

That's a little truth bomb right there. And that is why we want the 'enable empathy' initiative. It is only a dream at this point but the peas would love to talk to schoolkids, teachers and parents and explain what empathy is and why it is such an important thing to learn. If we teach the kids, maybe it will rub off on the teachers and adults.

 I have worked very hard at teaching my twins, aged nine, empathy. I have made small advances and they seem to have more empathy for me, they surprise me at times and other times frustrate me, perhaps the speech delay, the trouble reading faces and emotions and the processing speed doesn't help. *Pea friend Robyn*

Look at this! Pea parents everywhere trying their hearts out to teach empathy because they realise more than most the value in it!

Kate says

Empathy sometimes is an elusive rainbow. I get close to finding it, but it always seems to evade me at the last minute. Growing up I knew what it was like to be pitied because one of my four brothers is a heroin user. Such simple words: 'heroin user' – but those words change lives and families, and they can never be 'unchanged'. This isn't a story of addiction but rather how it taught me to have empathy for something I don't really understand. I don't know what it is like (and I hope I never will) to parent a child with a serious drug addiction. But my mum does and she will often say to me, 'You don't know what it's like. I love him!' She is one hundred per cent correct: I don't know. I know what it is like to have a brother who is an addict but I don't know what it is like for her. I have to say, 'You're right, Mum, I don't know.' I can sit with her and watch *Pride and Prejudice* or *Miss Marple*, I can listen and I can learn. But I cannot give her advice! Please don't give people advice unless you have the same or a very similar experience. Let's leave advice to the professionals, shall we, or maybe one of those guys on talkback radio? (Kidding!)

One day we were sitting at an airport after a horrendous international flight (don't live in the southern hemisphere and have children who love the snow, hot tip right there!). We were sitting at 'AREA B', which was quite clearly written on our itinerary. Luckily it had a coffee and bagel shop right next to it; unluckily it wasn't Melbourne coffee. We sat there with a million bags, skis, snowboards and big puffy jackets in plenty of time to meet the transfer to take us up the mountain. Along came an airport employee. He said 'Hi', we said 'Hi' and all kept talking and trying to sit upright and awake. After a while he inquired where we were from, where we were going, the ususal airport chitchat. And then he informed us, 'You are in the wrong place. No transfers ever leave from here.' We showed him our 'AREA B' paper and he shook his head. 'That's wrong,' he said.

Of course we immediately panicked. We were already stressed and it's true that we couldn't see anyone else who looked like they were heading up a mountain. But then there were so many of us we figured that the bus might just take us. While we scurried around looking for someone to help us, Woody came over to me and said, 'Mum, I was so glad everyone spoke to that man. I was worried maybe you wouldn't listen to him, or talk to him – I hate it when people do that to me – but you really listened, even when it was hard to understand him.'

I should point out at this point, as it now matters to the story, that the airport employee had Down syndrome. I admit I cried in that airport when I thought of all the kids (and later adults) with knowledge to impart and to whom people don't listen. But most of all, because Woody has lived with sometimes being ignored, he understood why it's important to never do it to others. It shows that when you get it, you really get it! Oh, and the airport guy was right by the way. We missed our connection and had to sleep at an airport hotel.

I really believe that empathy is a big game-changer for the world, but maybe that change is beyond Mandy and me. Even if everyone reading this book thinks about it a little more, that will help to bring about change. What do Paul Kelly and Kev Carmody say? Something about big things growing from little things?

Mandy says

I think empathy has been drilled into me by my mum. 'Always think of others, Mandy; do unto others, Mandy; look out for people who are different to you, Mandy; include them; look out for the shy people; you are confident, so you can help others.'

She was relentless in teaching me to look at how other people are feeling. But that doesn't mean that I truly understood pain. Of course I didn't, and it has taken time and reading and learning and listening and being so broken in heartache that I could recognise it in others. I am sure that I have and do stuff up a lot. I look back at my career and wonder what the hell I said to parents whose babies we were teaching to sleep, or the home visits to women who were abused and impoverished, seeking asylum, refugees, traumatised and tortured. What on earth did I know? How did I talk to them, teach them about parenting? Did I listen? Did I empathise? I like to think I was kind and respectful, interested in them, encouraged them, told them what a great job they were doing, despite the world that was surrounding them.

When we received my daughters' diagnoses I remember that was when the lights went on in the world. In the words of James Alexander Malcolm MacKenzie Fraser in *Outlander*, 'It was as if I stepped outside on a cloudy day and suddenly the sun came out.' I saw people. I saw pain, I saw hurt, I saw everything. I recognised pain in people's eyes when they spoke and I never ever would return to that old Mandy. I am so grateful for this. I am also grateful for the people in my life who understood this too. Family and friends who have stood by my side, even after many times of my pushing them away. That takes some fortitude: to be pushed away and then say, 'I am staying by your side.' I am sure there are people I have pushed away who have stayed away and I am sorry for that. At the time I didn't really have or show empathy for them, so I am sure that took its toll.

Empathy from teachers who themselves had walked the path of difference, nurses and doctors who acknowledged me, listened and gave me strength. Kind physiotherapists and speech pathologists. If a person could have too much support, then it's me. I have had the very best people around me, people with incredible skills, and they tried, they really tried. Friends who called me each week and listened and asked me how I was, friends who looked after one baby as I went to appointments with the other. My loyal and kind friend Charlotte arranged meal trains for us. I was so touched by her organisational skills (she had spreadsheets and everything!) and care for me. Others coordinated mowing lawns, babysitting and cleaning my house. People picked up my daughter and carried her for me, drove me places, sent presents and flowers and balloons and cards to hospital and texted me during surgeries to distract me. My brother Adam bought the two biggest teddy bears you could possibly find and brought them into hospital. I remember laughing at the huge smile on his face as he walked into the room with these enormous bears. I couldn't wait to get rid of them. Other family members came to appointments, cuddled babies, toddlers, little girls in hospital, followed ridiculous present requests (cue seventy-six Barbies), brought chicken nuggets to the hospital bed, new PJs and beautiful clothes, sitting with my children in hospital so I could go and eat. I will never forget them.

This makes me cry as I write this. This is empathy in action. It's saying, 'I see you, and I will do what I can.' I now try to pay this forward and do the same myself, even at the risk of pushing someone away. A simple text message never goes astray, as long as it is accompanied by the words 'You don't need to reply.'

Perhaps because I have had so much support, I am still kicking and able to have started this podcast with Kate. The empathy that has come back from our listeners has been stunning and something I never imagined. We have been cheered on from the beginning and to know we are showing empathy in return to our pea tribe is a huge source of pride for us both. Sitting in silence, otherwise known as generous listening, is a skill I have been practising for twenty years. Sometimes I nail it and sometimes I don't, but you know what? When you do it and you allow someone to speak their truth in a friendship or in a family, it is one of the most powerful moments: you hear people transform their thinking right in front of you. Try it.

3

Guilt

If the Kate from 2021 could go back and chat to 2004 Kate about the guilt she would feel as not just a mum but a mum of five children – well, we would need cheese, crackers and an entire bottle of wine. Mostly she would say, 'Talk it out with a professional. You are too tired, too stressed, too busy to take up any little slivers of your time with unwarranted guilt!'

Mandy would tell the 2004 version of herself, 'Don't let guilt steal your time. It's the last emotion you need and will take your time and attention away from your life and all you need to get done.'

What does the dictionary say about this lovely emotion?

A feeling of worry or unhappiness that you have because you have done something wrong, such as causing harm to another person.

It's hard not to worry that we might have caused harm to our children while we were pregnant. That it was something we did or didn't eat or drink, or the way we slept, or because we walked too fast – you name it, we have thought it might have caused harm to those babies in our belly. Of course, our rational brain knows this is all bullshit, but the non-rational brain can be loud, bossy and, to be honest, a bully.

When it is your tiny baby in the NICU, or you are on bed rest, fighting to stay pregnant for a few more precious hours after a steroid injection to strengthen your unborn babies' lungs, it is so hard not to feel like a failure. This, pea friends, is no way to start a parenting journey. We have had a fuck-tonne of counselling over the years and we know this to be true. It takes all our strength to tell this guilt bully to fuck off out of our minds, but it creeps back when we are not watching!

Here's the thing about guilt: sometimes it's useful and properly founded, and can inspire us to do better next time. It helps us to learn and grow and incites action. But we are made to feel guilty for so many things that it can be hard to tell what is founded and what is not, and so we end up conflating everything and creating this enormous mass of guilt, patched together from snippets of conversations, things we heard at the doctor's or on morning television. It all merges into one messy lump of playdough. You know when all the colours squish together because the kids refuse to keep them separate? It is impossible to get those colours back. It's a sort of grey-purple-brown now, and no one wants to touch it.

Like the playdough, chuck that guilt away. Have a look at all the fresh new colours, play with them for a bit, roll them around and see which ones stick. Guilt is like that: some is founded, some is rubbish, some is useful. Pick through it and then chuck most of it away.

Here is a non-definitive list of ridiculous – though very real! – things that the peas have felt guilty about! Feel free to tick them off, too.

- bottle-feeding vs breastfeeding (nipple confusion, friends!)
- cloth vs disposable nappies (please add in guilt about climate change here too)

- organic, homemade baby food vs store-bought jar convenience
- day care vs being minded at home by a parent or family member
- attending a music session with toddler vs a walk to the park via a coffee shop
- working mum vs non-working mum vs working-part-time mum
- iPad vs only wooden toys in this house please!
- school committee parent vs drop-and-run mum
- Pilates mum vs 'let's-do-an-extra-lap-of-Westfield-and-call-it-exercise' mum
- homemade vs takeaway food
- store-bought eggs vs having your own chooks
- Aldi vs local artisan grocery stores
- homemade sourdough bread vs Wonder White High Fibre
- late-night cupcakes for birthday party vs Woolies mudcake decorated with Maltesers
- medication vs no medication
- intensive therapy vs once-a-week therapy
- private school vs public school
- mainstream school vs specialist school
- only child vs half a soccer team
- dressing twins in matching clothes vs 'why would you want clone children'
- homework vs fuck homework, we need down time in this family
- religion vs no religion
- names with vowels vs names with no vowels
- school holiday medication breaks vs no medication breaks
- divorce vs staying unhappily married
- long day care vs family day care

- birthday party at home vs birthday party at the play centre
- Barbie dolls vs dolls with a realistic body shape
- wine on a school night vs calming peppermint tea
- ethically sourced kids' clothes vs cheap clothes from Kmart
- letting your kids get their ears pierced vs 'God, no – what are you, a sadist?'
- surgery vs no surgery
- public vs private hospitals
- public vs private surgeons
- pets vs no pets
- Diet Coke vs Coke Zero.

Kate remembers

Guilt robs you of joy and laughter, two things you need the most in life. Guilt can dull happy moments and makes you constantly wonder 'What if?' Well, I say to that, what if I didn't bloody feel guilty all the time? And you know what? Mostly it works. I mean, I am no super human – I have emotions that I cannot control all the time. I feel guilty writing this as I am spending school holiday time (during a pandemic lockdown, mind you), writing a book instead of doing educational puzzles and games with Buzz and Woody. I feel guilty for being sad that I can't get a manicure right now. People are sick, my business is under stress and yet here I am thinking about my bloody fingernails! Guilt is always around, friends. It's just a 'Hey, Siri!'-level shout away! But I'm getting better at being able to unpack that guilt, work out where it's coming from and throw it away if I need to. If it is something out of my control, I handball it either to the 'universe' or a teacher or doctor or someone who can help me. Lying awake at night makes worrying about things I can't change worse, not better!

I feel guilt as a woman who didn't pursue a career early enough, guilt that I have given my children very different parenting styles as I grew and learnt and changed. Guilt that I don't hold the same religious beliefs as some of the people I love the most. Guilt that I don't give my friends enough of my time, even after they have supported me so much in life. Guilt for working, guilt for feeling impatient, guilt for sometimes speaking harshly to my kids. Guilt for hiding in my room watching *Normal People* instead of making muffins for my family. Guilt for not being a good-enough feminist role model for my kids. The list is endless.

Mostly I feel guilty that I have made wrong decisions about things that may affect my offspring for the rest of their lives. But guess what? I am not a doctor, teacher, lawyer or therapist; I am just a mediocre mum who is doing her best. And I have one solid belief that wins out over guilt every time and that is this: I love my children unconditionally. I might get stuff wrong, but they know I have their back. I always will, and love trumps everything! You know what else? I have amazing peafessionals in my life, whom I trust. Why should I feel guilty when I am following medical advice? Do I feel guilty because uninformed people are giving me an opinion on educating my kids, on whether or not they should take medications, or whether I should (God forbid) have a few nights away each year to remember who I am outside Mummy Kate? Nope. They can take that guilt and just gossip about it behind my sizeable arse. I don't need it.

Maybe these people are making these comments to make themselves feel better, to try to feel less of that guilt themselves by pointing out my failures. After all, we all have the guilt monster on our back, don't we? Why do we waste time on guilt? It takes up too much time – time better spent dancing, my friends!

I don't want to live a life with guilty feet and no rhythm. Scholarship says I only have one 'mum dance move' but I love that dance move anyway. There are enough things in life that come along and try to rob you of joy; I don't need guilt muscling in. Let's take a moment here, shall we? Join with me, pea friends and all the hands that are reading this book, as we look to the sky and say, 'Fuck off, guilt!' Then grab your dancing shoes, pop down to the podbar and let's dance, baby!

Mandy says

As a parent, I have grappled with guilt almost constantly. Mainly to do with my body being unable to keep my babies inside until term. That was a doozy. I suppose the feelings aren't as intense as they used to be, though, so that's something.

I often feel guilty about school. Did I choose the right one? Am I doing a good enough job navigating the ones they are at? Are they the best choices? Should I be sending them to private schools and eating fewer avocados?

I think I also felt the need to not 'be that pea': the mum constantly up at the school, demanding this and demanding that. I didn't want to be labelled that way and I was convinced that if I was polite, then the teachers would respect me when I did come to them. Mostly this is still true and I think there is room for this kind of approach. I also think, in the early years of school, I was so tired − and, with a new baby, distracted − and ultimately just relieved that the twins were at school, that I didn't step in enough. I have a lot of guilt about that: sending them into the firing line of school every day and often not stepping in to advocate for them. I mean, they had enough diagnoses to warrant me being at the school every day, but I wasn't. Ironically, I had spent ten years working in early childhood and parenting, so I'm not sure why I didn't know how much I could go in to bat for them. I had certainly been around families who did. Hindsight is something.

I feel guilty I couldn't go back to work sooner after having children to provide an income that would have helped my family. Even now, I am so proud of my business and the fact that the money I bring in each week is generated by me, my reputation and my pride in my work – but I still feel guilty that I haven't pushed my work to the absolute max.

I feel guilty that I haven't done my best with NDIS. That I have support coordination because I just don't have it in me to do it alone, that I have someone managing the finance (although that guilt is not that bad), that I haven't fought tooth and nail for everything. I feel guilty for having therapy fatigue, and sometimes just giving up and not doing it.

I feel guilty for leaving the church, for observing others who have managed to keep their faith and navigate lives far trickier than mine. For upsetting my family, whose faith is very important to them, to my friends who also can't share that part of their lives with me anymore. But not attending meetings for hours on end each week, *that* I don't feel guilty about. That part is so freeing.

I do feel guilty for the times that I haven't provided the best food for my family, and I have said, once again, 'Tonight it's a freezer dinner' – to which they have always cheered. Food isn't my thing. I bake and cook from scratch, but I admit to cooking to get the job done, as opposed to enjoying it. The chore of weekly food shopping on a budget has always been a drain.

The guilt I haven't felt, though, is not being there for my family. Because I have. I have been at nearly every appointment, every surgery, every rehab appointment; I have cooked and cleaned for years. Now I have a cleaner to help, my beautiful friend Kim, and I one hundred per cent do not feel guilty about that. I hug her each week when she comes to my front door (although this practice ceased in around March 2020 – thanks, coronavirus!).

I have asked her, 'Do your other clients hug you when you arrive?' and she said, 'No.'

I went back to seeing a psychologist in the severe lockdown in Melbourne in 2020. Home learning, isolation, fear, curfews, exercise limits and trying to stay upbeat for my daughters got to me. I took myself off to hospital after about four weeks of chest pain. I couldn't physically get to a GP, so I went to Emergency. I told them, 'I know it's anxiety, but I just need you to check my heart.' Which they did. It was fine.

I confess: the roast dinner in a bed in Emergency had tears rolling down my face – someone was cooking a meal for me. It was an expensive check of my heart, and a night of 'rest' in Emergency, but I was so desperate. Off I went to talk to the psychologist about my beating heart and she saw me every week. She said something I had never heard before: 'You are parenting from a place of guilt.' I was stunned, and then not stunned, as I have been guilty since they were born prematurely. Of course this is my narrative, and I need to work on it.

I don't feel guilty for taking time out, for being in a book club, for joining a choir and travelling for competitions, for the years I went to the gym, for when I started a podcast, for doing a live show. And I wrote a freakin' book!

4

An extended faith crisis

There is nothing designed to make you feel more guilty than religion.

So what is religion? Let's see what it says when you Google it, shall we?

> Complete trust or confidence in someone or something. Strong belief in the doctrines of a religion based on spiritual conviction rather than proof.

The 2016 Census of Population and Housing found that three-fifths of the Australian population (61 per cent, or 14 million people) are affiliated with a religion or spiritual belief. Christianity is still the dominant religion in Australia, with 12 million people, and 86 per cent of religious Australians, identifying as Christians.[3] It is strange because we don't think we live in a religious country, but there is at least one church in every suburb, plus temples, mosques, gathering halls ... call them what you will, but the truth is we are a country with a lot of religion and religions. There is religious instruction in many schools; there are theological colleges, and growing numbers of Christian schools. Religion is all around us, and for lots of us our formative years were spent perhaps going to Sunday school, or youth group, or hearing about a god at our grandparents' place. While a lot of Aussies don't identify as following a specific religion, most of us have had someone in our lives who does or has. You get to tick it on the census, on medical forms, on surveys. But do you ever take the time to really examine what you do or don't believe? Have you ever had your faith challenged? Have you ever lost faith in a religion? Have you radically changed your belief or belief structure in your life? Maybe you have never thought about it and don't care to. Maybe this chapter isn't for you, but hey, you might learn something, you might unlearn something. One thing for sure is that the question we most often get asked is something along the lines of, 'Why don't you go to church anymore? What do you believe?' Most people are very bloody interested in our church/religious experience.

It is a good question but, as with lots of good questions, there isn't a simple one-sentence answer. The truth is that we haven't worked it all out yet ourselves. But life within the church and life without the church have both been pivotal parts of our lives and our times as mothers.

Mandy says

Here's what I would tell 2004 Mandy about what's to come.

You probably won't believe that this will actually happen. Moving away from your church will hurt, and you might hurt people. But time will ease feelings, and you will realise that you might not need the church to be a person of faith in the world, and you can still be inclusive, kind, stand up for injustices and find stillness.

You won't sing for many, many years and that will be a huge loss. But then you will find a choir and sing beautiful harmonies again. You will have to work on your friendships, and your friends will miss you being at church, but they will stand by you, regardless. Then, in around 2017, you'll hear a whisper in your ear and a persistent feeling about beginning a revolution; creating a place where parents of twins, and higher-order multiples who live with disabilities and additional needs can belong. You have lived in no-woman's-land for thirteen years by then. You won't even know what a podcast is, but it's your perfect place. It's a ministry in a new way.

I spent my whole life in the church, and knew no different. I had ministers on either side of the family, both uncles; Mum and Dad loved belonging to our church and my sister and brother and I knew that church on Sundays was non-negotiable. As a child I loved it, and have such vivid and fond memories of standing and singing next to my parents. We would always sit in the same-ish spot each week. It's funny how people have a very strong connection to their spot in the church. We would laugh about how if you sat in old so-and-so's spot, she would go up to you and tell you to move.

I also remember church dinners, where you got an ice-cream scoop of mashed potato and pumpkin alongside your meat and three veg, and I loved being a part of church musicals (Psalty the Singing Songbook comes to mind!). We were assigned parts and then we learnt the songs and attended rehearsals with kids of all ages. Dad helped make costumes.

Being a good companion (or a 'goodie') was also a big deal in the Church of Christ faith and I made my pledge: 'As a good companion I promise to do my utmost, to cherish health, seek truth, know God and serve others.' I got my badge and I faithfully did cooking, craft and made hospital gifts each week. Mum had been a goodie (I always wondered where the bad companions were and if they were called baddies). I was a teenager of the Hillsong revolution. I sang all the songs, had the CDs and went to the conferences. I loved the music and the harmonies and power of collective singing. I prided myself on being a worship leader in my church, organising services and teams, and spending all day on Sundays at church. I was juggling shift work and rosters and spent many a time on the stage feeling what Christians explain as the Holy Spirit fill my body and the church.

One of my most embarrassing memories was when I emailed the senior minister to ask him if he could please move me on the monthly roster because each time I was on I was premenstrual. Gasp, but I knew I had to do it because I was so lethargic and I had migraine headaches. I never got a reply, but I was swiftly moved to another weekend and that makes me laugh to remember it.

The congregation was always so encouraging; people didn't mind when I forgot words or cried when talking about the realities of life. It was a precious time but I had to give it up when I was pregnant with twins; have you ever tried to sing while growing two babies?

I gave birth to the twins at twenty-eight years of age. I went back to church as soon as they were home and we could manage getting out of the house, but it was like going somewhere completely different. I was completely different. The church was being renovated so I barely recognised the place, plus my life changed drastically, not only with the babies but we had also moved house and suburb.

It might be different now, but at that time the church had a room called the 'cry room' and this is where women (and sometimes men) and babies and toddlers were given the option to sit during a service, listening in through crackly audio and feeling extremely apart from the rest of the church. The cry room had existed when I was a child, but that version of it had been big and light and airy and was just off the chapel. The cry room in the church I attended as an adult was up the back of the church, separated from the rest of the space by glass windows, and was dark and not very inviting. The sound system crackled and people walked in and out. There was not a chance in heck that I was going to be able to breastfeed twins in that room while I gazed at my old life from outside the glass windows. Cry room for babies indeed, but who was actually crying?

It's a funny room, because you don't really care about it until you're asked to use it, hence the fact that they are usually awful. Imagine organising two babies to be fed, nappies changed, dressed, yourself dressed, breastpads on, stop to change a dirty nappy or two, pack a bag with double everything, get in the car, drive for twenty minutes, get out of the car, unpack the pram, two babies, walk in the door, and head to the dark room with the glass windows and sit in there. I would sit and talk to the other women, while jiggling babies, changing nappies on the floor, trying to keep them quiet, sing a few lines of a song I used to sing from the stage, miss the entire sermon because I was distracted and couldn't hear a thing anyway, and then make all the post-service small talk, bundle the babies back in the car, cry because I was so tired and go home. And then repeat the next week. Many women have done this before me and after me, and I admire them for that. I just found it stressful.

Then came diagnosis time. I can't even remember how or where or when I ventured back to church after that intense sad period. Some members of the church really loved us and tried their hardest to support us, with meals and gifts and even painting our babies' room from the eye-piercing hot pink it had been, but not one of them could change the fact that our babies had a brain injury.

Some things they said just stabbed my heart. Nothing made any sense. It was like they were speaking a foreign language. I think then we just floated away. I remember praying to God (begging, really) and hearing the words, 'You don't have to go to church, Mandy, just be like me in the world.' Remembering I have the spiritual gift of discernment (I took the test, you know) I decided that I would follow that voice and try my best to do that. In the podcast I joke about the gift of discernment meaning that I know when I meet people if they are a dickhead (that's not the technical term) or not.

I can't explain why, then, for the next few years, every attempt to re-engage with church – trying to enter the buildings or even just driving past – was an extreme trigger for me. I had panic attacks just thinking about going there, seeing people, answering questions, deflecting pity, having to face pitying head tilt after pitying head tilt that accompanied the question, 'How are the girls?'

What could I say? 'They still have CP [cerebral palsy], we are still up to our eyeballs in appointments, I still cry every day. The only difference is that instead of being tired because of my baby twins, I'm tired because of my toddler twins.'

Lots of my friends had babies at this time and were taking part in the community and the women's groups that the church was offering. I was acutely aware that I was missing out, but the narrative in my head was strong: 'I can't go and sit with women whose kids haven't sat in doctors' waiting rooms, and endured endless therapy, MRIs, scans, surgeries, etc. – even though some of them are my oldest friends and I know they want me there.' The thought of sharing in a group, or pretending to pray felt impossible and inauthentic. I realised that if I did go, I would probably cry the whole way home, that's how different I felt. In order to protect myself from that, I just didn't go.

When I did try to go to church again, the twins were around three years old. I dressed them as nicely as I could and sat up the back of the church. People welcomed me back like a prodigal daughter. For the twelve months that I attended church regularly during this period, they did try to make an effort but it was no use. I was so anxious. I tried to get the twins into Sunday school, but panicked that the fifteen-year-old girls looking after them would never understand how precious and vulnerable they were. I couldn't sing the words of the songs, because I just didn't know what they meant anymore. I was shocked at the pictures of Jesus on the cross in their drawings and vowed never to take my girls to church at Easter time ever again. My ghost stared down at me from the stage; the Mandy that might have been and used to be was throbbing in my head constantly. I stared at families and I couldn't relate to what I saw. I began to understand why people who didn't fit the mould either stayed away from churches, or found their small circles of people within their churches who were like them. Single people, divorced people, widowers, people who wanted children but couldn't have them, LGBTQI people, people with lots of children, disabled people – it was like a torch was on their heads. How on earth did they believe in God, give so much of their time to the church, and not feel what I was feeling?

I remember a time towards the beginning of the year, when all the children who were starting school got to go up on the stage and everyone would pray for them. This was a standard ritual and a lovely tradition. My girls were a year younger than these kids, so they stayed with me, but I sat there looking at all the precious children, shaking my head inconspicuously and saying to myself, 'There is not one child even with glasses on that stage.'

Every child had white skin, beautiful clothes and matching shoes, and their parents were so proud. They were rushing around, setting the children up on the stage before sitting back down to hold their spouse's hand and praise God for the health of their beautiful child. That's when I felt the panic start to take over, thinking, 'Well if I stick it out, imagine next year. I get my two up there, they might be overwhelmed. What if the microphone or speaker is too loud for them? What if they get pushed over in all the rush? I can't do it to them. What am I doing here?'

I think this is when I was really beginning to understand that I needed to build a life of inclusion for my children so that they could grow up in a world full of people of all abilities, from all walks of life. I was searching for children like mine, families like mine, wherever we went. I am that mum who sees a child with AFOs and I go up to their mum and talk to them, much to my girls' embarrassment but I can't help it. And once we talk AFOs and shoes and socks, we are basically BFFs.

The painful process of withdrawing from the church began a second time, and would become permanent. I had to learn how to introduce myself when I met Christians in the world. I could always recognise them from their language, and I didn't know what to say to them anymore. 'Hi, I'm Mandy. I used to be a Christian, like, big time, and now I don't know what I am. I understand your lingo and please can we be friends, but no I won't pray for you. I have no idea who I am any more.' I came up with line 'I am in an extended faith crisis'.

This helped in a few ways. It gave hope to the Christians that I might yet find my way back (and I think I wanted this too for a long time), it shocked the hardcores into staying away (literally, I would see them backing away as I said it), but, best of all, I would hear the words 'me too' and then I immediately had new friends.

I met some lifelong friends this way – my friend Karen and also Marg, who was the chaplain at the girls' primary school. Marg could handle me; she laughed and cried with me, and, at a time of feeling so disconnected from the church, she was an anchor. She was our minister. She was particularly helpful the morning we discovered three stillborn guinea pigs and had to hold a funeral and burial all by 8.27 am. I managed to coax everyone into school and they went straight in to see Marg, whom I knew would care for them beautifully.

Being blunt and talking about my faith crisis became a funny little game with myself to find my people, and it eventually led me to Kate! We would sit in the car after a dinner out with the twin mums and talk about leaving our churches – what we missed, how our friendships had changed, how people didn't know how to talk to us any more or deal with our brashness, or our pain, or our sheer fatigue.

As time passed, it became less painful. It was still a bit of a wrench to observe all my friends living life together and to know I wasn't part of it, but my friends remained my friends and I am very thankful to them for that. They listened to the new Mandy, swearing and angry and upset and blaspheming (although they still recoiled when I did). I could see it in their faces and they stopped using words like 'blessed' or saying that God had answered their prayers in front of me. I'm certain that when I wasn't around, their Christianese was still flowing, but I knew and they knew that it was a language I simply did not speak anymore.

I knew it was sad for my mum and dad, and for that hurt I was sorry. They love their church and are very sad their granddaughters have not been brought up in it. Mum used to implore me, 'Mandy, the church will support and accept them.' But I couldn't quite share her certainty about this.

Once the girls were teenagers, I tried again to join a local church. I had reached a point where I was unsure how to navigate the girls' teenage years without the kind of support and fellowship a church can offer and that I had experienced as a teen. I could tell this local church had good bones. There were all sorts of people attending: it fitted the criteria of inclusion that I could see. I knew quite a lot of people there already, and no one put any pressure on me. They accepted us, although I did feel like the mysterious mother with the three girls who were uninitiated. We sat in the pews and my girls would say things like, 'What is that bath? What is that drink?' at the tops of their voices. I would run away as soon as the service was over to dodge the families who were all standing together.

The girls and I were of course accepted there, just like Mum had said they would be, but I could see that for Molly and her intellectual disability it was probably not going to work. Was I introducing her to a life of standing on the sidelines again? It wasn't for the lack of trying by people; that was never the case. Once Molly said she didn't want to attend, I accepted that and didn't push her. I am extremely conscious of listening to her telling me when she is not comfortable, as that will be a skill she will need for the rest of her life. I am actively teaching that.

The magic about this place, though, was that it led us to Amy. Amy is a gorgeous woman in her early twenties and she was a youth group leader. She went out of her way to talk to Molly and make her feel welcome, and they got on very well. At that time, we had our first NDIS plan and we were given hours to use to employ a support worker, basically a person who can help Molly access the community as a teenager would like to do. Amy was studying youth work and so I approached her and asked her if she would consider working with Molly and effectively our entire family. It has been absolutely wonderful to have Amy as a part of our family support network. She has been with us through surgeries, and Molly escaping from the house and running down the road after school. Amy has picked up Molly and driven her to school, bought frozen Cokes at the drive-through, attended a camp with Molly twice (for four *looong* nights) and, most importantly, she has been with us during the pandemic. Amy took over Molly's home learning and provided another pair of trained eyes to observe how my girls were coping. She was flexible, fun and firm, and I am so thankful we found her. Eight months of online learning and lockdown here in Melbourne and I categorically can say that the only way we made it out of there was with Amy's help. She observed our family, warts and all; she saw me in all my glory; she was kind and supportive and did everything she could at a horrendous time in her life too, to support us.

Singing has always been a huge part of my life. Singing harmonies in church with my friend Matt and recording music together was so incredibly special and formed a huge part of my identity. But when I went back to church, I could not sing anymore. The sound just would not come out. I was devastated about it. Singing was so closely connected to my heart and when I was in pain, I lost my voice. This was one of the biggest losses I experienced while I tried to stay in church. If I tried to sing, I would cry instead, so if I didn't go to church at all, then I wouldn't cry, thus protecting myself.

A few years ago, my friend Kym and I were at home searching for a local choir to join, as I thought if I could sing again in a space that wasn't attached to faith, maybe that was a way forward. We found Vocal Vibes, a local women's barbershop a cappella chorus. They were part of the Sweet Adeline's International movement and we were equal parts in love and overwhelmed at joining.

After some time getting to know the specific parts (I am a baritone) we were welcomed into the chorus. Kym and I held hands with our director Lorraine and we were 'sung in' (the term they use for initiation). The chorus stood in a circle, and sung in a four-part harmony while she gently moved us around to watch every woman singing to us. Boy, did the tears stream down my face at the sight of multiple generations of women singing harmonies to me.

I belonged to Vocal Vibes for five years, competed in three national competitions and made lifelong friendships. (I also couldn't believe that we didn't pray at the end of the night!) My voice came back, and it was an enormous part of my healing.

How do I feel now about my faith? I don't know. I don't want to give up on it. Maybe it's just the going-to-church part that I find tricky. I think now, after lockdowns, the church is probably at a really big crossroads itself. People are realising that giving so much time and energy to a place is a big deal, and the idea of the bricks-and-mortar church isn't what it used to be. I try to find all the parts of my old faith and put them into my life, but I know I fail them daily, especially as a daughter, a wife, a mother, a friend, a sister. I listen to faith podcasts and deconstruction podcasts; I love the Facebook group Raising Children Unfundamentalist. I've read Rachel Held Evans's book *Searching for Sunday*. I try to listen to that whisper in my ear that I always believed was God and pay attention to it. I tend to look to the feminine, use words like spirituality. I try to attune myself to loving people in the best way I can.

It is also not lost on me that Kate and I speaking the truth with love into our community through *Too Peas* has hit a nerve, and if it is the hand of God that has done this, then how wonderful. I am thankful, and so proud that we are able to be voices for so many women who would otherwise be incredibly lonely. I think that God said, 'You could be singing on a stage in my name to 300 people a week, or you can speak to more than one million people this way. Go for it, ladies.'

I will do anything that supports my girls in exploring faith and church, and I will encourage and show and teach them that faith in my extended family has been extremely important and special. It's their choice.

I am pretty sure God is a pea – in fact, the leader of the peas – and I can't wait for the end of my life, when I sit wherever I end up and we can have a great old laugh about my life and all the stages of my faith, faith crisis and ultimately peace in my own understanding.

Kate says

If I could turn back time, what would I say to 2004 Kate? I would tell her this: 'Thou shalt not lie ... this remains true, and you will stop lying to yourself and in that moment be more honest than you have been for years.' Phew, this is a big topic! It's one I have avoided talking about for the last fifteen or sixteen years of my life, but it is actually one of the biggest things about me and defines me in a lot of ways. I can (only just) remember my life pre-religion; I was five when my mum joined 'the church' and nine when my dad did. After that, I probably only missed two or three weekends of church till I was thirty-two years old. The specific brand of Christianity that my parents felt held the truth came with a very tight-knit community, and our religion influenced everything I did. We had our own schools and colleges and after that, if you wanted to, you could work for various arms of the church, which most of my friends did. And nearly all of them went through the church school system. Rightly or wrongly, all my friends were from church. I don't mean some: I mean *all*.

Growing up in a church can be really fun. There are loads of people to be friends with, constant organised activities, a little bit of brainwashing and lots of volunteer work. There are some real advantages to church life – you learn to think about other people, to 'count your blessings', to share your money, you often get to learn a musical instrument and you learn how to do public speaking. Many people I love deeply love the church. I know organised religions have done some pretty shit things in the name of God and I won't defend any of them, but religion has given us some cool societal structures too. I would never hate a belief system; I love that we live in a country that has a diversity of beliefs; I love that I can think differently from someone and still be their friend – I didn't always think like that.

It never entered my thinking that I might one day 'leave the church'; I just loved it and lived it. True, parts of it were judgemental and as a young wife and mother, I felt a lot of pressure to be a 'good housewife and mum' (gee, 2004 Kate is very different from me now!). But leaving is not something you do on a whim. It's like changing who you barrack for in the footy, but way more intense.

But leaving is what I did. So how did I get to that point? It was strangely quick and profound; it happened in the shower, and it was definitely a result of being pregnant with the twins.

I had twin-to-twin transfusion syndrome (TTTS) with the boys and hence had a lot of scans once we were 'viable' (don't even get me started about how much I hate that word). We had to have three scans a week, which amounted to something like forty scans all up. I built up quite the relationship with the doctor who did the scans. He had a lovely nature, and Buzz even has his name as his middle name. I felt calm with him, and was lucky that my obstetrician sent me to him for that all-important second opinion after we received the initial advice to terminate. He had lovely rooms in a big old house in the very leafy suburbs of Melbourne, but some days he worked at Monash Medical Centre and, because I needed oh-so-many scans, I also saw him there. This was a hospital, an amazing hospital, but a hospital all the same – more women in the waiting room, more high-risk babies being monitored, more stress all round.

After one of these scans at Monash, I came home to cry in the shower (shower cries, by the way, are the best!). When I finished crying I started talking to God about my twin baby boys. And all of a sudden, I couldn't make sense of a God who would maybe answer my prayers and 'heal' my babies only because I asked Him. What about those other frightened mothers in the waiting room at the hospital? Would God not heal their babies because they didn't ask? In the Bible it says, 'Ask and it shall be given to you' (Matthew 7:7. I still remember Bible stuff; I am pretty fab at a trivia night, just saying!). But what if you don't ask? Will it not be given? Does God not want to help all the babies?

Right there, with the shower water flowing over my big twin belly, I realised I could not believe in a God like that, who will only offer help if we ask. If you are my friend, you should not have to ask for my time because I enjoy giving it to you. And you definitely don't need to beg me to help you when you are sick, or really need help.

This was the moment when the house of cards that was most of my life came crashing down, the moment in which I realised I didn't believe what everyone I loved believed. Add to that a very high-risk pregnancy, and three other children ... life was intense, friends! I had all the head miles! But even so, I never went back to church. Such an easy sentence to type, such a hard sentence to live.

All my friends were there, in that church world, and that is where they stayed. Imagine moving overseas, to a country where you don't speak the language and the religion is foreign to you ... that is pretty much what leaving a religion is like. Sounds a bit dramatic (how dare you suggest I am dramatic), but it is true! I didn't really have friends outside the church: I had a couple of 'coffee friends' from the kids' school, but no bosom buddies. I was going through the scariest thing I had experienced and walking away from what is undoubtedly an amazing support structure. I will say, though, that the church did cook for me three nights a week for three months after the twins were born! This was pre-Uber Eats, so I don't know how we would have survived without that food. I will be forever grateful for that. (Side note: church food rosters are the best. They are, of course, organised by women, because – let's face it – it is the women of the church who make things happen. They may not be allowed to be ministers in that particular church, but they really know how to support a community.)

I grieved for church; I grieved when I realised that many church people only loved me while I was there. It is hard. Hard to start again in your thirties. Luckily for me my best friend Rachel left too. Together, we navigated this new life. I had never shopped on Sabbath before (Seventh-day Adventists believe in the biblical Sabbath on the seventh day, so Saturday not Sunday). I know that sounds like it isn't really much, but it is. I had never set foot in a shop on a Saturday! It was new, scary and liberating. But the downside, the huge landslide, is the people I love the most, my mum and dad: they were sad. I was hurting the people I loved; it's not easy. Believe me, it's actually shit. But it is also glorious; now, the only person to judge me was me. Even though my new life was a weird, lonely chaos, I didn't feel that I fell short any more, didn't have to be a super wife and housewife anymore! I felt free.

And then one day I met Mandy, who was going through such a similar isolating journey. We were able to share our funny church memories and our sadness at not belonging anymore. We could laugh and cry, reminisce about worship leadership, progressive dinners and welcoming foyers. I was hesitant to trust and let people into my life post-church, but she wormed her way in. Man, am I glad she did! It does say in the Bible, 'A man who has friends must show himself friendly' (Proverbs 18:24. They don't talk about women much in that book). Mandy was friendly, and that friendship gave me hope. I am now perhaps, as they say, blessed to have her in my life. What an awesome friend she is. She shares my love of some Christian songs. 'Shine, Jesus, Shine' – that is a tune!

I think back on 2004 Kate: she went to church each week; she was so different from me, but you know what? She made the decision that made me who I am today; I love her for her bravery. She walked away and gave me freedom. I am still amazed!

But what do you believe now, Kate? That is what everyone asks. I find it strange how much people want an answer to that. Truth is (and remember, 'thou shalt not lie') I don't know, but what I do know is that I am no longer defined by what I do or don't believe. I have five beautiful kids, raised mostly outside the church walls. They are awesome humans and I am proud to know them. Together we have learnt what it is to be kind, brave and full of empathy (we aren't perfect, by any means).

My mum – and I love her more than anything – loves her God and her church. My dad, who took a part of me when he died, also loved that God. Maybe if God is real he loves me despite what I do or don't believe. For so many reasons, I can't say much more about that – hey, a girl has to have her secrets! Right here, right now, all I can say is I believe we all have the right to believe what we want, but we don't have the right to be a dick to anyone! That's about it: I'm a firm believer in the 'Don't-be-a-dick' religion!

PART TWO

I LOVE YOU EXACTLY HOW YOU ARE

5

Just a healthy baby

When we released the *Too Peas* episode 'Just a healthy baby' in June 2019, we wanted to unpack the meaning behind that exact phrase. Almost all of us have heard or uttered a variation of it; it is one of those things we say without thinking. You know how it goes . . .

'*You're pregnant! Do you want a boy or a girl?*'

'*Oh, we don't mind. We just want a healthy baby.*'

When we were toying with the idea of a podcast, at the very beginning (which is, of course, a very good place to start), we had some topics that we were just busting to talk about – ideas, phrases and sayings that had eaten at us for years – and this was one of them. If you haven't said it or heard it we would be pretty shocked. Most people say it at some point, and it does come from a good place. For peas, however, it can mean something else.

Before we recorded the episode, the phrase grated on us on a good day and pissed us off on a bad day. Over the course of our discussion, we dug a little deeper and we found that it bothered us in so many ways we'd never really considered before – and clearly, it bothered the pea-verse as well. We had no idea how strongly it would resonate with our audience, but after the episode we received an outpouring from listeners who had similarly fraught experiences and reactions to that phrase.

We can break our discomfort down into two things. Firstly, the question that usually precedes it, that assumes you care about your baby's gender, and that further assumes that if you don't get what you're hoping for then you won't love your baby. Well, to that we say, who cares about gender! So far, we're with you. And secondly, the response that suggests that having a 'healthy' baby is the ultimate goal is hugely problematic.

Kate says

I watched the spectacular rise of gender-reveal parties with an almost detached curiosity. I don't understand why we are so obsessed by the gender and size and even potential IQ of our unborn babies. This might seem weird to some but I didn't find out the gender of any of my babies until they were born – except for Buzz and Woody, which was inevitable, really, with three scans a week. I also was very aware the only time these babies might have been alive was when they were nestled inside me and I wanted to know as much about them as I could.

I had no gender preference, which I know may be an easy thing to say when you already have a mixed bag at home. But even before I had the older three back in the '90s, I didn't give two hoots about gender-specific clothing or wallpaper in the nursery. I loved little Bonds wondersuits and those irresistibly tiny socks (who doesn't!), but the colour was never important. I suppose I was just such a raging feminist that I couldn't quite come at the whole girls-in-pink-boys-in-blue jam. And here's the thing: babies don't give a fuck what they wear. Sure, they like to be warm and clean but they have no colour preference for their clothing. Also – and lean in if you haven't had kids – once they get a bit older, your kids actually have preferences of their own. Some want to wear dress-ups every freaking day for about a year, some only want to wear two T-shirts and one pair of shorts on repeat, and some love pink and sparkles. Scholarship, for example, loved stripes and dots and patterns and would only wear those combos! So don't get too hung up on the colour of the clothes you think matches your child's gender!

If you are cool enough to not have a gender preference (I mean, it is not a choice!), the line that will fall out of your mouth will sound something like this, 'Oh Janice, we don't care, we just want a healthy baby.'

Look, don't get me wrong: no one wants anyone they love to be unwell, but to me, that isn't really what that phrase means. To me it means, 'I want a normal baby'; and to take it further in my mind it means, 'I don't want a child who isn't neurotypical. I don't want a child like yours.'

Do you know how hard that is to write? Why wouldn't you want a child like mine? My kids, all five of them, are bloody awesome. Besides, who decided that the 'best' people are those with a high IQ? Who reach milestones early? Does that make you easier to love? Does the word 'Mum' mean more from a child who has been in speech therapy for three years or the ten-month-old who says it early? What about the child who gets the hang of their communication device at seven and types 'Mum'?

There is nothing wrong with wishing that the life of the child you give birth to (or foster or adopt or step-parent or care for – we could even extend this to your niece or grandchild) won't be hard. There is nothing wrong with wishing that they will make friends, that they will love your cuddles, that they will find someone to love if they choose. There is nothing wrong with wishing that their life won't be a road full of shitty potholes, but some things don't go to plan. Some things don't happen in the way that you – or society – wish they would. And that's okay!

Maybe what we should wish for is this: that our kids have amazing support structures, have unconditional love to fall back on, have an awesome medical system, have schools that they adore, and that adore them. These are lovely things to wish for. Wishing your baby has a penis or is really good at problem-solving . . . ah, over-rated. Look at me: I have no penis (which is apparently important to a lot of parents-to-be) and I am pretty shit at problem-solving (also very important to some people) and I'm okay (mostly).

Disability

Did you know that one in five Australians has a disability? Also, while we're at it, do you know what a disability is?

> A disability is any condition that restricts a person's mental, sensory or mobility functions. It may be caused by accident, trauma, genetics or disease. A disability may be temporary or permanent, total or partial, lifelong or acquired, visible or invisible.[4]

That equates to more than 4.4 million people in Australia living with some form of disability. That is a lot of families – awesome families with amazing lives. They may be different to yours, but then is anyone's life the same? Get this: I am friends with people who have boxes of shoes at their front door and everyone's – everyone who lives in that house – stinky shoes have to go in the same box and live there till they get worn, all getting stinkier together. I would prefer that my kids don't grow up to do this, but I don't go around saying that to everyone, because people who love the stinky-shoe box love that stinky-shoe life!

Mandy says

I think once I started really sharing my feelings with other pea women, I realised that the words 'I just want a healthy baby' must have come up. Someone else must have said that they find the sentence hurtful as well, like a physical reaction or the feeling of being punched in the guts. I mean, I was convinced I was having boy–girl twins. Don't ask me why because, like Kate, I didn't find out my babies' genders during my pregnancies. I told myself, 'This is the only surprise left in this world.' Plus, my Myers-Briggs personality type is ESFP (Extraverted, Sensing, Feeling, Perceiving) and I am totally okay with that big P on the end. I wasn't fussed with setting up the nursery in certain colours or designs (which was lucky, because I didn't get to). Don't get me wrong, I love a beautiful room. I just didn't need to find out for those reasons. Although I will admit to loving the colour pink! I always have and I probably always will. I dressed the girls in it any chance I could get, mixed in with purple and sometimes aqua to differen-tiate. I think it was also about dressing them in colours that suited them (I have been a little obsessed with this for twenty years, ever since I had a professional colour consultant teach me about which colours suit me). I guess if I had had boy babies I would have dressed them to suit their eyes and hair as well.

When I gave birth to the twins and the doctor said, 'It's a girl and it's another girl,' I was so happy. Not because of their XX chromosomes, but because they were alive. I also remember calling my mum to tell her I was now the mother of two girls and she was shocked and then said, 'Oh Mandy, wait till they are teen-agers,' which is funny now, because I am right in the thick of it!

The babies' premature births meant that I didn't have a scrap of anything organised for them, but boy, were we showered with love in the form of gifts. You name it and we were gifted it (twice!

And matching!): beautiful clothes, embroidered singlets and bibs, beautiful dresses and cardigans, bonnets and beanies, handmade blankets and dolls, bracelets, and even the most precious clock to go on the nursery wall. I was so thankful. I kept every piece of clothing and dressed the girls in them whenever I knew we would see the person who gave them to us. Honestly, those presents helped me start to celebrate the girls while they were so far away from me in hospital.

I sit here writing knowing that many of my friends and family would have loved a certain gendered baby and I don't ever want to dismiss their feelings. I have joked with friends who have three sons that we should have swapped husbands. I know having my third daughter I just could not believe that I had given birth to a baby at term and I could hold her: no one was going to take her away from me, that was all I had dreamt about. What a moment of rejoicing and thankfulness and transformation in my birthing story. I knew that having a live baby – let alone two – in my arms was extraordinary. So many women (and men), long to have a baby, and infertility cruelly takes that away from them, so a little squirmy baby to hold is a gift to cherish.

When I was in groups and people said, 'I just want a healthy baby,' I would internally be screaming, 'It does not matter; you are just so lucky if you even get a baby in your arms!' But instead I would politely listen, trying not to let my face give away what my heart was pumping. I wasn't very good at that. Friends have told me that they often saw a change in my face and the trauma was there for all to see.

I don't think I made a point of asking people if they knew what they were having when they were pregnant, mainly because I knew the answer 'No, I just want a healthy baby' might be coming for me and I couldn't handle it.

I always celebrated a pregnant woman, even though every single time I would fear for them having a premature birth, but they didn't know that. I would hear 'healthy baby' and feel like a knife had pierced my heart, or a hammer had hit my stomach. I had never known the physical pain from people's words, but it is real. I smiled from my mouth, not my eyes, and thought, 'So you mean you don't want babies like mine, like my precious children who are the loves of my life, who have made me who I am, who are miracles, who show me what love is really all about.'

I usually tried to get away from the conversation or just stood there silently. Anyone who knows me knows that standing silently is not the real Mandy, so then it would probably get awkward and people back-pedalled or filled the space. It would take a while for my body to calm down and usually I would just go and kiss my girls as many times as I could, just to show them how much I loved them. It's like our *Hunger Games* Mockingjay symbol to other mums: kiss your children with disabilities and additional needs when you are hurting. You may notice it now that I have pointed it out. I notice it, and do it all the time. It's my instinct to protect my children and maybe it's just my heart reminding me that nothing is more important than them, so I bring them in, grab them and kiss and cuddle them. If people don't want babies like mine, then they do not know what they are missing: the deepest love, and a fierce protection and the making of me.

It might come from a harmless (and thoughtless) enough place, but this phrase – both of these phrases – can be toxic. We want people to unthink, unlearn, un-assume and pay more attention to what they are asking and how they are responding. And we want to celebrate that all babies, no matter what gender, are perfect little miracles we will cherish and nurture and love. We've done some community service here and created some responses to the question, 'Do you want a boy or a girl?'

- 'As we have no say over the gender of our baby, or even how that baby will want to live within that gender, we really haven't given it much thought. Which gender babies sleep through earliest, though? We might choose that one.'

- 'Mate, I don't give a flying fuck; I just wish it would stop giving me heartburn 24/7.'

- 'Look, to be honest, we have had a good think about this as parents, and decided we just don't want our offspring to be a dickhead.'

- 'Thanks for that awesome question, Prue; we have decided we just want a baby who makes us laugh.'

- 'Oh well, as we don't get a choice and my partner's sperm just does its own thing and swims to the egg without caring if it is XY, or XX chromosome, we decided just to be grateful it penetrated the egg and we got pregnant.'

- 'Well, to be honest, we are just hoping by the time this foetus gets to school, they will be accessible to all children, penis or vagina notwithstanding.'

- 'Look, we really wanted a puppy but I am allergic, so we are having a baby. Not as exciting as a puppy, so we don't really care about the gender, just hoping it likes walks in the pram.'

- 'Um, I don't know. What do you think we should have?'

- 'What? Do you get to choose? How does that work?'

- 'The thing is, we really want a baby that pops out knowing what the Special K breastfeeding lips are!'

- 'We don't care one bit what gender this baby is born with, but we are going to try with all we have got to make sure this baby is kind, empathetic and barracks for St Kilda.'

6

The NICU and the SCN

It is a truth universally acknowledged (our apologies to Jane Austen) that parents would do almost anything to protect their children from struggling or suffering. No newly pregnant mum dreams of NICU, or SCN, CPAP or intubation. Most pregnant women only think of midwives and obstetricians, not neonatologists and paediatricians. NICU–SCN is a world that most of you may never even glance at, but if you do happen to walk those hallowed halls, if you do have to leave your baby in the care of strangers for weeks on end, if your first experience of breastfeeding is via a breast pump and you are not allowed to cuddle your baby till a nurse can help you . . . well, you become a different person and your view of pregnancy, childbirth and the fragility of life will be forever altered.

Here's the thing: everyone gets something shit in life. No one sails through without an unexpected and often terrifying life event. Maybe it is a car crash or a cancer diagnosis, the death of a loved one, a late-night trip to the Emergency room with a burst appendix, broken limbs, a break-up of a relationship, or a miscarriage after a much-wanted pregnancy. These can have lasting effects on people. Maybe one day there will be enough space between events for them to become nothing more than a good story told after dinner, but nevertheless they change you. For some people (like our babies) this story starts with their very first minutes of life, their first breath, which they may literally struggle to take. This story impacts not just the mother who, if her baby has been admitted to NICU or SCN, will be traumatised, but the mother's partner, siblings of the baby, grandparents, close family and friends. While the babies going into NICU are often very tiny, their ripple effect is huge. And right then, their lives change, as do the lives of their parents.

At Monash Medical Centre, where Milly and Molly and Buzz and Woody were born, there are thirty-two NICU cots and thirty-two SCN cots, so when they are full (which they often are), that means there are sixty-four babies who are fighting for survival, being nursed and cared for, but not by their mums. NICU has its own unique soundscape, which, if you have experienced it, you will never forget. Machines beeping and whirring; parents and medical teams talking in hushed tones; hands being constantly washed and sanitised; milk being expressed and placed in fridges. It is a special place, a place of tears, of loss and of hope. NICU and SCN meant that our babies survived. Without these spaces, we would not have taken them home. It is an integral part of who they are today. Even though they will never remember it, we will never forget it.

If you google how important bonding is when you have a newborn baby, there are pages of information at your fingertips. (If you are currently pregnant with a high-risk pregnancy we forbid you to google this. Google Nigella Lawson's Sweet and Salty Crunchy Nut Bars instead; it will have a much healthier outcome for you, we promise.) But if your baby (or babies) goes to the NICU, those precious newborn moments for both mother and child are completely ripped away from you. Your mother-hood story, while incredible, will be different, and you will feel alone and terrified. You will still bond with your baby, but it's not the way most mums do. You will have to touch your baby through a little window in a plastic box, but don't let anyone bloody tell you that little touch is not bonding. Have we ever felt a love so fierce? Never! True, we couldn't nurse our babies and sway them to sleep, but if babies can sense being loved, they bloody sensed it!

Infections come and go in places like NICU and SCN. Jaundice, little sunglasses, IVs in tiny arms; some babies are so unwell they are on the cusp of death every day. The sound of the machines: the constant reminder that your baby's life (or babies' lives) is in danger. The nurses nonchalantly giving them a shake when they forget to breathe. The beautiful names on the cribs, written by a nurse to show the world that these babies are loved. Butterflies on some cribs.

The butterfly is the symbol put on a crib to signify that the baby is a twin or triplet, part of a multiple birth. This initiative is so touching and necessary. Having twins or triplets next to each other in SCN is perhaps one of the most wonderful moments in a mummy's life; finally your babies are back together. Or for some families, never back together, as they take one twin home first and then make the trek back into hospital every day for weeks and months, while having one baby at home. The exhaustion is not comparable to anything.

The day you bring those babies home, either together or separately, is the most wonderful and frightening time. Getting on with your new life, with the traumas of the NICU and SCN sitting right by your side. The traumas of the NICU and SCN sit right on top of your babies: feeding traumas, touch traumas, pain, the loving of kangaroo care (holding your baby under your shirt, skin to skin), and then the fear of sickness every single day.

There is another place many people don't know exists: the expressing room. A room just off to the side of the NICU; cold, stiff couches and chairs; a coffee table; a bench for a place to put your water bottle or if you are lucky maybe a cup of tea. Pumps to express with. Disinfectant to spray on the couches and chairs and then wipe down with paper towel. What an unexpected room of shared pain. It is a most profound space that actually needs to be treated like a palace. If the walls could talk, you probably wouldn't need our podcast. The tears, the grief, the fear, the smell of breast milk, the smell of soaked pads of blood from after birth. Women bravely trying to sit on an uncomfortable chair after tears and episiotomies and caesarean sections. Slowly putting their bodies down on the seat. Pulling open a T-shirt or jumper (not easy for premature mums; they haven't got the right clothing yet). Getting the pump and curling their toes as the machine brutally sucks on their breasts and nipples. *Shhh pump, shhh pump, shhh pump* goes the sound. Women try to smile and say hello to other women, some with milk streaming out of their breasts into bottles, others barely getting a drop. The women facing diagnosis, the women who have had babies die, and then are continuing to get milk out for their remaining twins and triplets: it is a sacred, sacred place.

Here in this room Mandy came up with a new phrase: 'Prem Prejudice'. It's a term she uses to explain how she felt talking to women who had babies earlier than she did. 'Oh, thirty-one weeks, that's good, you're lucky. Mine were twenty-four weeks; we've been here for six months.'

You refrain from speaking your thoughts; act grateful, be grateful. I am lucky. Our babies are lucky; they are alive. Don't be sad; you have no right, not here, not now. A new mother comes into the room: 'My baby was thirty-nine weeks; he wasn't breathing at birth. I don't know what's going to happen.' Once again, refrain: my babies are well. Don't say anything, don't tell anyone if you have good news. This isn't the good-news room.

Some babies are moved from the hospital where they were born, spending the beginning of their lives in a NICU in the city away from their mum in the country, or worse, in another state. That's a family that is not sitting in the expressing room sharing stories, or sitting in silence. Their story is instead a story of car trips and planes and doing whatever it takes to be by their babies' sides.

Lots of premmie babies move hospitals so they can be closer to the family home. Moving to a new hospital often also comes with new and fresh anxieties. Bringing babies from 'dirty hospitals' or big tertiary hospitals to smaller hospitals that may call themselves 'clean hospitals' feels pretty scary.

Family members have to learn the new rules: wear gowns, be polite *again*, meet new doctors. You have more hands on your breasts. There is no expressing room, but rather a chair behind a curtain. Getting your breasts out in a new place, without the privacy of a room, is really confronting for so many mums. But quickly you adapt and learn as, at three-hourly intervals, you use the new pump and follow the new way of disinfecting. A smaller hospital means fewer of your prem people. It can be torturous to be in a smaller place with so many wonderful stories happening every five minutes. You walk down the hallways without your babies, past rooms full of people laughing and celebrating. Balloons, flowers and presents fill those rooms you walk past as you go home to an empty house. You get out the pump as soon as you arrive home, dreaming of the day that you can bring your babies home. You can get those tiny little matching outfits on and the babies will be finally yours! Yours to dress, change and bath. Yours to hold, yours to feed on your own couch (soon to be covered in milk stains), as you watch your own TV, listen to your own music. This day never felt like it would come.

Mandy says

My experience of NICU and SCN as a first-time mummy was profound. Those seven weeks changed me forever. My eyes were opened to so many things: to the pain of childbirth, pregnancy and birth loss and trauma; to the new Mandy, the new woman who felt like the old Mandy would never be seen again; to the marriage that would never be the same again; to the family relationships that would never be the same again. All alongside the most amazing two little babies who forever changed me and made me a mummy. The love I have for them (and Miss Ten, my singleton) is like nothing I have ever felt before. The pride in every single move they make. Every noise (yes, even crying, because that took a long time to happen) wasn't taken for granted. Every smile, every breastfeed that 'went well', every bottle that was drained, every beautiful outfit I dressed them in that they actually fitted, and having our family home all together. I never took any of it for granted. One of the most unforgettable moments of being in NICU was when my friends Lisa and Darren came back from a (child-free) holiday to be by our sides after the girls were born. They too were NICU parents, and to have them rush home to be with us is a treasured memory and one I will never forget. We are forever bonded by this shared experience at the beginning of our parenting journeys, and it helped me enormously.

Another significant moment was when my beautiful friend Maryann, who is a healer, sat with me when I had mastitis for the umpteenth time from the expressing pump. I had a huge lump in my breast and was in excruciating pain and very unwell. She pulled up a chair, sat next to me and gently massaged my breast. We both laughed, but I was so relieved and the milk started to flow out into the bottle. I could cry remembering this moment, as a friend literally laid her hands on me and helped me.

The NICU–SCN had lasting effects on me, some of which I will talk about later in Chapter 12. I am so grateful the twins don't remember it, but I sure as hell know that their little bodies remembered it for a very long time and the fact that they had a traumatised mummy could not have been good for them, as best as I tried. I will always feel guilt and disappointment that I wasn't the mummy I thought I was going to be because trauma wove its tentacles into our lives every day.

The day we brought them home was one of the happiest days of my life. We played 'Home' by Michael Bublé on the CD player in the car (it was 2005) and took such incredible pride in bringing them into their home and starting the rest of our lives.

Kate says

If I could go back and talk to pre-NICU–SCN Kate I would tell her this: you are going to be fucking exhausted, but you will be okay at expressing milk, you will find time to cry, and holding twin babies in your arms is the greatest experience you will ever have; be grateful for that. The old gratitude attitude will help you a lot!

I knew from the day we had the first scan that if these little tiny baby boys were going to survive, their birth would have almost nothing to do with me. Sure, I would have to be there, but that was about it! Teams of doctors and nurses would fill a room; I would lie paralysed from the waist down and hope that they all knew what they were doing and that the boys having made it this far would continue to defy the odds.

Truth is, I never dreamt we would actually have them; the odds of survival were so low that I soaked up every pregnant moment I could, while I still had these two little boys inside me. I didn't like going out; I didn't like the questions I couldn't answer. How could I answer a stranger without crying? I wore sunglasses for months to cover my tear-induced bloodshot eyes. I couldn't allow myself to buy cots or prams, but I talked to my babies (talking a lot is a gift of mine), named them and loved them so much it hurt. Who knew someone telling you that your babies would not survive would increase your love for them in an unfathomable way? How I wanted these babies, Twin 1 and Twin 2 or Baby A and Baby B as they were called. I was desperate to stay pregnant long enough to get them to NICU.

Because Buzz and Woody were my fourth pregnancy (well, sixth if we count miscarriages), I went to the twelve-week scan on my own. I had been down this road before (but a word from the wise to the not-so-wise: don't do this; take your partner or a friend!). I had a weird feeling something wasn't right – or not the same as my other pregnancies, anyway. I felt that my usually wobbly mum-tum was too firm for a twelve-week gestation, and there was some nagging feeling something was different.

I am no psychic but turns out I was right. I remember my OB/GYN saying, 'I always trust that Mum instinct.' After the scan, I was told, 'Your babies have twin-to-twin transfusion syndrome. It's got a high mortality rate and we shouldn't see it this early. You seem like a sensible person, so I think you will agree you should terminate this week.' The reason was that it is unusual; babies don't present with TTTS at eleven weeks. I was informed, 'You might remain pregnant for a few more weeks, but that means you will have to give birth to babies without a heartbeat.' It was implied that this was much worse than having a termination.

Spoiler alert: we didn't end up taking that advice, and for some reason we beat the odds. My football team never achieves this (thanks, St Kilda), but Buzz and Woody did. They survived! It was without a doubt the most stressful thing I have been through. I had to have three scans a week, just to see if there were two little heartbeats, and after the magic twenty-four weeks' gestation to check if they needed to be born. Were they better out than in? This was the constant question for our most divine medical team. Before every scan I would have diarrhoea and vomit (sorry if that's TMI, but perhaps this isn't the book for you then). A very wise midwife said to me, 'Of course you do, Kate. You can lie to your body, but your body won't lie to you!' True that! So true!

We had a few close calls and near hospital admissions. When I was twenty-eight weeks and the boys were very nearly born, we were told one would go to Canberra and one to Hobart. Oh yeah, you can imagine how I took that news.

I remember the day the boys were born. The lovely doctor who did all our scans came to see us and he said, 'I am so glad they are born. Those babies caused me so much stress.' It wasn't just me stressing, Prue!

Our journey through NICU and SCN was relatively easy. Buzz and Woody did not need any emergency surgeries; they didn't develop infections; they just needed to meet the parole conditions of the nursery. Gain weight, maintain their temperatures and suck on a bottle: things taken for granted by me with my other babies. But I am profoundly aware we got through SCN and NICU 'lightly'.

I have friends who spent months and months in that very sacred ward; even my beautiful Mandy had a longer and tougher journey than me. I think about NICU–SCN every time I see a pregnant woman, every time I hear of someone expecting twins and whenever I drive past a maternity hospital. Occasionally when that good old middle-of-the-night insomnia comes rudely knocking, I think of the little babies all over the world, in NICU without their mums. You are not the same parent after you have spent time in NICU–SCN.

This change in my experience – although I suppose it was forewarned during my not-so-routine pregnancy – still took my breath away. While I was thrilled that my tiny baby boys were alive and it wasn't my body's job to keep nurturing them, my arms literally ached to hold them. My breasts were full of milk with no babies to hold and feed. Instead a machine rhythmically and clinically sucked the milk from me, to be stored in a fridge or freezer, reheated like a dinner lovingly cooked but not eaten, instead left to be microwaved long after the dinner party is over and consumed alone. Nothing felt right; I missed my big kids while I sat with my babies and I missed my babies when I was home.

Loneliness: that is what the NICU and SCN are to me, even though I had friends and family and lovely medical staff. It is so lonely sitting with your babies, when you want to be holding them, lonely when the babies are at different ends of the hospital. I felt wracked with guilt when I had to choose one baby to visit first. When we had the boys, Buzz was bigger (being the recipient twin), and he went straight to SCN. Woody was smaller and more fragile, and he went to NICU for a week till he finally made the journey down the long hospital corridor to be in his little beeping isolet beside the brother he had up until a week ago shared every moment of his life with. In fact, no one took me to see Woody; I am crying big fat tears as I remember the slow, painful shuffle I made down the very long halls to see him, only to have a NICU nurse say, 'Oh, we thought he didn't have a mum,' when I arrived.

What? You thought he *didn't have a mum*? I had just spent seven-and-a-half months stressing about him, and he had not been out of my thoughts since he was born, but I had had a catheter and an epidural and I couldn't get to him any earlier. And this is pre-smartphone, people. I didn't even have a picture of him. By the way, that is a Class A rectum comment. It may have been meant as a joke, but it came with judgement and wasn't funny. Fifteen years later it still makes me cry . . . be careful what you say, peafessionals.

Every NICU–SCN story is different and I can only speak for my own, but we probably all share the terror that every incoming phone call is from the hospital. If you were like me and awake at 2 am pumping milk 15 kilometres away from your babies, you probably rang the hospital, just to make sure that your babies were okay. I spoke to nurses who were kind and made you feel so at home, the ones who were loud and funny and broke up the monotony, or the ones you sadly remember the most: the ones with little care, who said hurtful things like, 'You should be glad your babies are in here. You got a preview. Most people have to wait for the movie to be released.' Or after spilling very-hard-to-come-by colostrum: 'Oh well, no use crying over spilt milk!' There will be rectum comments everywhere; really, if I could go back, I would tell myself to ignore them, but I know I would never be strong enough to speak up.

When you have kids who are not 'typical' you will get so many rectum comments. I wish I could tell you that one day they won't bother you, but they will, always. Some rectum comments, especially early on, cut deep; you are not at all ready to hear them, and are shocked that people say them. I wasn't ready for the SCN staff to be blasé. These people literally had the lives of my babies in their hands, so I would never call them out on what they said. I wanted to be the best mum, the best patient, and for them to really want to take care of my boys. I had to be on their team and, more importantly, they had to be on Team Buzz and Woody!

Like I said, we were lucky. Buzz and Woody 'fattened up' enough to almost fit into size 00000 clothes and after only five weeks in hospital they came home, bringing glorious, life-changing chaos with them. I got to walk out the doors of that hospital with two babies. Wheeling them out was like winning the lottery. I felt like no one had ever felt this way when coming home with their babies before. The doctor said to me, 'Just imagine they were born three days ago. Forget the moments of apnoea, the weight loss, the inability to stay warm; forget it all happened, imagine you never went into the nursery.' Yeah right, mate! That, while good advice, was impossible!

7

Diagnosis

First, let's get the official diagnosis of diagnosis:

The identification of the nature of an illness or other problem by examination of the symptoms.

Do you remember when you first realised COVID-19 was going to really affect you? I mean actually *you*, not some person on TV, or some blogger in France. It wasn't something happening overseas or interstate; it was everywhere. Your life was about to change in a lot of ways you had no control over. The spread of the coronavirus was the only news, and political media conferences were the most watched things on TV. People stopped working – stopped everything – to see what our prime minister or state premiers had to say. Every friend, partner, shop-owner and Uber driver spoke of nothing else. Would we get sick? Would we still have jobs? Would we be able to play sport? Go to the footy? Talk to a friend over a glass of wine? Go to a wedding, party or funeral? And the most terrifying: would someone we love die?

Perhaps you, like us, woke at night feeling terrified about what would be said at those press conferences the next day. Did you stockpile food? Were you afraid of losing a career you had fought hard for? Did you google and then google again? *How long will I be at home? How many people will get sick? Do we have enough ICU beds? Is my mum at risk? Will I get to visit family overseas? Will we get a vaccine? Why are the people not taking it seriously really annoying me?*

We wanted to know what our future was going to be like. We needed to know. People cried, baked, slept, bought copious amounts of toilet paper and felt simultaneously very alone.

You know what? That is sort of what life is like when you or someone you love gets a life-changing diagnosis. It's all you can think of. It wakes you at night. How will life look? Can anyone tell you? Dr Google sure gets a good bashing! You go through so many different stages: fear, counselling, education at a massive rate, tears (of course), and then one day acceptance and an entirely new way of looking at life. It isn't all bad. Lockdown was pretty awful, but there were some delightful moments, too. Remember how you worked out what mattered to you; your kids, your relationships? While some stress went up, other stress went down: bras became optional; mornings were no longer wholly consumed by the stress of getting the kids ready for school; we discovered some cool things about life we had for-gotten. Well, the new diagnosis way of life can be like that, but it takes a while to wade through.

The shit thing about diagnosis and human nature is our tendency to instantly launch ourselves into the worst-case scenario. What is that even? What is the worst case? No person is the same, no scenario is the same, so why do we immediately start to worry about how bad it will be? It's probably something to do with self-preservation and preparation, kind of like how, when you're running a marathon, you don't just turn up and start jogging, you spend time beforehand training (or so we have heard). This is a slightly different training regime, involving more doubts and wine, but you get the idea, yeah? I mention running a marathon because, although it's something you usually do in the company of others, you have to rely on yourself to get through it. Facing a diagnosis can be a little like this – sometimes you want to keep the news to yourself for a bit before you open up to everyone else. You have to be able to rely on yourself before you can allow others in. If you are going through this, we really recommend lovely pea mum Melanie Dimmitt's book *Special*. It is perfect!

You know what else will come out of diagnosis? You will find out who your real friends are. And the best bit? You will make new ones. One of the very best things about having twins was the new and unexpected friendships it gave us, and the same thing happened after diagnosis. We made new friends through support groups, people we met at the shops and immediately bonded with, secret Facebook groups – you name it.

A diagnosis can bring relief and validation and can open up your world, but to get to that part you do need to sift through fear and loneliness, and fight the worry that it might lead to your world closing off. As well as new friends, you will meet the most amazing doctors, occupational therapists, speech therapists, teacher's aides, teachers and sports coaches – awesome people, whom you might never have met otherwise. A diagnosis can throw you in the deep end, but we say far better to be in the deep end than spend your life wading around in the shallows.

Kate says

I think the most intense diagnosis time was during the pregnancy. During that time, my mind did head miles that reached beyond the moon and back. I lived in constant fear that my babies would not live. And then we beat the bloody odds. They are here, running up and down the hall as I write, so my journey and theirs is different from lots of families when they get an additional needs or disability diagnosis.

For me, the boys' diagnosis times have always been 'expected', and while some of them changed my life, they didn't change the boys' lives. They are who they are! So funny, so nimble, so unruffled about what other people think of them. All these years later I still look at them in awe. I cannot believe they are mine, and that they survived. I just love who they are and I wouldn't want to change anything about them (that's a lie; I do wish they peed straight). But I hate that the world doesn't celebrate diversity. That is, when I have felt sad or overwhelmed: when I think about hurdles or challenges they have faced and will face, just because they are who they are.

After a new diagnosis, I have always read and researched. *What does this mean? What does that mean? Can we change things, or should we accept this? Do we need another opinion? Are we happy?* I scroll through blogs and read books, some of which I throw across the floor and others I cherish. I allow myself a day or two to sit with the realities of the new diagnosis, then I get the fuck up, and I get on with it. I finally talk to my friends and my kids – people whose opinion I actually value.

Now, this is only my story. It's not yours and it's not right or wrong. The diagnosis doesn't change who we are; it just gives us lots of insights from years of research. I know it brings labels that are often shit, but that is only because people are ignorant or rude or uneducated, or don't listen to *Too Peas in a Podcast*! I can't fix that, but I can let everyone know how awesome and funny my twins are. Imagine laughing with your kids every day! Now, that is a life-changing diagnosis if we ever had one!

After diagnosis there is no 'magic wand', as the boys' paediatrician used to say to me. You don't walk into the paediatrician's office and come out with all the answers. The diagnosis, while making things less complicated at times, doesn't change day-to-day life.

You get to learn loads of new skills, though, because now that we have established what the new normal is, you have to work out how to move forward. I don't want to suggest that coping with a diagnosis is easy; life post-diagnosis is extremely difficult at times. All parenting is difficult, but this is a different difficult. I am not going to share all those stories, because, for one thing, why dwell on them, and, for another, lots of them are not mine to share. But I think I am so much better at working out what matters and what doesn't, when to back down and when to stand firm-ish (there is no solid line in our family). Diversity is a gift. It ain't easy sometimes, but who said life was easy?

I also want to take a moment to acknowledge our beautiful peas who have had a diagnosis for their pea shoot that is life shortening. My story is nothing like your story, but I just want to say: big, big love. Life is supremely unfair, and I wish with all my heart you had never had to live with those soul-crushing diagnoses. And I'd understand if you just threw this book across the floor.

Mandy says

If I could turn back time, I would tell 2005–6 Mandy, who was in the thick of diagnosis time, that everything will be okay. I am sure many people did say that to me at the time and I completely ignored them, so I'm not sure I would even listen to myself. I would also tell her:

The time of diagnosis will be a profound one and a reckoning within yourself, coming to terms with the prejudices that you carry as an able-bodied woman. You will need to confront that head-on, and quickly. Look out for all the women who come your way; they are going to shine the light for you. You will be very compliant with doctors and hospitals and therapists and teachers because you want what's best for your girls, but work on your boundaries. Have as much time to be a mum as possible – that's the most important part. Take up offers of respite (why didn't you?). Know that this isn't the first diagnosis. You will have two more life-changing ones to come and each one will knock you sideways for some time. 2021 Mandy, though, knows that shower-crying or on-the-bathroom-floor-crying with your daughters, listening to them pouring out their own heartache at feeling different from the world, is actually a sacred time in parenting that not all experience. Each time you go through this together, it gets a little easier.

Your love for your daughters is bigger and more powerful than any diagnosis. You will go through so many feelings (many in one day!) but your life and family will be incredibly rich with diversity and experiences and people. You will be so incredibly proud of all three of your daughters and each day you will feel fortunate to have them (even through a pandemic and homeschooling – yes, you are going to be a principal in 2020!). No words will define your beautiful girls, and the enormous change in your own self will be something to cherish. You can do this, Mandy! Keep going, get up off the floor, wipe your tears away and keep going. That's all you have to do.

8

F*ck you, milestones!

Wゝhat does the old dictionary say about milestones?

> **Milestone:** an important event in the development or history of something or in someone's life.

How often do you think about milestones? If you don't have kids, probably not that often. When was the last time you achieved one? Maybe it was moving out of home or getting your driver's licence, or getting married or perhaps finishing your apprenticeship. Well, my friend, the first two years of your life were jam-packed with milestones. You had no control over them, but your parents were certainly aware of them. Everyone around your parents probably commented or obsessed over them, and mothers' group members bragged about them (the first baby to sleep through the night pretty much is equal bragging rights with your child getting into the Olympics!). If you have been in new mums'/parents' group you bloody know what we mean!

Would you like to see some of the milestones that you had to reach? The milestones that everyone watched and ticked off in a little book your parents were given when you were born, the milestones most of us have no memory of completing? Let's have a quick glance at the first twelve months, shall we?

Disclaimer: we understand how crucial these milestones are to health professionals, but seeing as we are mere peafessionals, we say loudly and proudly *FUCK YOU, MILESTONES!*

Milestones[5]

At birth:

- holds hand in a fist; grasps a finger when placed in their hand
- lifts head and turns to the side when lying on stomach
- communicates vocally by crying
- can be startled by sudden noise
- watches mother/carer
- follows things over short distances with eyes
- responds to needs by crying and usually stops when picked up
- varies sleep patterns.

At six-to-eight weeks:

- follows an object by moving eyes and head
- raises head to a forty-five-degree angle when lying on stomach
- starts to move fist to mouth
- hits at objects with hands.

At three months:

- develops awareness of surrounding sounds
- recognises parents' voices and responds with coos and various patterns of pitch and cry
- displays more deliberate behaviour

- begins to repeat enjoyable chance movements; for example, thumb sucking
- shows a particular type of temperament; for example, placid or excitable
- may extend sleeping time beyond four hours
- longer waking times
- can be unsettled in late afternoon or early evening.

At four months:

- moves more deliberately as reflex movement decreases
- lifts head and chest by supporting weight on arms when lying on stomach
- increase in neck and head control
- may roll from stomach on to back
- clasps hands together and takes them to mouth
- attempts to pick up object using both hands
- laughs and babbles with increasing tone and intensity
- enjoys being read to and looking at picture books
- takes greater interest in surroundings
- tries to prolong interesting happenings discovered accidentally
- starting to develop wariness of strangers and parent separation anxiety
- sleeps less during the day
- may be ready to sleep in a cot
- seventy per cent of babies sleep through the night.

At six to eight months:

- accepts variety of foods with varying textures and flavours
- breast or formula feeding reduces as solids increase
- the child may start to feed themselves, under parental supervision

- usually has two to four teeth, lower central incisors
- progresses from sitting supported by arms to sitting alone
- pulls to standing position and takes steps with alternate feet when held
- moves by creeping, rolling or attempting to crawl
- claps hands. Transfers objects hand to hand.

At twelve months:

- eats most of the food the family eats (three to four meals a day)
- appetite decreasing
- uses fingers to eat and can hold a spoon but is not ready to self-feed
- can drink cow's milk
- weaned completely from the bottle
- average weight: 9 to 10 kg
- has six to eight teeth
- pulls to stand, walks forwards and sideways holding a hand
- may stand alone or walk alone
- uses thumb and forefinger to pick up small objects
- points with index finger
- builds a tower of two blocks and bangs two blocks together
- uses most sounds in the language
- says three recognisable words
- understands several words and simple commands
- reacts vocally to music
- searches for a hidden object
- shows great interest in surroundings
- shows sensitivity to approval and disapproval
- developing ability to trust
- settling into routine sleep and wake times, but may still wake at night

- has one to two daytime naps
- continues bedtime rituals, including stories.

That is a lot of things to accomplish in twelve months, isn't it? And as pea parents we are very, very aware of milestones. If your baby or babies were born prematurely then you are so aware that every milestone is late. You are constantly correcting back the age they were born, while everyone is watching, to see if the little boxes get ticked, and the milestones are met.

But here's the thing: lots of kids don't meet these milestones. Some children don't catch up or tick all the boxes. So how do you sit at a new mums' group and listen to all the milestone chatter? How do you join in? Where do you and your family fit?

The peas thought we might add some more entries to the milestones list (actually we prefer the term 'Smilestones'). These ones aren't age-dependent and we don't have to say 'fuck you' to them. Imagine if you got asked some of these questions:*

- maintained my temperature so the doctor said I could leave SCN
- slept in Dad's arms
- made Grandma smile
- went for the first ride in a pram (made Mum cry tears of joy)
- went up a size in clothes
- was able to stay at kinder by myself, without Mum or Nana
- made Mum laugh
- made Dad laugh

---

* As well as, not instead of, the other ones, of course. We do get how important they are! We don't like them, but hey, we don't like sit-ups either.

- made Grandad laugh
- made the paediatrician laugh
- had a therapy session with no response behaviours
- charmed everyone at the shops
- ate a new food
- ate an old food
- communicated that I loved my mum
- swore at exactly the right moment
- kissed my aunty
- cuddled my sister
- ate nuggets
- named all the *Thomas the Tank Engine* trains
- laughed
- had a therapy session with only six response behaviours
- skipped therapy and went to the beach.

Kate says

Ah, milestones. So necessary and so horrid! And they go on and on! Once the newborn milestones and the Maternal and Child Health milestones end, you move on to the bloody school reports. But after that, they do get less and less important, and I can assure you that one day they will be nothing but a memory. I have given birth to five babies and I don't remember any of their milestones, but I remember late-night feeds, tiny hands curling around my finger, Bonds wondersuits and first cuddles. I can't remember when they first ate solid food, or crawled or rolled over, but I still love and rate as the greatest Mum Smilestone every single time they say or demonstrate that they love me!

And let me tell you, as an adult, apart from asking how many glasses of wine I drink a week, there are not really any milestone questions asked of me. Unlike with my boys, the doctor is not impressed when I gain weight. Any achievements (like going for a walk every day) are milestones I set for myself.

I love the support team we have around us, the educators and health professionals who think that any progress whatsoever is an incredible achievement. They are my kind of people. You know those personal trainers who say, 'No matter how slow you go, you are still lapping the people on the couch'? Well, it's sort of like that, except we don't give a shit about lapping people. Coming first or last means nothing anymore. Perhaps our motto could be 'the only way is up', as long as we are happy to have dips along the way. Having these amazing, incredible boys in my life, when we were told they wouldn't make it, is still today worth more than any fucking milestone!

Mandy says

I had no idea the statement 'Fuck you, milestones' would resonate with our listeners. I just said it in an episode as I was expressing how little they meant to me and to my family and also how offensive they were at times. I had those blue books (which used to be yellow and are now green) from my babies' births, which doctors and nurses would write in. I had Mary Sheridan's *From Birth to Five Years* sitting on my shelf. I first had to adjust to having premature babies and then adjust again to the milestones that were not being met, or took a lot longer than Mary suggested they would.

The trickiness in twin mummying is the celebrating of one and the worrying about the other. I suspect this is universal in multiple-birth parenting, amplified in our stories. Cheering on the toddler who is walking, while cheering on the toddler who is learning to sit. Both in their own right equally as amazing and incredible. This is the unique situation of multiple-birth parents and perhaps one of the reasons I wanted to do the podcast. I noticed differences in my friends who had singletons with physical disabilities and it wasn't until they had another baby that they would go through some of the emotions that I was going through every day. Joy and worry sitting side by side.

The best part about having children who don't fit the mould is that I now know what to celebrate and what doesn't matter. As I write this, due to the NDIS and a new temperature-controlled tap, my daughter got herself into the shower for the first time in fifteen years. That made me cry. That deserves to go in the book that no one writes. That is a milestone that I want to scream on Facebook and, you know, I could, and people would say, 'Yay, go her,' or my least favourite: 'Hugs.'

I saved it for this book, so that you, the reader, can imagine what that feels like; such pride that the average person whose five-year-old can do that will never understand. More importantly, the pride my daughter feels, and that is the Smilestone that makes a mum's heart sing.

9

Surgery

Surgery: such a little word for such a world of pain. Not that the dictionary mentions that:

Surgery: a medical specialty that uses operative manual and instrumental techniques on a person to investigate or treat a pathological condition such as a disease or injury, to help improve bodily function or appearance to repair unwanted ruptured areas. The act of performing surgery may be called a surgical procedure or simply surgery.

There are so many scenarios around surgery that we at *Too Peas* are not qualified to even explain in the slightest. What we are certain of is that our pea families know more about surgery than most and they live with the dread of it, for some families every day. Every experience is different, and it's impossible to speak for everyone. For this chapter, we are handing the mic straight to Mandy.

Mandy says

Below is an account of what the lead-up to a typical leg surgery looks like for my daughters and me. It's a mishmash of the many surgeries they have had in their fifteen years. I must remind you, dear reader, that this is from my perspective. I'm thankful that my girls have different memories; they can tell them if they want, one day.

The years when we have had scheduled surgeries have been some of the most distressing years of my parenting journey. They have involved months of sleepless nights, fines from the police for not even noticing that I was speeding right past their marked car, not being able to concentrate or plan anything or read or join in on life. It's as if a huge chunk of the year disappears for me as I come to terms with what my daughters will endure and what I must do to protect, aid and help them thrive in their recovery.

It is the hardest thing in the world to hand your precious child or children – whether they are tiny, medium or large – over to a group of strangers in masks and gowns, in a hospital or clinic and try to be fine with it. It's the ultimate in the unnatural feelings of being a mummy. If you could swap and have the surgery for your child you would. You would endure the fasting, the gas, the IVs and the recovery if it meant not putting your child through any pain, discomfort, fear or anxiety.

The lead-up to surgery (if you are 'lucky' and it's not an emer-gency) can be particularly torturous for pea families. Meeting new doctors and specialists, waiting for letters to arrive containing the details of D-day, planning how the family will cope during the surgery. Depending on the type of surgery and the expected length of recovery and rehab, life can come to a complete halt. No holidays are planned. Family celebrations are put on hold.

Preparing for the surgery also means liaising with kinder or school – the time out of the classroom required, the work that needs to be completed while they are recovering. Teachers wanting to visit in hospital, little friends not understanding (and I don't blame them: it's a super-confusing time).

The surgery day is looming. The bags are being packed, the siblings are being allocated family members to stay with, or getting dropped at school with a quick explanation to the teacher of what's happening, your breastfeeding baby is going to stay at your mum's for a week. Maybe some new pyjamas are being bought (I always buy new PJs for my children and myself for hospital, anything to give you some dignity for the 7 am bedside meeting when ten doctors suddenly appear in the room). What PJs or clothes will be able to cater to the rehab? Is the iPad charged? Back in the olden days of the 2000s this part of my preparations involved ensuring that the portable DVD player was ready to go, and that none of the DVDs were scratched. Do we have the special teddies, dummies and food that our pea shoots will actually eat? We promise them nuggets as soon as they are up to eating, and that we will visit all the exciting attractions the children's hospital has to offer: the meerkats, the fish tank, the Starlight Room, the whatever-the-frickin'-room-you-want to make this time easier on you. You want Subway? Sure. You want ten Beanie Boos? Done. The spoiling can get out of control, but who cares? This is shit. This is hard. If you have some spare money, why not spoil your precious children, who already have a tough time in life?

The night before. We make them a nice dinner that we know they will eat, filling their bellies before they have to start fasting. Then they have a shower before bed, as it might be the last one for a long time. You watch them standing in the shower in their wholeness, look at their precious bodies and gulp down that huge cry you have in your throat knowing that this time tomorrow, they will not look the same. Scars are coming – new big scars that will change the landscape of their bodies forever. That's okay, you tell yourself, everyone has a scar somewhere. A funny story, a little incident. Try to tell yourself that this scar is going to be a reminder that the world tried to 'fix, enable, help'. You show your child all the scars you have on your body. 'Look, this one was when . . . Dad has this one because . . . And Grandpa has this one . . .'

Normalise, normalise, normalise.

The morning of. Say goodbye to the rest of the family, drive along the freeway and arrive in pre-admission. Butterflies in everyone's tummies, which are not helped by hunger from having to fast. Facebook Messenger is going berserk with well-meaning messages. Introduce yourself and your child, keep them calm, sit down, look at all the other pea families who are waiting. *What surgery are you having today? Do you have lots of bags, or are you in for day surgery?*

They go into a little room where they have their temperature taken (please don't have a fever, we can't cancel this), they are weighed and we chat about how we are all doing (fake it, fake it, Mummy, we are fine, this is fine).

Into the room with the beds, getting into a gown, pulling the curtain, lots of coaxing and encouraging and kisses and cuddles. Lying on the bed; where do we stand, can we sit, who's coming next?

Here come the doctors and the anaesthetists. Maybe some medication for the child or children to relax. Wheeling into theatre, only one parent from this point on, who will it be? In this situation you're 'lucky', if your twins are having surgery on the same day, you can have one each. In we go, into theatre, the lights, the staff, keeping my child calm. Look them in the eyes and tell them how proud you are of them, kisses, cuddles, try not to look too needy, try not to cry, be brave, it's for the best, please do your best, don't hurt them, *hurry up*. Chocolate-smelling anaesthetic mask, please (as if that is going to make it all better). Remember pink cast for one and purple for the other please? Coloured plaster makes all the difference. Do they have their special toy to cuddle? Bright lights, so many bright lights.

Your child at this point might be crying, fighting, staring, begging, pleading with you to make it stop, but then they get sleepy and their eyes roll into the back of their heads.

You leave and then immediately collapse; either on your own or in the arms of someone else. Once you regain composure, you walk away and put all thoughts of what they are doing to your precious child out of your head. Head to the cafe, maybe eat because you haven't been able to eat all morning, maybe all week. Drink Coke, message family, friends, gratefully receive distraction. Take every prayer, every good wish, even every 'hug' and keep being brave. Check your phone. Have they called? Has it been five hours yet? How on earth can someone operate on my child for five hours safely, surely this is not right?

Walk back up near recovery, sit in the waiting room, flip through magazines, check your phone, smile at other parents who are waiting for their child as well – some quiet, some loud, some friendly, some volatile. When is my child's UR* number coming up on the screen?

Finally, the number comes up. It doesn't feel like freaking Powerball, that's for sure, but it's still a relief. That's my child's number in recovery. Okay, still some time before we can run to see them, but don't run, pretend to be fine, pretend to be brave, be polite.

Finally, the nurse calls you and you pick up your bags, and follow her as swiftly as you can. You scan every bed to find your child, and then you see your precious person, who is still sleepy. The tears sting your eyes. If you are with a partner you both squeeze up to get your heads in the line of your child's eyes as soon as they wake.

---

* A UR (Unit Record) number is a unique identification number assigned to a patient while in hospital.

Nothing else matters in the world at this moment. This is the only place you want to be – except, of course, if your twin is now in surgery too, in which case you stay and recover with one and then run to recover with the other. Juggling, soothing, kissing, crying, relief, such relief, *it's over, the wait is over* we tell ourselves, knowing that the next few days, weeks, months will be just as hard, if not harder, both physically and emotionally. But this bit, the torturous bit that has haunted our dreams and our waking nightmares at 3 am for months on end is over. Relief, even if we are going to be 'resting' on the world's worst bed tonight, we will be right there, hoping our child's pain is managed. We are a step closer to getting home, to this whole thing being over.

Text message the family members, do a post on Facebook and Instagram and be discreet, do it in black-and-white so there is no blood in the photo, pack bags, walk alongside the bed to the ward, which room will we get? Will it have a window? Will it be in a dungeon? Will we have a bathroom, or will we have to share? Let's start unpacking in the hotel that no one wants to stay at. Put some things away, check out the families you might be sharing the ward with, immediately know if you are going to get a moment's sleep at night.

Breathe, listen, learn, become a nurse, help, change sheets, re-position pillows, offer jelly, ice-cream, juice, sips of soup they never eat at home. Beg family members to pick up some nuggets on their way to visit, please bring balloons, presents, cuddly toys, anything to give us something to look at, to think about, to feel like we are being thought of.

Escape downstairs even for 20 minutes on your own, scoff a cheeseburger and eat your feelings, cry, or be numb.

Change into your PJs or collapse on the bed. It's dark now and the ward is quiet, except for the constant beeping of the blue machine. Kiss your child constantly, know that the first night is usually relatively peaceful as medication is the key. Know you will be seeing nurses all through the night, be polite, be kind, be brave.

Kate says

To be honest, I am a bit of a rectum when it comes to children and surgeries. The closest I got was when Buzz and Woody had to have grommets (little drainage tubes in their ears) at sixteen months of age. I remember leaving Buzz with my mum and walking Woody in with the nurse. The terrifying fight-or-flight response as he went under and the beautiful anaesthetist singing to him . . . only to repeat it all in about fifteen minutes. Then having two screaming babies in recovery, both wanting me, and the screaming was next level! Finally being able to give them a bottle, thankful that they were just a little armful and I could juggle them both, before strapping them in the pram and leaving. I am not going to pretend I can really contribute to this chapter; I saw my beautiful friend go through it and all I can add is this: if you have a friend going through surgery with her precious offspring, help out, pea-ple!

10

Toddler twins

Here's the definition of toddler:

A young child that is learning to walk (to toddle).

And, in the words of Jerry Seinfeld:

Having a two-year-old is kind of like having a blender without a lid.

As the saying goes, there are two things in life that you can never be prepared for: twins. We would like to add that nothing in life could have prepared us for toddler twins. We hope that sharing our memories of the chaos vortex of twin toddlerdom might help any readers who are currently parenting toddler twins. But then again, if you have toddler twins now, how have you even found the time to read?! Wow! Well done!

If you have had newborn twins and coordinated feeding, expressing, bottle feeds, bath times, nappy changes and somehow managed to shower ... what a star you are. Having baby twins was the most profound time of our lives. We cannot believe we survived, and, to be honest, we have repressed most of the memories, but we've tried to dredge them up here. If your twins are not toddlers yet … maybe you don't want to read what toddler twins are actually like.

Mandy says

Toddler twins, what can I say? I remember at my ultrasound at twelve weeks when we were told we were having twins and I just kept saying, 'Two two-year-olds, two two-year-olds, how are we going to have two two-year-olds?!' I had longed for twins; I had worked in childcare; I had run rooms of fifteen two-year-olds (with two other staff members) so surely I would survive this? 2005 Mandy had no idea what was coming her way, but she did know that it would not be easy.

So many days, weeks and months I sat on the floor with two toddlers crawling over me at 6.52 am and thought, 'Is the day over yet?'

Breakfast and bottles, a huge tub next to the highchairs with bibs and face washers (the childcare organiser in me took over in my own home), were how we started every day. Nappy changes and getting dressed while wrestling children was a sport.

Never would I ever have imagined that I would start the day with a phone call to a friend at 7 am. My friends with toddlers had no problem calling for a chat that early in the morning, because we had usually been up for a few hours already. We met for walks at 7.30 or 8, and talked about our new lives; either a walk with another twin mum and our double prams, or friends with singletons who marvelled at the way I was pushing those two up the hill in the pram. I had never been so fit – or so tanned, from spending so much time out at the washing line.

I lived for the twins' morning sleep around 9 am when I knew I would have an hour or two to get some jobs done. I tried to sort my day into sections. Morning sleep = jobs, washing, picking up toys, hanging out washing, cooking dinner. I did as much as I could while they slept. I marvelled at how on the days that I had appointments or wanted to go out they slept for hours. On the days that I was at home with no rushing they woke early. What on earth is that about? Can someone please do a study on this?

Once the girls were awake, I would feed them, clean and sweep around the highchairs (boy, did I envy friends with dogs) and then give them some playtime or we would drive to an appointment. I tried so hard to schedule appointments around their sleeping. Sometimes it worked; other times it didn't. My girls were awesome at car sleeping and pram sleeping. I was pretty determined that they would be flexible sleepers, but even I was surprised at myself and how well we managed. Every single moment I had spent learning to teach babies and toddlers to sleep while I worked at QEC was a huge advantage for me. I knew what they needed in terms of routine and tried my best to stick to it. I believe this gave them a great advantage when it came to all our therapies, as they were not battling overtiredness as well.

During their afternoon sleeps I sat down with either a sandwich or a tub of ice cream and ate in peace. I then watched Oprah or Dr Phil (remember, this was 2006–7; there was no Netflix to stream) and fell asleep on the couch. Even fifteen minutes of sleep was enough to power me through the next hours, which were always more difficult.

Once we all woke up it was on for the afternoon: trying to get out for a walk with the pram if the weather was okay, packing snacks, drink bottles, nappies, wipes, spare clothes, bibs for saliva, going to the local park and hoping I could get the two swings so I could sit the girls in them. Trying not to be sad watching all the other toddlers who were up and running and climbing. I'd kiss my girls a hundred times so they knew how much I loved them amid my worry.

Home to dinner, and more cleaning up, baths for them both, water everywhere, can't leave them alone – whoops, all the towels are now in the bath – tiredness, often sickness and clingyness, PJs and clean nappies, hilarious talking and singing and wonderful cuddles and kisses, reading books, and dancing and incredible cuteness, alongside wishing for their dad to walk in the door. I sat in the lounge room, waiting for his car to turn the corner so I would have someone to help me. He walked in the door and just stepped over toy after toy after crushed biscuits and sultanas. No matter how hard I tried, I could not get on top of the housework. I look back on home videos and my word, there was stuff everywhere.

On a good day, my parents or Darren's parents turned up at the back door and I nearly cried with relief that they could help, especially if the girls were unwell. Two sick toddlers are not easy.

Night time, and snuggling in for a bottle, and then a story. On the good nights, a story on my lap or their dad's lap; on a hard night, both girls in their cots and me reading a token story over the bars of the cot.

I sang them the same night-time song and marvelled at how much I loved them, their cute sucking noises on dummies and cuddling their blankies, and knew that of course I would see one of them again overnight in some way, but for a few hours I would get some peace. I could go out for dinner with friends (cue Kate and the twin mummies) or I could watch TV. In retrospect these times were the best, knowing that I had the evenings.

I know not every twin mummy has this feeling and in my work this is what I strive to help them do. I never worked harder in my whole life than when I had toddler twins. I had never been busier with therapies and the constant thought that brains are super flexible until around age three, so I had to do whatever it took to get those synaptic connections happening. The botox, the casting, the AFOs, the shoes, the speech therapy, the OT, the physio, dietician, paediatrician, maternal and child health nurses, every hospital in Melbourne for sickness and MRIs and diagnosis, never been so sad, never been so happy, asking for help from everyone in the family, attempting holidays (or as I called them, 'changes of scenery'), packing the car with two highchairs, two porta cots, the double pram, the clothes, the toys, the food. I was an expert. Probably riding high on anxiety about getting them to stay within their schedules, and I am sure people thought I was inflexible, but I chose routine and their sleep over everything. It was the only way I could cope.

Once we moved to one big sleep in the middle of the day – somewhere around sixteen months, I think – life opened up. We could do therapies in the morning, we went to playgroup with my mothers' group, Mainly Music with all the twin mums and playdates with friends. I *loved* this time. Socialising in the morning and then a big peaceful afternoon sleep for all. I powered through chores as soon as they hit the cots and then I could sit and close my eyes, or eat. I loved inviting people over to my home at this stage of life; I loved having twins eating lunch on my deck, making up platters of food and welcoming tired women into my home. One day we had three sets of twins all sleeping in my house in porta cots and fold-out couches and my two friends and I feeling like queens eating our lunch in peace. I love and treasure these memories.

I also had strangers arrive at my back door, often from the Australian Multiple Birth Association forum. I really knuckled down to find my tribe and so inviting twin mummies with toddlers with disabilities, additional needs and who were medically complex was wonderful. I had a great ramp up to my back door built by my dad, so no one ever went to the front door. I found people peeking into my laundry and then wheeling their prams into my house, where we were immediately friends. I hosted for many reasons. I loved it and I knew that my girls were safe at home so I could relax. Going to other people's homes was equal parts relief to not be hosting and also high alert to where my girls could fall (I tried never to go to people's houses with stairs, my worst nightmare). I also belonged to Essential Baby, another online forum where I found so many friends who had children with all the types of CP that you could find – a few with twins, as well. These friends were wonderful and still are. Even though all the ways our children were affected were different, we were similar, in that we felt we didn't fit in. I am thankful for these women, the way they included me too, when often my life and the way the CP wand had weaved was easier on my daughters than theirs.

The week my girls turned two years old I had five other women and their twins in my house. In my concrete driveway to be exact, where children could toddle up and down my ramp and my driveway, with the fence locked to the dangers of the world. I cooked nachos, brought them out and placed them on the rubbish bins for the mums to stand around and eat. We didn't even question that eating off a bin was probably a bit yuck, we were just so happy to be together. The legend lives on and we even hosted a Nacho Bin Day during the first lockdown in 2020. We had around forty women from around the world on Zoom with their nachos on their bins. It was fantastic. My favourite story of all was the woman who made the nachos, put them on her bin out the front of her house and ate them alone because she didn't know there was a Zoom she could join. I still laugh so hard at this. That is the power of belonging.

Also . . . picture lots of undies at toilet training time. Lots and lots and lots of My Little Pony and Dorothy the Dinosaur undies on my washing line, and for Kate, Bob the Builder and

Thomas the Tank Engine. We both confess that, sometimes, when they were filled with poo, we threw them out! Do not tell our mums!

This time was also filled with much sickness, doctors appointments and hospital admissions. In fact, the girls had never been so sick: colds, bronchitis, croup, gastro, ear infections, tonsillitis, falls – and many ambulances or visits from the on-call nurse. I always had a bag packed ready for the overnight drive to the Emergency department. Each time, the worry of weight loss and how to manage two toddlers in hospital was very real.

I was more alert to breathing difficulties than anything else and spent many a night sleeping on the floor in between the cots, giving medication and listening to every single breath. Croup was particularly harrowing. Never have I been so frightened about children and their breathing. I learnt all about the tug in the throat and the pull in at the side of the chest. And I noticed that, often, when I got the girls into the cold night air, their croup cough would improve, so sometimes I sat outside at 3 am with them and got them through it.

I was acutely aware that other families weren't going through this as much as we were, and I often think about how tired I was. Being a full-time mother to sick toddler twins was the most exhausted I have ever been. Sometimes I would lie on the floor among the toys and they would both sit on my head and jump all over my body, but I didn't care because at least I was able to close my eyes for five minutes.

This was also a time when going to playgroups or music groups and observing all the typically developing toddlers was a real challenge. I wanted the girls to have the same experiences as their peers, but I knew that some days, just walking into those rooms was like a knife in my chest. I had to be really brave and focus on my girls and how a morning of play was more important than my heart. Some days I couldn't do it, though, but I knew that I could try again the next week.

Kate says

Batten down the hatches, friends, this is a storm warning. You know when you watch the news and they say something like, 'A big storm is coming. Don't leave anything untethered on the front porch, put the trampoline away and make sure you have some bottled water'? This is also the advice you should get from the government when your twins turn two! (And for those of you with triplets: I bow before you. I am not worthy.) Every day is a freaking storm – or it was around here. The thing is, even after having three toddlers, nothing prepared me for toddler twins. If you have a friend with toddler twins, check on them right this second; they are not okay! As I have mentioned, when I am not recording podcasts, mothering five kids or hanging out the washing or eating cheese with friends, I am a home stylist. I like nice things – cushions and candles and uneven pottery bowls. Well, forget all that! Our house looked like we were just about to move out and going to have the carpets steam-cleaned. Every day of the week, every chair up high on the table, with not an ornament, not a photo frame, not a tissue box lying around (have you ever seen a toddler with a tissue box? They can empty those things faster than a politician dodging a question about public housing). We were stripped of all the things that made our house look like ours, but we were given these two climbing, crawling, running little tornadoes that gave us no time to care about soft (or hard, for that matter) furnishings. You probably think I am prone to a bit of Irish exaggeration here, but read on, pea friend, for a very accurate depiction of a day in the life of Toddler Buzz, Toddler Woody and Frazzled Mum Kate.

5.30–6.00 am   The twins are awake. This is easy to tell as they somehow thump out of bed. Cue an adrenaline surge as my sleep-deprived mind realises *SHIT! The twins are awake!* This is like the opposite of an orgasm, but equally as effective at increasing your heart rate. Some people have to bungee jump; I just had twins. Same-same.

6.01–6.03 am   Buzz runs into the doorframe of their shared bedroom and Woody crashes into him. Both get lumps on their foreheads and I grab one of the 180 cold packs we have in the freezer to prevent bruises. The huge egg-shaped bulges do not make them cry but the cold pack does. I wrap the 'bruise buddy' in a slightly dirty tea towel and now it's hardly cold and isn't really effective but I feel better as a mother. Due to the amount of screaming and crying, the four other members of the house are now awake.

6.04 am   The twins are doing laps of the house because we have the absolute joy of having a 'round and round' house, with a hallway that links the kitchen with the living room. This is one of the worst architectural designs of all time, but you may not be aware of this until you have small children. Ours went through the kitchen as well. Early toddler days were pushing little carts, later days were riding little cars. I mean, it took up time, which was almost a blessing. They could do this for about twenty minutes until we forced them into highchairs to eat/drink their breakfast.

6.23 am   Highchair time, baby! You better believe we have hacked the harness so there is no escaping! It's a good day, which means that the soggy Weet-Bix get eaten, and also somehow gets all through their most angelic curls and eyebrows. The all-in-one PJ suits have a lovely soggy Weet-Bix collar. There is no time to deal with this, though, as the three other children aged thirteen, eleven and six need to eat, find sports socks, library books, clean teeth and put on ironed school uniforms. So highchairs are loaded with books (cardboard of course, no page ripping), blocks, dummies and bread crusts. It's Go Time, team – we need to walk out that front door at 8 am.

6.25 am   One adult showers, the other adult has already showered. (It's not our first toddler twin morning!)

6.27 am Scholarship remembers it's Bring a Flower to School Day (I mean, who fucking invents these days? Why is it the parents' responsibility to have to do these things? Fairy Day, Harmony Day, Red Day, Country of Origin Day, Easter Hat Day, bloody Book Week Dress-up Day . . .) I am hoping it's a real flower; please don't make me cut the Weet-Bix box up and make a flower!

6.28 am Ignore food and books on the floor around highchairs, give new books and all the Tupperware to buy more time.

6.29 am Continue to gently nag older children to eat, clean teeth and wash faces.

6.30 am Continue to gently nag older children to eat, clean teeth and wash faces.

6.31 am Continue to gently nag older children to eat, clean teeth and wash faces.

6.32 am Dash to bathroom to clean teeth and put mascara on so people stop asking if I am sick.

6.33 am Bugger singing 'Happy Birthday' (the tip a dentist gave me to make sure I brush for long enough) to myself – if the toothpaste covers the coffee breath it is a win for dental hygiene.

6.34 am Continue to gently nag older children to eat, clean teeth and wash faces.

6.35 am Begin Operation Wipe Down Buzz, realise they both smell like that rewarding morning poo smell.

6.37 am Free Buzz, hope he doesn't have poo all down his legs. Begin Operation Wipe Down Woody and realise nostril hair has somehow been infused with poo smell.

6.40 am Continue to not-so-gently nag older children to eat, clean teeth and wash faces.

6.41 am Catch Woody and remove every article of clothing, as they are covered in poo, milk or Weet-Bix. Hold child with one hand while folding dirty nappy and placing on shelf (note to self: do not forget this nappy is here!). Place new nappy on child, remember I haven't got today's outfit out of the child-locked wardrobe, put Woody under my arm and wrangle child lock, find clothes (mentally high-fiving myself that I grabbed clothes for Buzz, too). Dress Woody, use baby wipes on his hair to remove Weet-Bix. Release him, go hunt for Buzz.

6.48 am   Hunt for Buzz and continue to nag older children to eat, clean teeth and wash faces and get dressed. Have a very strong sense of deja vu as I repeat Woody's undressing and re-dressing.

7.00 am   Realise we have an hour until we need to leave – heaps of time! Put kettle on and make a cup of tea.

7.01 am   Go outside with Scholarship, who has school dress on and has made her lunch, to find a flower. Buzz and Woody doing laps again. Sound Engineer is flicking Number One Daughter with a face washer, and sounds of siblings fighting filling the house. Spend way too long deciding on a flower; end up choosing a very cute seaside daisy.

7.18 am   Put tepid tea in microwave. Buzz and Woody have emptied every bit of plastic out of the big plastic drawer, tipped out all the Lego and found a cup of water and very creatively made a puddle under the table. They are now very wet.

7.19 am   Loudly nag older children to clean teeth, wash faces and get dressed.

7.20 am   Remove tea from constantly beeping microwave, place on bench. Catch Woody, wrangle wardrobe drawer with child lock, grab clothes for him and Buzz, completely strip Woody of clothes, spy morning nappies festering on shelf and berate myself for leaving them there. What sort of a human have I become?! Re-dress Woody, place him on the ground, but he wants to be held and koala-holds my leg. Pick him up again and go find Buzz. Feel grateful I can lift both boys and that Buzz was doing laps and easy to find. Put Woody on the ground and he stops whingeing – phew! Get Buzz changed, see that Woody was playing with the dirty nappies, swear in front of twins.

7.43 am   Yell commands and bark questions at Scholarship, Number One Daughter and Sound Engineer: 'Do you have your library bag? Is your lunch in your bag? Put your lunch in your bag! Are your teeth clean? Does anyone need a ponytail? Do you have your recorder? And your reader? Is your hair done?'

7.44 am   Wipe down highchairs and put twins back in them to keep them from getting dirty, wet or tripped over. Pile toys, books and old jar lids on highchair trays.

7.47 am Glance at now-microwaved tea, take a sip. Hmm, not bad. Plait Number One Daughter's hair, and decree everyone must wee.

7.50 am Make it to the toilet to wee before I wet my pants but realise I don't have time to poo as we have ten minutes to get everyone out of the house. Wonder where husband is, then remember he had to leave early for work. Wonder if I will ever work outside the home again, glance at toilet roll to realise it is empty. Decide to shake off wee and jump to the cupboard with underpants around knees to get more loo roll rather than asking kids for help. Will just delay the morning.

7.51 am Wipe, wash hands and try to fluff hair into some sort of style.

7.52 am Stand in the kitchen and see Buzz and Woody back in highchairs, Number One Daughter playing with them and the three of them are laughing. Heart soars. What an amazing mother I am. Sound Engineer cannot find one shoe; spend six minutes looking before finding it in the bath! Thank God bath is empty. Scholarship waiting with backpack and flowers at front door.

7.58 am Do a final check of daily planner (or first check, if I am honest), realise Number One Daughter needs her violin, hurriedly place it in its case, then see the bow still on the bed, place that in the case and hand it to aforementioned offspring.

7.59 am Basically scream that it is 8 am and we need to be in the car, see tea on the table, ignore it, put my backpack full of nappies, dummies, Cruskits, etc., on my back, command children to follow, grab a twin in each hand, walk painfully slowly down the hallway, glance in twins' room, see those bloody nappies on the floor! Oh, for fuck's sake, Kate! How hard is it to put nappies in the bin?

8.04 am Click final child in seatbelt, remove backpack, wonder how I became a People-mover Mum but also, how much room is in this car?! Drive up the driveway, become overwhelmed with the feeling the front door isn't locked, ignore feeling, drive to school.

8.11 am   Drop Sound Engineer at Kiss-and-Drop point, tell him 'make the right choices and be kind' and feel smug for remembering to be such a good parent.

8.11am   Twins hysterical after seeing a rubbish truck and me not following it due to needing to get the girls to school.

8.24 am   Circle the streets around the school, desperate to find a car park, as school has a rule that Scholarship must be walked in and I don't want to feel like the ordinary mum I am. Plus, it's Bring a Flower to School Day! I must walk in for Bring a Flower to School Day. Curse the mums happily chatting in the playground in their activewear – why don't you fucking leave? Go to the gym already! Spy mum in a suit leaving school, stalk her to her car space; she is on her phone. I fist-pump: she is not stopping to chat, I can have her car space.

8.28 am   Car parked, pram out of car, twins into pram, girls out of car, walking to gate, might even get there before the 8.30 bell! Kiss Number One Daughter, remember to tell her I love her, forget to tell her to make the right choices. Enter Scholarship's classroom and wonder if someone has died. Flowers everywhere: staggering numbers of floral arrangements. Is that a weeping cherry in a pot? My heart sinks. I mean, come on, I was so good at this shit once. I look at Scholarship, who is still very proud of her daisies. She happily places them with the wreath that looks fit for a royal wedding and I squeeze her very tight and tell her how much I love her. But I have got to get the twins home before 9 am otherwise they will fall asleep in the car. And I need them to nap at home!

8.29 am   Twins grabbing their dummies out of each other's mouths as I beeline for the car. I am stopped by a wonderful friend whom I truly adore, but I am on the clock. She loves Bring a Flower to School Day, so lovely for the kids. I won't give her my 'stupid fucking dress-up and theme days' rant – wrong crowd, Kate, wrong crowd. She has to go take photos of the flowers. Shit, I should have done that. I ask her to take one of Scholarship and I head to the car. Overhear two women chatting about the struggles of getting their one child to school, walk the long way to the car. I can't hear that today.

8.34 am Both boys in car seats. Have to do the gentle hold-stomach-with-elbow manoeuvre to get Buzz in. Pram in boot, radio on, windows down, gotta keep them awake till we get home. Reach behind me and tickle them, remove dummies and do all that is humanly possible from the front seat of the car. Feel proud as we pull into driveway that sleep has not happened!

9.01 am Twins in cots, dummies in, little exhausted eyes closed (having a sleep consultant as a friend has really paid off with the dynamic duo). Pick up those bloody nappies, put them in the bin that is high on a laundry shelf to avoid twins!

9.02 am Laugh loudly at the 'Nap when your child naps' advice. There is washing billowing out of the laundry, half-drunk cups of tea in three rooms, every piece of plastic Tupperware we own strewn down the hallway, Lego all through the living room, breakfast plates on the bench, pyjamas in piles at the ends of beds, beds to be made, floors to be swept and for the love of anything holy, I would like a cup of bloody tea!

9.03 am Put the kettle on and as a little reward for surviving the first three or four hours of my day I might even have a shit! As I wash my hands in the bathroom I realise my jumper has toothpaste all down it . . . *great!*

9.05 am Make a cup of tea and drink it while doing the most basic yet undervalued and beautiful dance a person does: restoring some sort of harmony to our little home. There really aren't words for the feeling of satisfaction that comes from tidying up and hanging out a load of washing while your toddlers sleep. I admire the books, which are now back on a shelf, the Lego in the big plastic tub. Wow!

11.03 am Thump! Buzz and Woody are awake, and a hug cyclone is coming my way . . . Anyway, I am going to Mandy's to eat nachos off a wheelie bin, which we won't even think twice about.

I could go on, but you get the idea. Life was a sweet hurricane. I thought about getting a tattoo that said 'Never a dull moment' but why tattoo what you already live? Really, I needed a tattoo that said 'Dreaming of dull, baby, dreaming of dull.' I suppose I didn't even have time to wonder if the boys had too much energy, or if they were developing differently from the other kids. I was just flat out keeping them safe and trying to be a parent to the other three. This was pre-diagnosis time for us. 'Busy' can't describe it; if I hadn't been so busy, I might have realised things were a little too busy – does that make sense at all? I failed a little bit, but you know what, that's okay. Sometimes you thrive, sometimes you survive! Never beat yourself up when you are in survival mode. Bear Grylls has made a fortune from surviving – we should be more proud of survival than we are!

Food

We are pretty sure everyone knows the definition of food, but in keeping with the book, here goes.

> **Food:** any nutritious substance that people or animals eat or drink or that plants absorb in order to maintain life and growth.

Simple, right? Unless you have a baby who doesn't feed, is lactose intolerant, is peg fed or has been deemed a 'failure to thrive'.* Or you have a child who is 'fussy' or restricted in what they can eat due to allergies.

All parents dream of a baby dipping carrot sticks into homemade hummus; we might just have been baby food snobs pre-twins, too. We've all seen the Instagram influencer mums packing a lunchbox loaded with tofu, cucumbers, protein bars, olives and a mandarin, but there is another group out there too, who have been shamed into silence. Why wouldn't we be shamed? Feeding your children is one of the most important responsibilities a parent has. Food is

---

* It pains us to put this phrase in the book. Children are diagnosed with 'failure to thrive' when their weight or rate of weight gain is significantly below that of other children of similar age and sex. It is an outdated term, and it doesn't help that there are lots of different definitions for it.

not a choice, like deciding on the best pram or which swimming school you prefer, it is necessary for survival. True, you can choose to be vegetarian or to never let your child have soft drinks but everyone has to eat.

So what happens when your kids hate food? Or when certain foods seem to hate your child? According to the Australasian Society of Clinical Immunology and Allergy, 'Food allergy occurs in around 10 per cent of infants ... and around 2 per cent of adults'.[6] Everything in your life has to change, then, doesn't it? A certain food could kill your child. Sometimes it is not that 'simple' though (not that there is anything simple about an allergy!) and a child will refuse to eat certain food or will eat *only* certain foods, for seemingly no reason.

There is *always* a reason, friends. Is the very small food selection a preference or has the child experienced trauma associated with food? Do certain foods create a sensory overload? Are the child's oral motor skills an issue? Is it painful for the child to eat? Do they have reflux? You know what is painful? Other people giving their unwanted opinions on what your child eats! People get very annoyed if your kid only eats nuggets or pizza or Up&Go. We don't quite know why this is other people's business or why they give a shit, but give a shit they do! And it makes an already tricky pea life harder.

As a society we are obsessed with drawing uninformed conclusions about people's health based on their body shape. 'Have you lost weight?' or 'She has really let herself go' (this means you got fat!) or 'Did you see [insert celebrity's name here]? She looks so good' or 'He really gained weight after the filming of his latest movie finished'. We grow up believing it is our business what people weigh and what they eat. Ask any overweight person how guilty they feel if they ever have to stock up for a party.

We can trace food shaming and body shaming all the way back to birth. 'What a big healthy baby.' Or 'Oh, isn't she tiny. Are you feeding her?' Of course I am fucking feeding her. I think the question the person wants to ask is, 'Are you feeding her breast-milk? And how are you feeding her – breast and formula, breast but in a bottle, boob on demand?' The implications in that one question are many, so maybe that question shouldn't be asked in the first place!

Let's look back at that definition of food. 'Any nutritious sub-stance', hmm? Are chicken nuggets nutritious? Probably not, hence the food guilt and the harsh judgement we feel from others whenever we feed nuggets to our children. All we want is to serve our kids a big bowl of veggies with a healthy protein source on the side. Or a mug of soup with all those veggies plus lentils, chicken or beef! Salad on a burger; salad on its own. It's something we spend hours obsessing over, and believe me, we don't need any more advice on 'hiding' carrots. Don't think we haven't tried everything. And don't think we don't know that avocado and olive oil are good fats. Our children aren't eating chicken nuggets and crackers because we are 'un-food-educated'! We have spoken to every health professional we can about this, so please don't tell us what your friend's naturopath said. Actually, maybe don't tell us anything; just let us bring crackers for our kids when we come over to your place for a barbecue!

Mandy says

I spent nearly ten years teaching parents about food, and fed babies, toddlers and preschoolers five to six times a day. And I was good at it. Kind and firm, but not too pushy. I was all for healthy foods with treats here and there. Less sugar, more texture. Let's make food an enjoyable experience, never force feed, give choice, lots of colours, give it to them ten times. You name it, I knew it. Fast-forward to premature twins and Molly at this stage with undiagnosed CP. She had a mouth that certainly wasn't letting her latch and suck on the breast, and she was losing weight. Beginning my parenting journey with babies who were losing weight and being weighed every second day for seven weeks in hospital induces a certain amount of food anxiety, but I fought it at every turn. I pretended that it was fine that they had only gained 10 grams that day and so we weren't allowed to bath them – at least they had gained a little bit of weight!

Once we got home, I tried to downplay the noises that Molly made when sucking on the bottle, as well as the gagging and the vomiting. She continued gagging on her food when we started solids. *It's okay*, I told myself, *this is normal. Just keep an eye on her and don't show her that you are worried. And don't put your fingers down her throat to get the food out if she is choking.* This was the number one rule, but how many times did I panic and do this?

Even after her diagnosis, I don't think I fully understood how difficult it was for her to eat. It wasn't until a speech therapist told me that she had a huge ripple in her tongue, probably caused by the spasticity, that I really, truly realised the extent of the issue. We saw a dietician, who told me to add sour cream to everything. For Molly, who had been choking and gagging, the sour cream did not help at all – but Milly loved it. She gained glorious weight and started thriving.

I have done everything I can in the last fifteen years to help Molly gain weight. My attitude towards food is based on the saying, 'Our family is not black-and-white, we are a thousand shades of grey'. I could never say to my daughter, 'Now, if you don't eat this you will not get any more food.' *NEVER*. My husband eventually got through to her by saying, 'How do children grow? Water, food and sleep. These are the only things you must do every day.'

So many food restrictions, smell restrictions, cutting up meat into tiny pieces, milkshakes, smoothies. Don't have anything a tiny bit gritty in there, oh no, everything will be spotted from a mile away. Despite my best efforts, lots of food was scary for her. Going out for dinners or lunches at people's places – be still my beating heart: how could I have her sit at the table safely and be able to eat food without judgement or well-meaning offers to help?

The year after her first big bone surgery, Molly lost so much weight, almost as much as the time after a hospital admission for gastro at twelve months; kilos and kilos lost. I would look at her in the shower and think, 'How can this be my child?' I cooked and baked and bought the same foods so many times. I tried and tried; I tried not to make it a big deal for her twin or for her other sibling, but stress about response behaviours at the family table are real and all my dreams of having happy family meal times all but dissolved. She tried her very best, and I think the combination of tiredness after kinder or school and my anxiety may have made it harder on her; in hindsight, I feel terrible about that.

Going out for dinner can also fill our family with panic, so sticking to the same few restaurants worked: places that served nuggets, hot chips, roti bread, Chinese food, prawn crackers and a few other select items.

Have you seen the meme about blueberries and how each one can taste so different – sour, hard, soft, squishy – and the picture of a plain biscuit and how they taste the same every single time? No wonder it was easier for Molly to trust plain food.

In my work with parents, and especially parents of premature babies, I recognise food anxiety from a mile away. I say to the families I work with, 'Providing food and ensuring our children are thriving is so personal and sometimes it feels like it's a way the world is judging you.'

Different cultures also view food in ways that are diverse and for some parents of premature kids, the judgement from family is too much to bear. It feels like a direct reflection on your parenting; sometimes that sort of fear meant I didn't leave the house.

I could go on and on, but I might end here. I am writing from lockdown and I am a full-time caterer at the moment, and I have to go make dinner!

Kate says

Food! Don't start me, because you won't stop me. But just so this book doesn't end up being the size of *War and Peace*, I will try to hold back (the opposite of what I do in front of a cheese platter).

From the moment Buzz and Woody were born, feeding them was the only thing I felt I could physically do for them. They had little wires on them, they had to stay warm in their isolets, and they were tube-fed via a naso-gastric tube. They weren't supposed to be born yet – they should have been happily kicking around in amniotic fluid and living it up on the placenta. But here they were, and expressing breast milk was all I could do. At first, the nurses struggled to squeeze drops of colostrum from my breasts, but then within a few days I was able to express more than a litre of milk per pumping session (don't roll your eyes; I know I am a good cow and I will try not to brag about it, as it really is luck of the draw). I hated expressing. It didn't feel right, and I had never done it with my other babies, so it was something new I learnt with the twins, although, now that I think about, I re-learnt nearly everything with those two. I spent many cold winter nights pumping away at home, writing the date on the side of the bottle and choosing fridge or freezer, all while my babies were kilometres away. It was lonely, but that milk was liquid gold: I was feeding them what they needed. In all honesty, that was probably the last time they had a balanced diet!

The good thing about having older children was that I already knew what kids ate and when, and I had already dealt with a fussy eater (not pointing fingers, Mr Sound Engineer), a child who breastfed almost exclusively for a year, another who didn't want to be weaned, one who loved olives, and one who still cannot stand even the smell of them. Children are people too, it turns out, and they like and dislike certain foods. Mostly it all balances out. Some days it's nuggets and Vegemite toast, some days it's veggie soup and fruit salad.

To be honest, I was actually pretty smug at that point. My kids ate veggies and salad. I didn't get what the food fuss was about. What is wrong with people? Why can't they get their kids to eat? Won't they eat if they are hungry? (What the fuck, Kate, what a rectum you were!)

And then along came Buzz and Woody, and guess what? I get it now. I have experienced it all: the stress, the tears, the gagging, the refusals, the anxiety (for all of us), restaurant anxiety, family dinner anxiety . . . I hate food now! I mean, not me, I love eating, but my relationship with food – the way I view a 'good diet', the fact that I feel judgement when it comes to what my children eat – has changed. It has diminished my love of cooking, too. Why cook food that will never be eaten? Food has made me feel so much shame and I am ashamed of myself for feeling shamed. But when your kids have a limited palate, the judgement comes from everywhere.

You know where this shit really gets real? Primary school. All those lunchbox discussions, kids' birthday parties and class parties . . . ugh, I can feel my heart beat faster just thinking about it. The little snide looks from other mums, the constant comments about what my kids weighed! I mean, really?! Does it make you feel that much better to do that to me? It certainly doesn't make *me* feel better, nor my beautiful boys, who heard a lot of it too. Here is the thing: I can't call them out on it, either. I don't want my kids to lose friends, for the mums to alienate me, and I will probably cry, and my kids will see it. So how about you keep it to yourself, or at least gossip about me behind my back. Have some respect!

If I block out the haters and think about my family, my kids, if at dinner some of us eat a big vegetable satay curry and some of us eat a veggie sausage and two bites of broccoli, or a roti from Aldi washed down with a Milo and no one cries or has a panic attack at dinner (not even me!), then who cares? We all ate and we sat at a table together and we got to laugh. So what if my family dinners don't look like yours? In those moments the 'new' Kate feels so happy. Because we are together, and that is something I will never take for granted. True, the conversation is probably also nothing like you have at your house. I mean, do you have 'motherfucking kiss time'* before bed? See, now you are jealous of my meal times, aren't you?

---

* If you are not a listener to the podcast you are probably wondering what on earth 'motherfucking kiss time' is. To save you the hours and hours of finding that quote, I will give you a rough explanation. One night I was in my room and up the hall came Woody to give me my goodnight kiss. As he approached I heard his chant, 'It's motherfucking kiss time, it's motherfucking kiss time', and then he showered me in love! I laughed till I cried!

12

Post-traumatic stress disorder

The dictionary describes post-traumatic stress disorder like this:

> A disorder characterised by failure to recover after experiencing or witnessing a terrifying event. The condition may last months, or years, with triggers that can bring back memories of the trauma accompanied by intense emotional and physical reactions.

Here's another helpful definition, taken from the website of Life's Little Treasures, a foundation that supports premature and sick babies and their families.

> Powell . . . states that: 'Most people experience the loss of some-one or something of great importance several times during their lives . . . ['] When grief is related to loss of an experience, not a death, how does one grieve or cope? Boss . . . coined the term 'ambiguous loss' when studying the wives of pilots missing in action in Vietnam and Cambodia. They had no information and no official verification that anything had been lost, thus were filled with conflicting thoughts and feelings. This ambiguity aptly describes the feelings of loss after a premature birth. The parents have a live baby [or babies], thus there is no proof that anything was lost.[7]

When you begin your journey of parenting, and the pregnancy and birth are traumatic (many women experience a traumatic birth, even when their babies are well) that sets the scene. Of course, each person has their own triggers and we are not experts in this field. In fact, only Mandy was diagnosed with PTSD, and her triggers and responses are unique to her.

Mandy is going to share more of her story in a moment, but we wanted to just say that if you think you might be experiencing PTSD in any way, help is available to you and it's important to seek it. These are some organisations that are available to you:

- Life's Little Treasures
- Miracle Babies
- PANDA – Perinatal Anxiety and Depression Australia.

It's important to see your GP, too.

Mandy says

If I could turn back time, I would tell 2005 Mandy that having panic attacks is not 'normal' and that you need to acknowledge that you are suffering. I would tell her that the trauma of having premature babies is affecting your body, your mind and your life, and is absolutely something that you need help with. You need to be gentle with yourself, and know that when you move house in 2010, most of the triggers will disappear.

When you have a baby (or babies), the last thing you expect to encounter is something as debilitating as PTSD. Before I had the twins, the extent of my knowledge about PTSD came from watching *Born on the Fourth of July* and seeing Tom Cruise's character go through trauma after being in the Vietnam War.

War, sure, but PTSD after having babies? I had trouble accepting it at first, until I thought about all I had been through: a twin pregnancy, then the NICU, the SCN, diagnoses, surgeries, endless appointments, therapies, adding hardware to our children's bodies, brain injuries, MRIs, general anaesthetics, casts on legs, splints on arms, walkers, medications, family and friendships changing and leaving a church? It made sense. This is just my list, but everyone's looks different. Sit and list all the things that you have experienced since having a baby or babies prematurely or traumatically, or even miscarrying. Can you see some of the signs of PTSD?

One of the most common threads to the memory of NICU is the smell of the handwash. Most NICU mums will agree that any whiff of it after that, perhaps during a subsequent visit to a hospital, immediately brings back the memories: of seeing your babies on CPAP, tubes down their noses, beeping and beeping and more beeping, heart-rate monitors, doctors, nurses, paediatricians, cleaners, the expressing room, the breast pumps, expressing the liquid gold. Every experience, every moment, imprinted – and all brought on by something as seemingly simple as the smell of handwash.

I remember speaking to my maternal and child health nurse (MCHN) a year or so after the twins were born about something that happened one night when I was getting into bed. The simple act of shutting the bedroom door made me burst into tears and start to panic, as a memory flashed into my mind of the night that my waters broke when I was in bed with the bedroom door shut. And it wasn't just that. The *whoosh* sound of the ducted heating coming on took me right back to the long nights, expressing alone without any babies by my side.

The MCHN recommended that I see someone to talk about these feelings, which was the best advice I could have possibly received. I found a great psychologist, and it didn't take long for

her to see that I was suffering from PTSD. Some of the other
signs for me were:

- panic attacks
- sweating
- heart palpitations
- blanking out when people spoke about their 'normal' birth
  experience
- not sleeping
- withdrawing
- crying and anxiety while visiting friends who had given
  birth
- anxiety about visiting hospitals for appointments for the
  children
- ruminating
- the trauma in each room of the house with memories of
  specific times, like the diagnosis, or my waters breaking in
  my bed.

Pride and Prejudice's Mrs Bennet and her nerves had nothing
on me. I also spoke to my psychologist about how, when I was
watching my girls undergo general anaesthetics many times a
year for botox injections and MRI scans, I experienced the same
feeling I did when I was heavily pregnant and had to put the
family dog down. How could two completely different scenarios cause so much distress and fear? The green needle and the
moment of watching your babies having a mask put over their
faces, fighting it and screaming, to then going limp in your arms
or on the table.

We moved house when the twins were four years old and
my counsellor said, 'I think I might tell all of my clients with
PTSD to move house.' The experience of leaving a home that

had ghosts of memories at every turn was only something that you could understand going through it. Our new house was a fresh canvas that was all about the future, rather than the past. It was to there that we brought home our term baby a year later and I am forever grateful for those happy memories within our walls.

Being diagnosed with PTSD was an enormous relief. It helped me make sense of what I was going through, as I knew I wasn't depressed, but I knew I wasn't right either. I could email articles to my family and friends and explain how I was feeling and why I was behaving in a certain way. I knew that once I explained the PTSD people understood and gave me the space I needed. It was life giving. I also know that after seeing my counsellor every week for a year, I was able to shift some of the trauma and then I was able to contemplate another pregnancy and baby. Without this diagnosis and subsequent therapy, I am quite sure our Miss Ten would not be here.

Kate says

Once again I am a rectum here, as PTSD is not my story, although I do have strong memories of the pregnancy with Buzz and Woody that can make my heart race or my eyes tear up. I didn't like leaving my babies in hospital, but I think that knowing we were going to have a premature delivery – doing tours of the NICU and talking to doctors and nurses about it – made a huge difference. Even now, all these years later, I still look over at them and pinch myself that they are here and wrestling like naughty puppies! If the outcome had not given us living babies, this would have been a very different story.

The closest thing to PTSD I have experienced was when my beautiful dad and my mum were on the holiday of a lifetime in the UK before heading home to see my dad's family in Ireland when he had a massive stroke. My brother Shenanigans and I flew across the world, then took a train from London to Cornwall to say goodbye to our precious dad. All the hotels in Cornwall were booked out by tourists wanting to catch the last of the English summer weather, so I remember changing hotels every day, then walking along ancient cobbled streets, dodging hundreds of holidaymakers with ice creams to get to the hospital.

We sat in a little room eating pre-packaged sandwiches and watching one of the most important people in the world to me taking his last breaths. I had to watch my mother go through agonising anguish, too, and all while we were thousands of kilometres from the rest of our family and friends. It was a massive pile of pain and shit, and I remember every moment of it so clearly – the phone calls, the tears, the absolute shock.

Every day for about a year after my dad died I woke up early with a surge of adrenaline, thinking about my dad and those weeks in the UK. I had to sit with the memories for a minute or two, then regroup and go and be a mum, a wife, an employer and a friend. But the knowledge that life had changed was still there, waiting to resurface the next morning.

Everyone processes trauma differently, and it's important not to judge or comment on it. After my dad's death, I was reminded of how powerful friends were, and I resolved to always be that friend to others. Just offer your hand, a hug, a card, bunch of flowers or a packet of doughnuts, and let people heal in their own time. And also acknowledge that time does not heal all things; that is bullshit! But good friendship does help all things!

13

Therapea
Peafessionals in allied health

A note from Mandy

While we were writing this chapter, I realised that most of my early intervention time with my daughters was pre-NDIS. It might seem strange to think about a time in Australia before it, but just keep that in mind when you are reading.

Definition time! This time we've gone to a new expert, Wikipedia:

> A **therapy or medical treatment** . . . is the attempted remediation of a health problem, usually following a medical diagnosis. As a rule, each therapy has indications and contraindications. There are many different types of therapy. Not all therapies are effective. Many therapies can produce unwanted adverse effects.

Physiotherapy, occupational therapy, speech therapy. These are some of the first words pea families hear when they are either awaiting a diagnosis or have been handed one. These words usually appear on a leaflet, or these days, an Instagram account of the local therapist, with funky branding and up-to-date social media presence.

Then come the questions. How do we choose a therapist? Is there one close by? Do we ask our friends and family if they know anyone or are we allocated someone by the hospital? Is early intervention required? Will they make home visits? How do I get both my babies to these appointments? How on earth do I cope with toddler twins and therapy? How do I squeeze this in around my work? Is this our new normal?

Meeting therapists, especially in a public hospital setting, is like a marathon. Meet, greet, listen, agree, be polite, don't be rude, be friendly, wrangle the children. Oh wait, you've resigned? Pregnant, I hear you say? Moving interstate? Continuing your study? Wow, congratulations, and yes, we would love to meet the next physio who will also up and leave us in six months. What's your name again? What did you just say?

Grabbing diaries and phones and plugging in appointments for each week almost requires a Master's degree in logistics. To any rectums reading this who think working and raising children is hard – you know nothing, Jon Snow. This stuff is like the Olympics. If you lose your diary or your phone, you will have lost phone numbers and appointments for up to a year or more.

Even just getting in the room is a saga. First, there's the problem of the waiting list, where you find out that there's a month-long wait to get your child in to the speech therapist in your suburb. Then you're told that there's another therapist who has space next week – but they are an hour's drive away, so you have to make that decision. And then once appointment day rolls around, you have to get the babies organised (or if the appointment is only for one baby then arrange for the other one to be minded), then drive there and hope that the babies sleep on the way so that they are ready for therapy. Then you need money for the car park.

Oh, they offer subsidised parking, great. Can you make your way down to the security section of the carpark with your children who can't walk, and talk to the people there about getting a discounted parking rate?

Some pea families can access different therapies in the one place. For example, the Cerebral Palsy Education Centre (CPEC) is a one-stop shop and has a central philosophy of conductive education. Irabina is an autism early intervention services provider. The beauty of places like this is that you instantly feel like you belong, and you are sure to meet other people there who are on a similar therapy journey. There was no place for children with hemiplegia at that time in Melbourne. I remember visiting one of these places and they said, 'I'm sorry she is too able.' To which I cried all the way home and went through drive-through Macca's to try and make sense of where on earth we could go.

In the beginning, most families will move heaven and earth to get help for their children. They will pay higher fees or drive to a 'richer' suburb to access 'better' therapists, change their work schedules or give up their work entirely. But eventually some peas get tired. They get worn out, they begin to truth-tell or lie or miss appointments altogether. They ghost their therapists because the thought of answering another call, or driving another thirty minutes at 4.30 pm on a Tuesday for the child who is already exhausted and refusing to get in the car, feels all too difficult. Don't even get us started about being involved in studies. Letters asking our families to participate in studies that will give our children no benefits, but could we please attend an appointment in North Melbourne at 4 pm on a Friday? You quickly learn which studies to say yes to and which ones to give a firm no.

In the specialist primary school system in Victoria, students have access to onsite therapists. Not all children see therapists on a regular basis, but those who can, do. Imagine the sheer relief to know that your pea shoot is having hydrotherapy on a Thursday at 10 am, speech therapy on Monday at 1.30 pm and then when they come home from their one-hour bus ride they can rest or play or watch a movie or cuddle with Grandma or garden or ride a bike. They have time to just be a kid. The therapy is happening at the best time for the child: this is the peas' dream.

The specialist secondary school system does not offer onsite therapy, or at least Mandy's daughter's school doesn't. Granted, lots of pea shoots are at this point having less therapy than younger pea shoots, but if you went into a specialist secondary college you would be hard-pressed to find an adolescent who does not have any therapy funded on their NDIS plan. It may also be impossible for schools to accommodate this, as the amount of therapy time would eat into learning time.

But imagine for a moment that, say, twice a year your pea shoot's classroom teacher meets with their speech therapist, occupational therapist, physiotherapist and psychotherapist. You are invited too, and you bring along your pea shoot's NDIS plan, and then everyone sits down as a cohesive unit to discuss how your pea shoot is going. Everyone can see what skills the child needs to be working on and it gets done authentically throughout the school day. The art teacher, the drama teacher, the PE teacher all liaise. And then no one is surprised when the teenager with cerebral palsy is unable to use a knife in Food Tech. The OT has already gone into the Food Tech classroom and seen each child, and the teacher has already been told that this child needs a special cutting board so that they are not left frustrated from not being able to cut. It would be revolutionary! We think there is time and money to be saved here.

Let's even for a minute dream that this could happen in mainstream schools too, public and independent. The peas call for every secondary school in Australia and the world to have onsite therapists, whom the children are familiar with, whom they can even (heaven forbid) go and speak to themselves and start the journey of autonomy in their therapy. The sooner the teen learns how to start managing some of their therapies, the better, don't you think? Setting them up for a lifetime of advocating for themselves, if they are able.

We might be a while off from celebrating the complete integration of therapists into mainstream schools all across the country, but one thing we can all celebrate right now is our wonderful therapeas. These are the dedicated professionals who help our pea shoots and who make a genuine difference in our lives. They are also some of the podcast's most engaged and loyal listeners. How do they feel when they hear that some of us peas simply don't want to engage with their services, after years of doing so? How do they feel when we say sometimes all this therapy causes trauma? Shit, it's hard all round!

If we are late to an appointment (as annoying as that is), or if we don't turn up (also annoying) it is not because we don't value your time, it is because we are trying our hardest, but some days we fail. Never forget that we really value you!

Mandy says

If the peas were opening their dream therapy place it would look like this. Firstly, Kate would style it, so it would be beautiful. Secondly, I would lay out a red carpet from the front door to the desk, to indicate to the families that they are royalty (although Kate would probably say it has to be pea green!).

It will be called TheraPEA and will be a one-stop shop with easy and flat accessible parking and a giant sign with our faces over the door (again, subject to Kate's design approval).

When you walk inside, along that pea-green carpet, with your beautiful child/children, you will be greeted by someone who will, we hope, become a person whom your family gets to know. That person can also help with getting wheelchairs or walkers out of cars or carrying your bags so that you, the pea parents, can help your child. Imagine calling ahead from the car and saying, 'Hi Sarah, it's Mandy here, incoming with an upset child, can you please meet me in the carpark? I'll handle our pea shoot, but could you please give me a hand with the bags?'

The play therapist remembers your child's favourite toy from last week and comes outside to work their magic with a puppet in the car window to help your pea shoot calm down. Gosh, we could cry thinking about how awesome this would be.

Here is the list of peafessionals that Too Peas TheraPEA will have:

- paediatricians
- MCHN
- GPs
- psychologists
- speech pathologists
- occupational therapists
- physiotherapists
- sleep consultants
- psychiatrists
- play therapists
- dieticians
- social workers
- supervision.

You might be reading this list thinking, 'This sounds like hospital to me,' and yes, sure it does. But it's not and it never will be. There is no memory of traumatic births, NICU stays, surgeries, X-rays or admissions to contend with for the child or the parent. Less PTSD all round.

There will be no forms to fill out (you will have already done that at home), and you will only ever need one referral. You will *never* be made to go back to the doctor every year to get a referral for a lifelong disability that is not going to change. And don't even talk to me about parking permits, peas: all the car parking will be accessible.

There will be coffee or tea for parents who haven't managed one yet. And nice ones, not crappy ones. Heck, why not a beautiful cafe with roti bread and nuggets, plus dietician-approved snacks, plus fresh doughnuts every day! There will be comfy chairs and couches and a coffee table, and in the main room there will be a TV quietly in the corner, set to a program that might inspire conversations. And *Too Peas in a Podcast* playing on a never-ending loop.

I will set up the toy area, with books and playdough and all the play therapy you could want for a child waiting for their appointments. Outside is a sensory garden with tables and chairs for picnic lunches for dieticians to practise on, maybe even in little groups of like-minded pea shoots. Parents can talk, can listen, can laugh and cry.

MyTime, the Australian support group, could also meet there once a week, and a mobile lasagne business would come each day so you can buy your dinner to take home.

This place is open to every single pea shoot and their family for as long as they need. No one is kicked out at eighteen. It's not disability-specific, so that if you are like most children who don't fit in a box, it doesn't matter. You need it; you can access it.

There would also be a huge staffroom that is comfortable and welcoming to all the staff, an option to buy their lunch from the cafe if they have run out of time, potentially with their own children or pea shoots, or if they are simply tired themselves. Weekly staff meetings are followed by dinner paid for by the peas, giving an opportunity to debrief informally. Staff celebrate the wins of the families they have worked with, so that the team can cheer the family on together – as opposed to one person at this place, one person at that place, emailing each other.

By now you are probably thinking, 'You girls are dreaming.' Yes, we are, but every amazing band, building, support structure started with a dream . . .

Kate says

Now that you are here, would you like to accompany me and my preschool-aged twins to an occupational therapy assessment? I've opted for a morning appointment, as they are always better for the boys, but maybe I should have booked an afternoon assessment, to show the OT the raw honesty of what they are like later in the day. Which is better? I still don't know the answer to that one. I want everyone to see my kids at their best, but I don't want people to have unrealistic expectations of them.

Let's hope I bloody remember to turn up on the right day this time. I will dress Woody in red and Buzz in blue so hopefully everyone will remember which child is which. I do not want the wrong report given (it has happened, believe me). All right, let's get this show on the road!

I double-check that the bag has drink bottles, distracting toys (usually a new Matchbox car or similar), snacks, change of clothes (you never know!), pen and paper, colouring-in book and stickers (and don't forget to double all of these items).

Once we arrive, and while we are all still in the car we will have a chat, Mum to twins. It will go something like this:

'Now, we are not going to touch anything, we are going to sit still till it's our turn. We are going to not yell out, we are going to be super quiet, like, the most quiet we have ever been and we won't fight. Okay?'

'Okay, Mum.'

By the time I get to the back door of the car they are laughing and pulling each other's hair.

'What are you doing?'

Blank stares and then more laughter. They have already forgotten the Mum rant.

When you have preschool twins similar to mine, both car doors have the child safety locks on. You cannot risk for one second those very speedy (when least expected) twins escaping and running. There are systems in place: for example, you only open the car door nearest the kerb, you have to get yourself completely sorted and I mean *completely sorted* before you start disembarking those twins. If your shirt is pulled down and there is a boob halfway out, that is where it stays. If your skirt is stuck in your undies, too bad, sister. Once those twins have a hand each, you are not letting go, so get yourself together before you open that door.

Right, now we have to get into the building without tripping or collecting too many sticks. Generally, a small rock is better than a stick to take to an appointment, but you don't want to start too big a tantrum, so just put it out into the universe that small rocks be on your path and no sticks – and absolutely no snails!

You make it to the door and just as you think the planets are aligning you realise that the door's got a fucking handle. I shit you not. I mean, you can't let go of the child, he will bolt, but you don't want to dislocate his shoulder reaching his little arm up to the handle. Oh well, you've got legs for a reason, Kate, use that foot!

It's not glamorous but you at least made it through the door. The twins think it's hilarious so we are a pile of laughter and giggles until we look up and see a stern receptionist staring down her glasses at us. Your heart sinks. It's form time, bitches! Now, form time is not fun, as you well know, and it's even less fun filling out the same form twice, with literally identical information except for the names. The lovely receptionist, who thinks you are feral for kicking open the door, only needs the forms to enter them 'onto the system', so why can't we just fill one out?

But it has to be done. You get all the toys out of the bag and start filling out those forms like the first one finished gets a million dollars, because any time spent looking at the form is time not directly watching the twins, and for some insane reason there is a fish tank in this waiting room! Not only that but by the time we leave we will have one or two of every little pamphlet on offer in this waiting room, from domestic violence services to the local playgroup. I mean, in all fairness, it does say 'take one'; even though Buzz and Woody can't read yet, they get the vibe and we get the pamphlets.

The next ten minutes see us all shamed by reception lady, other patients and definitely the mum with one little child quietly colouring in, because we bring the much-needed fun and energy into waiting rooms. We climb chairs, try to get to the fish, go under the chairs, wrestle (every day is wrestle day), we spill crumbs and time stands still! Hot tip for receptionists: if you know you have twins with ADHD coming to see you, let their parents know if the practice is running late or pay the consequences. Or even better, get rid of the fish! And put the pamphlets above kids' reach! Come on!

By the time we reach the assessment, the twins are hyped and I am exhausted – just in time for all the questions and hopefully no judgement.

I don't want you to think for one second I am exaggerating anything above. If anything I am 'under reporting' here, people! It was really crappy, but also funny, and the boys and I laughed at so many things along the way. I knew people thought I was a bad mum, but they were wrong; see, I was mediocre. And as hard as those days were, we bloody did it! I always felt such a huge achievement when we got back in the car. Perhaps not so much when the domestic violence pamphlet fell out of my bag at Woolies, but oh well . . .

Mostly, Buzz and Woody dipped in and out of therapea. We saw a lot of the big list of therapies for assessments and diagnosis, or we saw them in the curriculum support area of school. For me, good therapy is the kind that makes daily life easier and helps with the future. It's not about changing who my boys are, I don't like that; it's about embracing their skills and strengths and teaching us all the best way to do things. A good OT or nurse can literally change your day and life! We love you, and thank you! And I am sorry for the times I didn't do what you said. Sometimes it's like rolling shit uphill. It's stinky and I just can't do it.

PART THREE
PRECIOUS PEA SHOOTS

14

School

Let's see what Google says 'school' is, shall we?

An institution for educating children.

Maybe we should delve deeper. Google, what is an institution?

An organisation founded for a religious, educational, professional, or social purpose.

Right, so school is an organisation for educating children. So what is education, then?

The process of receiving or giving systematic instruction, especially at a school or university.

The definitions sort of go around in circles, which is perhaps a great metaphor for how parents feel when choosing a school, or even just communicating with a school, so we suppose it will do just fine.

Picture this: a brand-new school year, a new classroom with cute posters on the wall, little chairs and little desks, embroidered chair bags hanging on the back of each chair, new pencils sitting on top of desks with names on laminated cards (does anyone love a laminator as much as a teacher?). Just outside the door, little legs line up in a row, ready to enter this room of learning. Excitement, nerves – they're all there. All the little round pegs, ready to fit in the round holes.

Can you see the problem yet? I mean if you are a round peg, or a round-peg parent, more power to you. But what about the square pegs?

'One, two, three, eyes on me!'

The pegs – sorry – *children* are asked to sit quietly on the mat with their legs crossed. Such a basic, easy request . . . unless you have an AFO and they dig into you and hurt when you cross your legs. Or you find it really hard to look into the eyes of strangers. Or you have ADHD and sitting still when you first enter a room is actually impossible. Or you have a vision impairment and you cannot see the teacher properly.

Think of the child who has separation anxiety. School drop-off is the worst time of their day and they're probably not going to be in the best frame of mind to be quietly sitting on the mat, staring at the teacher. Or the pretty awesome child who has diabetes and his mum thinks he might need to pop to the office for a finger-prick test. What happens to the student who needs that little bit of extra time to hang up their hat, put their drink bottle on their desk and find their reader in the bottom of their bag? The round pegs comply easily, but what about the rest? Imagine 'failing' on your very first day of school. A school you (and your parents) will soon learn is not for people who don't fit in round holes. But everybody is going to twist you and turn you and force you to try to fit in that hole!

'Okay, now, Year Pea, everyone get your writing book out of your tub, find a lead pencil and your eraser and sit quietly at your desk.'

Perhaps 80 per cent of the class are happily following the 'relatively easy' task they have been given, but some kids can't remember past the first command (and let's face it, some of us adults would struggle) so they are deploying their unique class-room survival skills: observing and copying, which work a lot of the time. There are others: quietly chatting to a trusted friend and asking what was needed; sitting quietly and doing nothing, hoping no one will notice what they are 'not' doing; joking and distracting loudly so the teacher repeats their task request; asking to go to the toilet, so that when they return they can cast their eagle eyes around the classroom and work out what the heck they were supposed to be doing, all the while mindful of the seven different-coloured laminated clouds hanging on strings on the front wall. Each cloud contains a different phrase. Let's start at the bottom cloud, shall we?

The first/bottom cloud is black. It says, 'Go see the principal.'
The second cloud is grey. It says, 'Loss of privilege.'
The third cloud is red. It says, 'Warning.'
The middle and fourth cloud is green. It says, 'Ready to learn.'
The fifth cloud is a lovely light blue and says, 'Good day.'
The sixth cloud is pink and says, 'Delightful behaviour day.'

The seventh and top cloud is a beautiful rainbow and says, 'Fabulous student.'

Twenty-two cute little raindrop shapes (also laminated, of course), each bearing a student's name, are all sitting on 'ready to learn'. For any round pegs, they rarely or never go below 'ready to learn'. But kids who take that little bit longer, or who have to use coping strategies to get through every minute at school ... well, they know what it is like to sit on the 'warning' cloud, and they know that everyone else knows.

Every mum who comes in for reading time, every dad who comes in to bring back a forgotten lunch or recorder, they are drawn to the clouds like Mandy to doughnuts, and they see which students are heading down the storm cloud on the classroom weather chart and have never touched the rainbow.

Can you hear that scraping sound? It is the peas getting on the soapbox. We know it's not 'all teachers', we really do! And good peachers are game-changers, whom we love fiercely. But public reward charts – come on! We might as well call them public shame charts because that's what they are. Imagine if your manager put one up at your work; you could make a convincing case that that's workplace bullying! Besides, who is getting rewarded anyway? Mostly the kids for whom the rewarded behaviour is easy.

This is happening right now. Today, as you read this, there is a classroom with this reward system in place. It adds to stigma and shaming. There are charts for kids who go up reading levels, kids who learn all their times tables – the list goes on and on. Of course, we love it when kids get acknowledged for doing well, especially when they have tried super hard, and there is nothing wrong with that! But it should never come at the expense or shame of another child, and children's achievements should never be publicly pitted against each other. If you are reading this and you are a teacher with a rewards chart system, perhaps you might consider changing your system. Students now and in the future will thank you for it; you will change lives!

The bell rings. It's breaktime! Surely this is a time of relief for everyone?

Um, hell no. What if you can't eat as quickly as your friends? What if opening your lunchbox is tricky? What if you have to go to the office to have a tablet, and you miss where everyone is eating and or playing today? What if no one told you that scrunchies were cool and you are the only one with a ribbon in your hair? What if all the noise is overwhelming and you need a quiet space? What if it takes you all recess or most of lunchtime to get changed into your sports uniform? (Hey, private schools, we are looking at you! Stop making kids do this!) What if your school values winning above inclusion so you never get invited to play Kick to Kick? Yep, it seems like whoever is in charge of breaktime needs to go read the chapter on empathy!

This topic is a tricky one. We all need school because we all need to learn. True, there is homeschool, but it is still *school*. It's the one thing we've all done at some point or another, and the one thing that all our kids will do. For many of us, our first real concrete memories are indeed of school. Without any proof or peer-reviewed research, we think we can safely say that school can make or break you. The last thing we want to do is attack teachers; in all honesty, we think the education system itself is outdated and probably needs attacking. But even with this outdated system, I bet every person reading this can remember 'that one teacher': the one who made you love Shakespeare or the one who gave you your love of geography or art or science. The one who finally got you to understand algebra; the one who was kind when your home life was a mess. And sometimes there was 'that other teacher' too. The one who bullied students, the one who was racist, the one who turned a blind eye to what was really going on, the one who had favourites. Yep, we probably all have those memories too. For some of us, school may have been the happiest days of our lives; for some it is also true that 'anyone who says schools are the happiest days of their life obviously never went to high school'!

If everyone has to go to school, you would think that in this day and age, school would reflect the needs of everyone, that education ministers and departments would be working their hardest to find innovative and inclusive ways for us all to learn. But we all know that the education system in this country is a little bit broken. You have kids with ADHD getting suspended in early primary school, not because they are troublemakers but because their little bodies have boundless energy and there is nowhere for them to channel it. They have executive functioning disorders, and need to move and fidget, run and talk and play. It's a disability that needs support, but instead they get shamed and excluded. Some children with dyslexia receive no extra support either.

Schools full of stairs, schools with inaccessible classrooms, schools with drink fountains that require two hands to operate. Schools where children in wheelchairs have to fight to get into the toilet because teachers are using the accessible bathroom as a storage cupboard. Schools that have no money to help students who need a little extra help. Schools and parents and students desperate for the 'right' diagnosis that will allow funding. An ableist society is running our school systems. Over the years the broken system has been patched up here and there, but if you were buying it, the sign would say 'renovator's delight!' It is outrageous, and history will judge us for how we are treating these students.

School is the biggest race of your life, and it's clear that it's all about who finishes first. Not who knows the most, but who finishes first with the most information. Who can write all their times tables in the grid first, who finished extra questions on the test, whose NAPLAN ranking is the highest. Everything is timed, and speed is equated with intelligence. Don't we all sometimes take a moment to make a decision? Pace around a bit before answering an email to think things through? Well, there's no time for that at school!

We understand that sometimes speed is of the essence, and that there are some situations that require speed and quick decision-making, such as if you work in emergency services. But children are not paramedics and a Year 4 classroom is not the Emergency department. It is a lazy education system that decided speed was everything and if you don't fit that mould, too bad, so sad!

And what about the magic numbers in Victoria that determine whether your child is eligible for a specialist school or whether they have to stay mainstream? Now, don't get us wrong: we are passionate about inclusion and want all kids to be able to attend whatever school works for them. But imagine this: your local school isn't a good fit for your child with a disability; however, the local specialist school is amazing and would be a wonderful place for them to learn and thrive. Perfect! Well, wait just a second. In Victoria, if you have a mild intellectual disability this needs to be measured by having an IQ between 50 and 70 (with 100 being the average) to be eligible for a specialist school, and to attend a special developmental school it is 50 and below. So, what happens if your child's IQ is 73? Well, they have to stay at mainstream school! That is what!

The absolute joy of specialist schools is that they are actually reforming the education system. In other words, the renovation is nearly complete, or is at least in progress. Why aren't all schools like that? This is a constant debate, and people smarter than us continue to have it.

Specialist schools are wonderful places but our final gripe about the education system within which they operate is about the fact that they are so removed from mainstream schools. Why can't every school have a specialist unit? That way, siblings and twins won't have to be split up, and they can share a canteen or lunchtime activities – be included, rather than not?

We wonder why some children have anxiety! And the thing that breaks peas' hearts everywhere is that not going to school is not really an option for your pea shoots, unless you have the skills and time to homeschool them, which many of us don't. So off they go, to face bullies, rewards charts, judgement, coming last in everything, not finishing their work, being left out of parties and group chats, having people ask them, 'What is wrong with you?' 'What is on your leg?' 'Why do you have those things on your ears?' The more inclusive education and society is, the less these questions would be asked. If everyone is a round peg, though, the squares sure stand out!

In an ideal world, this is how a pea shoot's school report would read:

Too Peas school report

Reading   Oh, how we loved reading with Pea Shoot this term! We loved hearing her laugh at Hairy Maclary, and her joy at reading a page on her own before we read a page together. The feeling of fulfilment was palpable when we all understood the story. It has been a highlight of the school term to watch this progress.

Maths   Again, we have had a great term with Pea Shoot. Her ability to solve maths problems in such a unique way is nothing short of amazing. Repetition with times tables was not enjoyed at all, so we laminated a times-tables chart and stuck it on her desk, and it has worked beautifully.

Writing   This term we took a little reprieve from writing and used the iPad to create stories with pictures and a few words. This ended up inspiring so much conversation that we are going to use a scribe to get these amazing stories on paper next term. To say we are excited about Pea Shoot's progress is an understatement.

Library   We were delighted by Pea Shoot's enthusiasm this term. Borrowing *all* the *Guinness Books of World Records* – that was the heaviest library bag we packed!

Kate says

Oh, 2004 Kate, if I could go back and tell you what I know now about sending the twins to school, I would tell you that you will meet the most divine teachers ever. These teachers will be your lifeline, even after your kids have finished in their class. They will tell you when you are overreacting and when you are right to put your Doc Martens on and go talk to the principal. Cherish them!

Also, it is okay to change schools. No school is right for everyone. Don't constantly second-guess yourself; deep down, you know what to do.

My boys' experiences at school were one of my main drivers for starting the podcast. The number of times students with disabilities or additional needs are discriminated against at mainstream school is unbelievable. For some it happens daily; for most it is over and over again – and it is difficult for parents and students to feel they can voice concerns. It fills me with rage. So many of my friends with kids who have disabilities or additional needs have changed schools due to discrimination, or have paid for extra therapy and tutoring, or have cried at specialists and allied health professionals because they don't know where to go or what to do. If you hear even a whisper about a school that has aides in classrooms, welcomes diversity and is less than an hour from your house then you are on the phone and hoping you can afford the fees or it isn't zoned.

We all know education needs more funding, but what gets me is if we don't fund it now, won't we pay for it later? Doesn't it cost us in the long run having such a narrow view of what education is? Of course it works well for neurotypical kids who can concentrate – Scholarship bloody loved school – but what about the kids who excel in creating, in building, in 3D animation, in puzzle-matching? Where is their VCE/HSC/senior course? What about the kids with processing delays, who are given a whole extra fifteen minutes to complete an exam? Fifteen minutes! *Fuck off!* Shouldn't it be individualised?

The only way you can get an ATAR is to sit an exam. But wait, there is more. If you think your child will need a scribe then be prepared to have to jump through several thousand administrative hoops. Why are we treating our vulnerable kids or kids with learning disabilities this way?

They might be out there, but I have never met a parent of a child with additional needs who feels their child hasn't been singled out or discriminated against while attending mainstream school. To be honest, if I hadn't witnessed it I wouldn't believe it either, but it happens every day. If you are a school parent and you take the blinkers off, you will see it too. Everyone has a story about a bullying incident, a teacher making a wrong call or a lunch order being messed up, because the canteen ladies didn't think the allergy was real or that no mum would just order her child a chocolate milk! But when you live in fear of seeing the school's number on your phone or you can't wait for Friday afternoon so everyone can get a respite from the education system, you understand the injustice so many students face. It changes them and it changes you.

They say – and I believe it – that no one is born racist. I also think that no child is born ready to judge another child because of a disability. But if you are a non-neurotypical student at a mainstream school, you will soon learn that parents teach their children how to discriminate.

Also, here's a little tip: school reports can be almightily shit! You don't have to read them the day you get them; you can wait till you have chocolate/wine/doughnuts. And remember, they are just a list of milestones that someone, somewhere thought mattered. And what do we say to most milestones? Yep! Fuck you, milestones! I often think back on what Dr Shane said to me when the boys got mobile and kept running and falling over. He said, 'Don't tell them to stop; tell them, "Little steps, boys, little steps!"'

It's harder to lose control when you are taking little steps. I think school reports are little steps. They're certainly not the be-all and end-all of anything. I prefer in-control little steps in the right direction anyway! Little steps, friends, little steps!

It's also important to keep in mind that for every rectum parent passing their garbage opinions on to their rectum children, there are also wonderful, amazing parents and kids who will be bright spots and allies in what can be a difficult space for you and your family. It made all the difference to find fellow parents who didn't judge, who loved to laugh and chatted for too long after school drop-off and made me late for work. As we know, it's not always easy to find your people, peas, but if you do, you can handle almost anything.

Mandy says

School. Where do I begin? Well, it kind of began on the day we bought a house across the road from a public school and moved in a week before the twins were born. I remember looking at the school and imagining my twins walking in together on the first day as I chatted with fellow parents out the front and laughed about not having to drive to school for pick-up and drop-off. It took another three years for me to realise that the school was riddled with stairs and totally inappropriate for my girls to attend, so we sold the house and moved, and chose a school that had no stairs at all. At the time, the school was falling to pieces and only a few other families in the area chose to send their children there, but I just kept my eyes on the no-stairs prize. I could also sense the community feel; it was like a little country town and I could tell its heart at the time was welcoming and willing.

The first day the girls walked in together was an exhilarating victory that had been five years in the making. We looked ridiculous, with both sets of grandparents, my sister and our six-week-old baby all walking to school with the girls and entering the classroom like a tsunami of family. What I wanted to yell to everyone who was staring at us was, 'You don't know what this

day means to us; we never thought they would leave the hospital!'
Instead I was friendly and polite and tried not to cry.

The planning for an aide began in kinder, with the filling out
of many forms, painting the 'worst' picture of my precious five-
year-old so that we could get funding for her. That's how we
began school. Then the years went on, full of misunderstandings,
wonderful teachers, tricky teachers, wonderful aides, tricky aides,
happy years, unhappy years, calls from the school, falls, trips to
sick bay, surgeries, recoveries, therapies, beautiful friends, tricky
friends, wonderful awards, no awards, understanding and humiliation. Every day could be a mixture of all of it, and I was on
constant high alert.

What wasn't an issue were Molly's friendships – she had lots of
friends and both girls were accepted, belonged, and were part of
the community. I remember the first week of school I drove past
at lunchtime so I could spy on them and I saw Molly standing
on her own in her enormous hat. My heart sank and then I
kept driving and then I saw Milly standing on her own in her
enormous hat and I was able to laugh and not think the worst.
They were just five-year-olds who were learning their way.

The decision to move Molly to the specialist school we were
allocated to in Year 5 was the biggest decision I have made in my
life. She was the one who decided. She was having such a hard
time and, as we were both crying on the bathroom floor one
night, I made a promise to her to find the best school I could.
Since she was the one who wanted to leave, that was easier but I
still grappled with the decision. Was I taking her away from mainstream people? Was I taking the pressure off her? Was I giving her
twin room to breathe? Was I ruining their twin relationship or was
I enhancing it? How was I going to manage the bus? How could
this happen just when I was finally getting all three girls to the
one place at the one time? How did other families get so lucky

to never have to go through this? Where are my people? Who are my friends now? How was Molly going to manage this change? What if she hated it? What if she loved it and I should have moved her earlier? The questions went on and on until I remembered a friend telling me, 'This is a marathon, Mandy, not a sprint.'

I realised she was right. I had poured so much energy into advocating for Molly's needs and rights to be met at a mainstream school, but I hadn't even stopped to think about the fact that school life is short compared to the rest of their lives. These are actually the 'easy' years for a child with an intellectual disability. These are the years they have somewhere to go and belong that is age appropriate. What on earth are we going to do afterwards? And if I'm already burning myself out during the 'easy' years, then how am I going to have any energy left for the rest of her life?

That's when I decided to bite the bullet and send Molly to the specialist school. It was a hard decision, and, to be honest, taking her out of mainstream school made me feel as if I was giving up on her. I know logically that isn't true, but it's how I felt, like I'd taken the easy way out. I didn't have to fight anymore, didn't have to worry about homework or NAPLAN or VCE. At the specialist school, she could learn at her own pace. She is safe there, and, for the most part, content.

Any school that starts the day with two hundred children with intellectual disabilities dancing, is a fantastic school. The times I could catch assembly were my favourite times. Children dancing, leading the assembly, all the body movements, all the acceptance – it just made me cry and cry each time. The small class sizes, the sheer number of staff on the photo wall, Nurse Rae and her cat and her lollies, the buses, the drivers, the support staff, the early mornings, all made it so different and such a lot to learn.

Molly thrived instantly. She went on camps, and I didn't have to spend any time in preparation; I knew she would be spending five days doing activities that she could handle. She would never be left out again. I truly relaxed for the first time that year when she was away from me. The new stories she had to tell. I will never forget receiving the phone call from Molly in the principal's office to tell me she was going to be a school captain for a term; it was spine-tingling. The day of the school captains' speeches. My heart. I have never experienced anything so incredible in all my life. The bravery, the hilarity and when Molly gave her speech the tears just dripped down my face and I thought for the first time, 'That is twelve years of speech therapy right there.' I was so incredibly proud of her.

The siblings' nights. These were a revolution for our family. The siblings were invited, and the teachers showed them around the school. They had a PE lesson, saw their sibling's classroom, ate dinner together and learnt some of the dances from the morning dance routines. Finally, my girls got to experience some sibling support and I just loved what those nights meant to them.

The school production. As the principal, Claire, said into the microphone, 'You will never see a better show,' and boy, was she right. All the children in costumes, singing and dancing and crying and scared and headphones and walkers and wheelchairs and hearing aids and AFOs and you name it, it was the first night in twelve years that my entire family felt like we belonged. I cried at my friends' children being brave, and we laughed at the children who were hilarious. We all cried and hugged afterwards. That doesn't happen in mainstream schools. I have been to my fair share of mainstream school productions and while there is always a funny kid or two, it's bland compared to a specialist school.

The Year 6 graduation was another beautiful night. Children so adored and dressed up to the max, parents and grandparents, aunties and uncles beaming with pride and teachers so carefully and proudly introducing our kids and giving them their moment.

We also had the challenge of the cognitive tests that we told you about and the immense worry of her 'failing' them. Thankfully Molly passed her test for specialist school. As we both walked into the room with the psychologist, the first thing she said was, 'Molly has qualified for her school,' and then I didn't hear anything else she said. I was more relieved than I could ever express to you on the page.

The specialist secondary school is different. It was a big transition and gave me all the emotions. I will write about that time when it's over, maybe *The Invisible Life of Us*, Volume 5. What I will say though is our Year 9 teacher, a pea herself, was an incredible support during 2020 and I can't thank her enough for her availability and kindness in listening to me at that time and helping me whenever she could in the eight months of online learning/not learning.

I can imagine that when we finish secondary schooling, I will feel every single feeling. But from where I sit now, and especially after the coronavirus pandemic and homeschooling, I think we will be at a stage to move on. I suspect 2024 Mandy will be reading this and shaking her head, saying, 'You have no idea how tricky it is out of school, Mandy.' And she might be right, so perhaps I best be quiet.

15

Awards

It's the last Friday of term at the local primary school. The kids are full of fidgets. Scrunchies are falling out of ponytails and there is a strange smell of dirt and Cheezels wafting through the school hall. Parents are either bragging about their upcoming Bali holiday or moaning about the fact school has to finish early on the last day of term, and the teachers can smell the pinot grigio in the staffroom fridge.

The kids are all sitting cross-legged on the floor, as quietly as is possible with two or three hundred five- to twelve-year-olds. They are fidgeting and picking fluff off the school hall carpet, nudging each other and trying not to giggle. The parents are up the back, sitting on plastic stackable chairs, thankfully not forced to also endure the humiliation of middle-aged hips attempting to sit cross-legged (except for the yoga mum, who happily and slightly sanctimoniously sits on aforementioned floor). The principal of this perfectly unremarkable primary school assembly is about to change someone's life! If you are an old hand at school assemblies you can tell whose life this will be. There are telltale signs scattered around the hall – probably both primary caregivers of . . . let's call him 'Owen', and maybe even an aunt or uncle or grandma are there too. The camera phones are poised, and for the first time all year, Owen is wearing the correct school uniform. If the class teacher is amazingly efficient, Owen may also be sitting at the end of his haphazard row, but hopefully not, as the small-child-awkwardly-stepping-over-everyone shuffle is a definite part of the joy of assembly viewing.

But why is Owen's life about to be forever and so magnificently changed, I hear you wonder? It is because the mighty seven-and-three-quarter-year-old Owen is receiving an award for . . . drum roll, please . . . remarkable work in comprehension!

Exciting, right? Or, rather, remarkable! Let's look up that word 'remarkable', shall we?

Remarkable: worthy of attention or striking.

That's right, folks, before he has even turned eight, Owen's ability to comprehend a passage of writing is worthy of attention, which is lucky because today at 9.17 am that is exactly what is happening. This truly momentous occasion will be on Owen's mum's Facebook feed by 9.23 am, might make the school's tree-friendly, online-only newsletter by the afternoon, and will definitely be showcased on a slightly blurry phone photo at Nana's next hairdressing appointment. It's huge news! Probably a precursor to Owen becoming the prime minister, or perhaps a political journalist, able to explain detailed policy to the masses due to his remarkable ability to comprehend. Or, of course, it might just be bloody stupid!

That's right, it's bloody stupid on so many levels, and the levels are going down, baby! Right here, right now.

Okay (and don't ask us to calm down), for starters, awards in primary school (actually, pretty much anything before Year 12) for academic achievements are bullshit. Yep, we see the bullshit, we smell it and we are calling it! Let's have a quick look at the actual definition of an award, shall we?

Award: a prize or other mark of recognition given in honour of an achievement.

Even without asking Owen and his amazing comprehension abilities for help with this one, we can probably all figure out than an award is recognition for a superb achievement. So, pea friends, the question I ask of you all is what remarkable work did Owen do above and beyond everyone else in 2D's comprehension lesson? Did he take extra comprehension home to do after homework tasks were completed? Did he explain the school's uniform policies and after-care procedures to a group of new kids at lunchtime? Did he ask the teacher for more complex comprehension to do instead of the age-old tradition sharing of 'nude food' (yes, nude food – food without any plastic wrapping, it's a thing!) from his mates' lunchboxes?

Sadly, Owen probably did none of the above. In fact, and this may blow your minds, Owen actually finds comprehension extremely easy. He completed his work, did no extra work, his parents did not have to help him at home through a curtain of tears, the teacher did not have to re-explain the comprehension activity and he was actually able to go on his iPad while the other kids finished! Yep, Owen's remarkable achievement was finishing first at an activity he was lucky enough to be naturally good at (which some may argue is reward enough!).

But, I can hear you cry, 'Peas, doesn't Owen need this? Won't it fuel his desire for learning? Won't he be more likely to achieve great academic success? Won't he more fully realise the power of finishing first? Won't he be driven to learn even more comprehension skills?'

Sure, it will make him feel good about himself, which is not a bad thing, but remember he probably *already* feels good about himself – the teacher has probably already given him some positive feedback, he has seen his marks and knows he finished first! And here is the horrid flip side to our young comprehension genius's award.

For the non-naturally-gifted comprehension-loving assembly attendees, those who couldn't finish on time despite trying, those whose dyslexia makes comprehension a real bitch, those whose ADHD means they need another ten minutes and a quick trip to the drink bubbler, those who have fine motor dexterity issues, or the child whose dog died today, whose mum and dad had a huge fight over who forgot to put the bins out and they are a bit distracted, those with an aide who always is on their team and facilitates learning, but they still don't finish on time . . . do you know what they learn about awards? They learn that effort does not equal school awards. Because, and here is a very badly kept secret, the amazing students we just mentioned actually *worked harder at comprehension than Owen*. (True, some schools give out awards for effort. That is not what we mean when we talk about effort. What we mean is the herculean effort – often exerted in every subject, recess, lunchtime and even sport – that our kids put in time and time again, even despite getting 'fewer' results!)

The bottom line? Awards suck!

But before we get off our high horse, let's not forget the most amazing award of all . . . attendance!

After the librarian announces the Children's Book Council of Australia Children's Book of the Year, the principal stands and is ready to call up the kids who have achieved the most remarkable feat of all (even more remarkable than achievement in comprehension – sorry, Owen!). You won't believe it, but it's true: these kids managed to not have a day off all term. Not one ear infection, not one day of appointments at the Royal Children's Hospital, no surgeries or hospital admissions, no mental health days due to stress and anxiety, no stomach aches, no gastro, no colds! These kids stayed well!

They line up, proud of their achievement, and once again the kids who have multiple hospital or doctor's appointments or who find a term at school with no days off impossible for their mental health sink a little lower. Through no fault of their own, they remain without that little laminated A5 piece of paper that, although it means very little, actually means a great deal. Once again, these kids feel ashamed for things they should not feel ashamed about. Most assembly patrons won't notice, but there will be one or two parents holding back tears. The bloody attendance award is a knife to the heart, and frankly it can fuck off!*

Each school may call these something else – student of the week, achievement awards, year-level awards, and on and on. Personalised, targeted awards. Sometimes they are given for academic success, sometimes sporting prowess, sometimes for improving behaviours or sometimes for musical talent and sometimes they are given for character traits the teacher applauds.

Sometimes – and we are all human, so we get how this happens – the awards seem to be a bit like another amazing awards ceremony: the Logies. Yep, a popularity contest. Sometimes, some teachers appear to have favourites, and this is never more obvious than at assembly. We understand that some kids are compliant, and have lovely, easygoing natures, so it is 'easy' to get them to hand out the programs for Mother's Day or help with the school flag. But we in the pea-verse all know that if you give other kids a go, who may never get a go, you will see their self-esteem grow before your eyes. Let's not forget that some people don't like being up front (believe it or not, they probably won't grow up to have a podcast), but they still have skills that are important to the school day, which can be acknowledged during assembly.

---

* We know that the attendance award was a brilliant idea to get vulnerable children to attend school, and we acknowledge how important it is for all kids to attend school on a regular basis, but in truth it rewards some but punishes other vulnerable kids, and also encourages parents and kids to attend when perhaps that runny nose they have should have kept them home!

For example, 'Bonnie put the PowerPoint together today' or 'George carried all the water to the footy team when they won on Thursday and he cheered the loudest.' See what we did? The footy team got their win mentioned but so did George!

We don't mind the awards that recognise kindness, empathy, social justice or environmental awareness. We much prefer them over an award in assembly for 'great NAPLAN success' (don't roll your eyes, we've seen it happen!), and we love that children are recognised for things outside academia. Schools are supposed to be inclusive, and that doesn't just mean aides in classrooms. It means every tiny decision and tradition at a school being re-examined, and parents, students and the brilliant educators voicing concerns about who these traditions are serving and who they are excluding, and then finding a way to make a positive change. It may make little difference to some, but for others it can change the entire course of their education and the way they view school.

Mandy has noticed a big difference in Miss Ten's public mainstream school in the last five years when it comes to awards. Teachers and peachers are really taking the time to make awards meaningful. That's what counts.

Mandy says

I think one of the happiest moments of my twins attending school was Year 4 when they won a Student of the Week on the same day. Granted, it was because one of the girls was at a hospital appointment the week before and so therefore missed it, but that's a minor detail.

I even have a photo of that day. Twin sisters in the front garden in matching uniforms holding their meaningful awards. What a day – no one feeling left out or crying because they hadn't received an award yet. An afternoon that their mum didn't have to spend comforting, explaining or consoling. We could just pretend that we were like any ordinary family who came home and had afternoon tea and enjoyed each other's company. That was the last time I got a photo of the girls in matching uniforms with matching awards; Year 5 was the year that our family decided to send Molly to the local specialist school.

The teachers at our local primary school did a wonderful job of making these awards meaningful. I like to use that word as I think it makes all the difference. They didn't hand out achievement awards to the children who could achieve things with their eyes closed while ignoring the kids who tried the hardest. (A tip for those handing out awards – these are the ones that hurt when you don't receive them.) Or maybe they hurt the mums and dads, sitting on the chairs, running from work, turning their phones on silent, shushing the toddler (or toddlers), taking the fifteen-month-old's shoes off so they can walk around the loud hall and not be a distraction. Setting the phone video up so they can send the footage to family who adore this precious child and think that every move they make is extraordinary, especially when they have seen them from birth, fighting for their lives in NICU, to now being a child in the matching uniform who is one of many, but the only one in their eyes.

Year 3 was the turning point for my family, after Molly had run the cross-country at school, with her AFO on her leg, and her twin sister doing the same. I was cheering both girls on, my body and mind on high alert, so proud they were attempting it. I was remembering every first step with the physio, every appointment, every botox injection and general anaesthetic, and casts and finding shoes, the femoral osteotomy at age six, when Molly's leg was broken and turned into her hip, followed by recovery for one whole year, panic attacks finding shoes – this was a big moment.

The next week, it's assembly time and Molly is called to the front. Video on, toddler quiet, heart beating out of my chest. I think, 'Wow, this is fantastic, she is getting an award for finishing the cross-country. Such an effort. I'm so proud of her.' Then, 'For throwing a pile of leaves on her teacher and making her laugh.'

What?

Molly takes the award, the audience claps, and then Molly looks at it and then me; we were both surprised. An award for throwing leaves? Talk about missing the point! I also know that when Molly laughs, it's pure magic and her smile lights up a room, as so many children with CP do, so I understood that; I just didn't think it was an appropriate public award as her only award for the year, when she had achieved something so remarkable just the week before. What a shame.

Kate says

My experience of school assemblies is in the private school system. My boys, like lots of children who cannot quite meet the ridiculous requirements for aide funding in the state government system, attend private schools to get support in their learning. There is a lot of diversity in a school that may have originally been set up as a place of 'academic excellence'. The thing is academic excellence means so, so much more than getting excellent marks (or working beyond the expected level). But sometimes it feels like the schools have forgotten this and continue to reward academic success above all other success!

What advice would 2021 Kate say to Past Kate? Well, she would say, 'You know student academic awards are shit and you will never *change* your mind! Dig in, girlfriend: it gets worse, not better, but you are right! Awards suck and guess what? You are going to find a whole podcast audience who mostly agree!'

16

After-school activities

After-school, or extracurricular, activities are activities that you do outside class. The common definition says that extra-curricular activities include arts, athletics, clubs, employment, personal commitments and other pursuits.

One of the common discussions with women of school-aged children since the pandemic and lockdown here in Melbourne has been the relief at the abrupt ending of after-school and weekend activities. No more parents – mothers – spending hours driving their children to and from afternoon activities, no more making sure their kids are 'keeping up' as well as having the opportunities to excel in their chosen sport or dance class.

Turn to the discussion for families of children with additional needs and disabilities, and the chat about extracurricular activities is usually another discussion that we are not a part of. Finding activities for our children is sometimes just impossible.

Ask any parent in the pea tribe and they will have many stories of the trial and error of finding a creative or sporting outlet for their child or children. For some, the adjustment of recognising that their child will not follow in their footsteps of playing for the local cricket club or dance studio is sitting in their heart.

They will be able to tell you about the money they spent on uniforms in the hope that this particular activity might be the one. Volunteering at the club so that their child will be accepted. Running alongside their daughter with CP while she was crying, after the gun, just to get her confidence up to cross the line. Standing at the finish line, crying tears of pride for their son who was born at twenty-four weeks and ran the 100 metres. Seeing a daughter on stage in a dance concert being brave in front of so many people. We can go on and on (and we do in the podcast!). Our *Too Peas* episode on after-school activities resonated with our listeners. You can listen to it if you scroll back through our episodes. It is called 'What to do after school', from 7 November 2019.

Another significant part of the story is trying to find businesses and clubs and associations that will prioritise our children. Take, for example, the local swimming pool and swimming lessons. These will often have some spaces for one-on-one lessons for children with disabilities and additional needs. Great start. But always after the neurotypical kids and almost always at the most inconvenient times. 'Okay, Sarah's mum, the only spot we have is 6.30 pm on a Tuesday in winter.' So Sarah's mum moves and rearranges everything in her schedule, in the hope that her child will be able to participate in swimming lessons but knowing full well that Sarah will be absolutely exhausted from surviving a day at school. She walks past all the other women leaving the swimming lessons, laughing and chatting together with children all showered (all independently) and ready to go home, straight to dinner and bed and thinks, 'How come they get the fantastic swimming lesson times, when my child is arguably much more in need of the earlier time slots?' After a few weeks of distress and exhaustion, Sarah's mum gives up and feels guilty anytime someone mentions swimming lessons thereafter.

With the introduction of the NDIS in Australia there was much discussion about whether swimming lessons would be able to be claimed. Rumours were circulating, from 'you just need to call it aqua occupational therapy, it's all in the wording' to 'one-on-one swimming lessons are not reasonable and therefore cannot be funded'. The arguments went on and on with each family trying to work out how they could make this work.

There is a ginormous spectrum of choices regarding extracurricular activities within the disability and additional needs world. Do you only go with groups that tailor for children with intellectual disabilities? And if your children are in mainstream school, how do you find out about these groups? Do you encourage them to be in the mainstream groups, even when you know that they absolutely cannot join in? Who has the extra energy to be the parent rep at Little Athletics and start up a multi-class group that requires much communication and discussion? And who takes over if that parent leaves?

For your child in the wheelchair who desperately wants to dance, how does a parent find the unicorn dance class that will accommodate this? They look hard, they drive for long distances, they pay lots of money, they buy the costumes – they will do whatever it takes, because seeing their child shining on stage is an incredible moment. Pea parents will show the world what it means to go that extra mile for their precious child.

Thank goodness for groups like Special Olympics, an established worldwide group that caters for children and adults with intellectual disabilities. Participants have the chance to represent their region, their state and even their country; and if you ever get the chance to go along, you will see it's a wonderful group of volunteers and athletes. Using softballs for shotput; standing long jump; no guns; athletes belonging and having responsibilities towards their club and the expectations of the athletes is so wonderful to observe as a parent. A place to sit on the bleachers and know that not one person is judging; everyone is cheering, belonging, finishing or not finishing a race, wearing a uniform that puffs the wearer's chest up with pride. Every body, every noise, every behaviour is welcome.

Dance and drama groups are also most visible for pea shoots with intellectual disabilities, and now some can even be funded by NDIS – or at least funding for a support worker to take the pea shoot to these, which means the teenager or the adult has the experience of attending these without their parents, similar to their peers.

The multi-class/para inclusivity that is happening here in Australia, especially in primary school athletics, is awesome. Children having Paralympic classifications is the perfect place for our kids with physical disabilities who want to participate, and do in fact meet the criteria; this is the place for them. Children can be in the same team as their neurotypical classmates, wearing the same uniforms, being a state captain, winning bronze, silver or gold for their school or their state, or simply being in a race that is fair. Once the athletes understand the complex system of the classifications and why being a T38 who finishes first over the line, but comes fourth to the T37, T40 and T35, for example, is a sight to behold. (T stands for Track and F stands for field, and the numbers indicate a specific diagnosis or group such as cerebral palsy and the different diagnosis within that.) The children all finish the race; the track officials put the times and classifications into a system and then they will come out and tell the children who has come first, second and third. This can be a challenging time; for example, the child classified T20 – intellectual disability – has crossed the line first in the 100 metres, now comes fifth, as the athletes such as T35 with cerebral palsy come up the rankings and win.

It's a lot to cope with. What Mandy saw for those three years at state and national levels was so much bravery and acceptance that it never ceased to amaze her. Talk about resilience! The children especially have to quickly come to terms with the rating system. On a state and national level, this can be pretty brutal, but most multi-class/para kids usually get a few blue ribbons at the local levels, so that helps.

A multi-class dad once told Mandy that he had to get a curtain rod and mount it on the wall for all the medals that his son, who was a T35 (cerebral palsy), won at Nationals. I bet, when his son was diagnosed, that would have never entered his mind. The Paralympic movement is brilliant, and it gives some of our pea shoots the visibility that they so deserve to see on our TV screens. Even if sport is not their thing, it gives them a chance to see themselves.

And then there are our most precious pea shoots, those with profound disabilities, for whom these activities are limited. Thankfully, some can access water and music and movement through their schools, and some children who attend respite at beautiful places like Very Special Kids here in Melbourne have wonderful experiences for all their senses. Thanks to NDIS, people can access art therapy in their homes, and for the very creative parents and support workers, the sky is the limit to their ideas. Resources, however, are limited, and it's not fair. It's unequal, and our beautiful pea shoots deserve the very best. They, in fact, deserve the very best times, the very best teachers and the brightest spotlight of all.

Mandy says

Well, we have tried it all: swimming, netball, basketball, piano, cello, singing, dancing, acting, Girl Guides. I have attended all the info nights and dance concerts, bought all the uniforms, wiglet attachments and make-up, the list goes on. I am so glad we gave our girls as many chances as we could, but gee, when I look back I can see we were all pretty exhausted, because this was on top of therapies and surgeries and school and working and family. We attended a Mothers and Fathers Night run by the Girl Guides and I was so proud of our girls, even after the time they had a sleepover in the hall in tents. Both our girls kept everyone up (what was I thinking?!) and I had to carry them home in the morning and put them straight to bed. We have explained about feet that can't help stepping in netball and legs that can't run as fast as others in basketball and hands that find learning the cello really hard. I remember when the OT at our local hospital said to me, 'She is learning the cello – wow!' and I thought 'Yeah, that is probably really hard for her, whoops.' But she kept doing it and I was so proud. Our family has been thankful for the groups who tried, who asked us how they could support the girls, who were welcoming, even if we were the 'first' they had had.

We as parents adjusted to the idea that the sports we played and the instruments we learnt would never be appropriate. Once we did this, it was easier. We just paid attention to the important part: what was going to contribute to our girls' self-esteem and sense of belonging. They were the only things that mattered.

Eventually it all became obvious that these mainstream activities were challenging, so when we moved Molly into specialist school we also removed any pressure that we might have inadvertently placed on her and gave her a rest. She kept up being a multi-class athlete in primary school and had the most wonderful times representing Team Victoria for three years. We have the most fantastic photo of her running with a baton. After more surgeries and recoveries, we joined Special Olympics. Of course, just as she was getting confident the pandemic struck, so we will eagerly await the day when she can return.

Kate says

I want to write this with positivity and light. I want to say that we were welcomed by so many different sporting and dance groups with open arms. But the truth is, after-school activities for Buzz and Woody were not welcoming and were not inclusive! Every activity we did, we ended up paying that little bit extra for them to learn alone, not in a group, not high-fiving an excited bunch of kids, not standing with other mums chatting, not complaining about the weather on rainy weekend mornings, we had none of that. I suppose we were lucky that they had each other, though – two little boys and one swimming teacher, two amazing boys and one tennis couch, two fantastic boys and one soccer coach.

Once the 'little kids' activities such as Auskick and grasshopper soccer have ended, well, then everyone wants to win! I don't care what you say; I don't care how great your club is – the truth is, if you are not good at a sport, you will get put on the bench, you will bat last, you will never go up with your age group at tennis, and after a while even the coaches you pay for one-on-one training will give up on you. You simply must get better at sport! You must concentrate, even if that is nigh on impossible for you after a big day of school, you must not fail! Buzz and Woody tried the following and here is their and my commentary . . .

Swimming

We all know that being able to swim is essential in Australia. Loads of people have pools; we live near beaches: we have to learn to swim. But do you know how busy and loud and confronting public swimming pools are, particularly indoor ones? One lesson was all we managed in a pool full of people. The noise, the water splashing, the teachers kindly barking commands – nup, not going to happen. We found a small pool and paid for private lessons for the boys. Did it cost more? Yes! Was that fair? Well, I don't know: everything we do costs more, but did we learn to swim? Yes! We can play in a pool, that's all I cared about. (Although we did shut the pool down one day when the teacher ignored Buzz, who wanted to get out; the teacher said Buzz was just trying to get out of swimming. Hmm, nup: code brown! Pool closed due to floating shits!) But water is great therapy for us all. Buzz, Woody and I, we love chilling, and splashing and jumping in the pool.

Basketball

We can probably all see issues here, particularly that it is noisy, but we didn't mind the noise that much. It was the whole never-sharing-the-ball thing, as well. Buzz and Woody are the most awesome little sharers; they have shared everything for their entire lives. If you gave one of them a biscuit or chocolate even before they could talk, they broke it in half and shared it. And then hello, basketball, where everyone snatches the ball off you. They just couldn't understand why people kept taking the ball, and then why everyone yelled at them. 'It just isn't fun, Mum. Why can't it be fun?'

In my humble opinion (and I know the haters are going to hate here, but bring it!), it is because the adults want to win. They want their kids' teams to win, they want to share it on Facebook, like their kid won the NBA Championship or something. I love seeing photos of kids playing and laughing, but mostly on social media I see photos of kids winning. Winning matters more than fun. Being in a team is super fun if you win, if you score all the three pointers, if you are hardly on the bench and if your coach likes you. But if none of the above applies to you, it's a big pile of shit! Other parents openly discuss your technical weaknesses in front of you ('Got distracted there did you, Woody?' 'Maybe try actually aiming for the ring next time'). We did what any parent would do – built a basketball hoop in our backyard and got the fuck out of there.

Some kids are awesome at basketball and will go on to be the next Michael Jordan, but when they are six or ten it would probably be far more beneficial for them to share the court with someone who has ADHD or ASD or another neurodiversity. Because they will all share the world together!

Tennis

We were getting wise and went straight to small group coaching here. Four kids, one coach, nice parents, and we could walk there. But the coach didn't like kids who didn't progress quickly enough, and he couldn't handle the huge, terrible issues of Buzz and Woody sometimes taking too long to pick up a ball or laughing at a silly shot! Oh no, that was too much, even though he was being paid, and we had no expectations, except for fun and maybe a sport they could play together as they grew up. We got palmed off and then we went to lessons with the two of them; we paid more, the coach was lovely, but in the end, he said, 'I just don't see this going anywhere; I don't think it is worth my time or your money!' You better believe I cried big, fat, tears about that. Buzz and Woody liked it; they had fun; it was only thirty minutes and we paid. Where exactly did it have to go? Why do we all have to progress at the same rate?

Hip-hop dancing

I am going to give this a win. We found the most divine dance studio near where we live; they were happy for Buzz and Woody and their cousins to dance, with no concerts, no costumes, just dance for the joy of dance! Other friends could join in too from time to time. We did this for a couple of years and I don't mind saying those kids have the moves! But the best dance teacher moved interstate. (How dare he!) And we grew up, and no other kids were doing hip-hop – believe me, I tried to keep them going. It was great, though. We were completely accepted, and the dance teachers understood dance for the love of dance.

Cricket

Confession time: I love cricket. Like, really love it. Like travel-to-the-UK-to-watch-the-Ashes love it. I know what being good at cricket looks like, but we were not aiming for a baggy green cap* here, friends! We just wanted to play. There is an oval within walking distance of our home, so we joined a local junior cricket club. And the boys were okay. I mean it's boring when you are fielding, and it is easy to get distracted, but the coach was kind and, as we know, kindness goes a long way. But those other pesky parents: they really wanted certain kids to bat first and bowl first (and let's be clear, most of these kids had no clue what they were doing). We lasted a season and I enjoyed watching the team play. But we knew it wasn't going to be long term. Even the kind coach knew that.

Gymnastics

Balance is something that comes naturally to Buzz and Woody – I think they must have been mountain goats in a previous life. But after sitting (or trying to) all day, their concentration was not so great after school! And I will let you in on a little secret, based on my not-very-extensive research: gymnastics coaches are serious about gymnastics. Have you seen the hours some kids train for that sport? I really wanted them to love it, and I wanted the gym to recognise their natural abilities, but it wasn't to be.

---

* For non-cricket people, a baggy green cap = national selection

I had to stop and think, 'If they are crying, why am I doing this?' But still, I ponder why every kid has to do every somersault and every beam walk. If they get distracted, does it really matter?

Lawn bowls

We played with people of all ages and genders and abilities and I still hold lawn bowls up as a gold-standard sport when it comes to inclusion. But it is old school. People who play lawn bowls – well, their parents played lawn bowls, there are unwritten codes that if you don't grow up with you don't understand. And my little tip to these lovely people? Maybe lighten up a bit. But we had the kindest coaches (all doing it for free), we had quiet practice time and for the most part we had real fun. We got to play with a wheelchair user and another additional-needs boy when we did competitions, and lots of times we actually won, so take that, other parents! We will join our local lawn bowls club and just go play for fun, but we might steer clear of the competitions for a while, and hang with the retired people. For the most part, they seem happy to have us down the end just having fun!

Skiing

If you listen to our podcast you will know Buzz and Woody live for the pow (for those who are not powder hounds, pow is soft, fresh snow). I think what they did was sit together to work out the most expensive way to enjoy sport – and they won! Once again, we had to pay for individual lessons because, in Australia, there are very big ski school classes, like twelve kids per class! Every extra dollar I earn goes to the snow; I work so they can ski.

The freedom of the mountains cannot be described. It is one of those places where if you give something a go you are applauded. Everyone looks out for everyone; people stop to help you up or show you an easier way down the hill if you can't manage, and they love to see other people ski. They chat with my boys on the lifts, telling tales of tree runs and near misses. The excitement and exhaustion at the end of the day is palpable. Little red faces, cold noses and sore feet and pure joy! Don't roll your eyes at me: I know it's rich people's sport, I know we are lucky to get there. And even though hurtling down a mountain on slippery sticks is not my idea of fun, I will go every year they want to and that we can afford to. It is our happy place. My brother takes them on massive adventures, followed by hot chocolates and hot chips, and they are free. Finally free!

I won't bore you anymore but I stand by my claim that sport is one of the least inclusive activities that kids are subjected to. I will point out sense rugby: we went for a while until COVID shut that down, but it was inclusive, as it is designed to be that way. It is amazing and the coaches are OTs and so fab, but there will always be a part of me that wonders why we can't at some level all join in every kind of sport if we want to. Mandy and I joke about making the Fun Sports League, where you come and play, have fun and go home. You run around, get exercise, or sit on the field and play with the grass and join in when you want to and no one cares! Everyone gets a sausage or just plain bread (or a gluten-free roll) and memories are made without judgement! I tell you what, Too Peas sports and after-school activities would be fun, not competitive.

I see you, if you have had any of these struggles. I see you: you are not alone. I know it's lonely and the last thing we want is for our kids to be lonely, so we will continue to look for that activity that is inclusive, the amazing coach, the parents who know fun trumps winning. We will never stop looking, but when you feel sad, we feel sad too.

Some very deluded mother of a very talented athletic kid once said to me, 'You just have to find their sport; every kid has a sport,

Kate!' She might be right but she didn't want my boys on her kid's Aussie Rules team! I should have said, but I didn't, 'You have to teach your kid that my kids are valuable and worthy of joining in too. You need to teach inclusion and empathy. You need to realise that for some kids all team sport is tricky.' If you are reading this and you are a coach, or a parent on a team, maybe remember that! Maybe we will all learn the value of diversity over winning one day. Oh, and if we ever see you on the mountain, come up, say hi, have a ski and a hot chocolate; there is always room for one more!

17

Advocacy

If you look online you will see that advocacy is:

Public support for or recommendation of a particular cause or policy.

Or, and more fitting for the peas:

A person who puts a case on someone else's behalf.

You may have seen the T-shirts that say 'Advocate like a mother'. We sort of added to it and made it more of our own: 'Advocate like a motherf*cker'. If you have a child you will have at some point in their schooling, sporting or after-school dancing life probably been an advocate. Maybe you have advocated for a relative in aged care, or a friend who is unwell. Most of us have to don the advocate hat at some point – and you know what? It is rarely a comfortable fit.

Parents often become advocates when we feel, rightly or wrongly, that our child has somehow been mistreated, overlooked or excluded. When you have a child with an additional need or a disability, especially in mainstream schooling, you become an advocate and a negotiator like no other. This is also true in the hospital system. What makes this extremely hard is that very few

of us are teachers, doctors, speech pathologists, occupational therapists or teacher's aides. With not much power or institutional
knowledge on our side, we are up against a system. But, believe
me, we won't be giving up any time soon.

After a while of constant advocating, you will get bloody good
at it, although it never gets any easier. You will stop worrying about
not being popular, although – and it doesn't matter who you are or
how old you are – it isn't nice going into a room where you think
people dislike you. You do it anyway. You will learn to think about
what you are going to say before you say it, you will pause before
you speak and you will get other professionals to back you up.
But it's a hard slog to get to the point where you're comfortable
doing it. No one is born with these skills, and they aren't taught
anywhere. You won't learn them at school, and don't expect to be
taught them at antenatal classes! But they should be, as they are
skills that you will need at some point, no matter who you are.

When you have a baby, you may assume that the first time you
will speak to an educator is at day care or preschool, or that the first
time you will speak to a doctor is when your baby has a temperature, and for lots of us that is true. But some children have been in
and out of hospital since birth, have attended constant therapy and
had lots of psychological testing done. Those parents are already
wary from having been subjected to rectum comments, hurtful
remarks and unsolicited observations. They are not the same as
the parent whose child was born at term, only went to the doctor
for an ear infection or routine vaccinations and is an acceptable
weight for their age. But they all walk in to school together, such
different journeys through the same doorway! True, everyone
who walks through that door will have to go in to bat for their
child at some point, but not everyone knows when to hit a six,
a four, a swing and a miss or to just declare the innings over. Some
of us go in to bat like a fruit bat – lots of noise but not the greatest

vision for what we want ... but wait! Just as our kids are learning at school, so are we. Motherfucking advocators we will become!

If you are a non-advocating parent because you haven't had to walk that journey, or maybe you are a teacher or principal, try to have a little thought for the advocator parents in your classroom. They walk into school with butterflies in their stomach, already worried about talking to the teacher, bringing up some issue their child cried about or needs assistance with. They don't want to always be chatting with the teacher, we promise they would rather dump and run and go have coffee with the other mums. They probably stayed up half the night wording emails and working out how to approach the school that morning. Sometimes maybe they get it wrong, but remember they are tired and scared and only want the best for their kid, like everyone else does. The difference is they have to fight for it.

Then there is the hospital advocate, who is often the same person as the education advocate (can you see how exhausting this is?). I bet you can also see how good parents get at advocating. Sometimes you're lucky enough to find a doctor who listens to you and acts on your child's needs. This is the greatest gift and it means that you can relax a little. But what about when you are bumped around, seeing different doctors each time as someone is always on leave or off doing a research project, or a new speech therapist who thinks you could go in a different way from the last speechie! Terrifying, really. This is when having a peafessional as a friend is priceless (and we apologise to all of ours, again, for the constant phone calls!). Or a really good friend who is slightly impartial, because, and we admit this here, sometimes it's easy to lose sight of things or misunderstand a diagnosis. (Here's a tip: if you can, sometimes it helps to take a friend along to an important medical appointment – someone who loves you and your child but who can take notes and remember facts unclouded by emotion.)

If you're a new mother with tiny baby twins who need medical support, there is a whole world about to be thrown at you. Even just getting to an appointment entails some version of the following: feeding the babies, changing nappies, packing the bags, getting them into the car seats, driving to the hospital without falling asleep, finding a car park, getting the pram and both babies out, strapped into the pram, finding the appointment place, manoeuvring around crowds of sick people and finally sitting on a shitty chair in a shitty waiting room. Better keep both babies happy, quiet, no crying, give them a dummy, their toys, cuddle them, jiggle the pram, wait and wait for the name to be called. Then wheel them in, smile and be polite while waiting for the barrage of doctors and nurses and physicians and registrars and students to pile into the room and take notes, as for them it is a day at uni. They are using your precious babies to learn things. You stay polite, careful that your responses don't appear be rude or sarcastic. You show them that you are willing to do whatever it takes for your children, agree to invasive treatments, let them draw on your children's legs, talk about them in front of them to their colleagues, use phrases you never thought you would hear like, '*the* mother' or 'put them under for GAs'. It is you and your babies versus all of these people, and you realise that you are the sole voice in the room that is speaking just for them.

Being an advocate is not easy, and some of us do it better than others. Some pea advocates are incredible truth tellers. They have no time for bullshit or appeasing anyone, they just come right out with something like, 'Yep, I see what you're saying but that splint on her hand to stop her from using her "good hand" is not going to work when her twin takes it off for her, seeing as they are two years old.' Telling the truth means not wasting people's time, so being a truth-telling advocate is helpful for all involved. Try it sometime; it's wonderful.

A while ago, a friend of ours whose child was being treated for cancer told Mandy, 'The mummy can say no!' This has always remained with Mandy, as she had never heard a person tell her that a mummy (or a daddy) can indeed say no to a suggested procedure or treatment. Most parents won't say no; they will do everything within their power to cling on to every bit of hope that treatment and surgery and medications will provide some relief for their child. But even if you don't want to say no, it's always worth remembering that you are entitled to get a second opinion or take a day to think it through.

If you live in Australia you will probably be familiar with the NDIS. Well buckle up, because navigating the NDIS requires that we be the absolute epitomes of motherfucking advocates.

The grassroots organisation Every Australian Counts began its advocacy for the NDIS in 2011.[8] Every parent of a child with a disability knew all about it. Petitions were signed, conferences were attended, and after a lot of conversations and rumours, in 2013 it was finally announced that the NDIS was going to be rolled out. Pilot programs popped up around Australia, with families moving houses so that they could be in the pilot suburbs.

The NDIS is a huge step in the right direction for people living with disabilities and parents of children with a disability – adults, children and families who didn't want to be told 'you can only access this therapy at 5.45 pm in the city' anymore. They wanted access to disability support made easier for them, person-focused and person-centred.

After the pilot programs were successful, the NDIS was finally made accessible to everyone. And wow. So. Much. Documentation.

First there were reports, then enrolling in the scheme, being knocked back, being accepted and learning the lingo. There was *so much lingo*. Self-managed, plan-managed, NDIA-managed.

What the hell was the difference? LAC, support coordination, support workers, respite arrangements that families had locked in for many years being cancelled; employ your own support workers; join this support worker company to help you pay them; sign these forms; sign those forms; get more evidence. Is your physio, OT, speech therapist NDIS-registered? What about a cleaner? Can you keep the cleaner whom the council had paid for and was actually such a positive contribution to your family's mental health? No, no, maybe, yes?

Going into NDIS meetings is the ultimate advocacy work until your child is an adult. Then after the meetings comes the guilt. *Am I skilled enough to do this, did I say enough, did I paint a terrible enough picture of my amazing child so that they can get the help they need? Did I explain myself clearly without crying? I don't know what my child needs: will they even comply with this?* Who knew when that baby was born the parenting journey we were going on might mean being a case manager for potentially the rest of our lives. But it's one of the most important hats that we wear as mothers of kids with additional needs or disabilities.

Kate says

Unsurprisingly, I have a lot to say about this topic. If I could go back and chat to 2004 Kate about this, I would tell her that being a fierce advocate won't make you popular but it will enable you to sleep at night, knowing you are fighting for what is right. Being popular with some of these people doesn't matter, and the people who really matter are the ones who also try to make a difference!

Maybe one day society will embrace the amazing and rich diversity that kids with learning issues, additional needs and disabilities bring into the world but until then, advocacy will be my life. Just call me advoKate.

I feel a fully justified rage that parents have to advocate so hard all the time. For example, it's not enough that, after several years and thousands of dollars, the therapist has finally handed over an important report that will help you access important services at school for your child. You will still have to present and justify it to every teacher, every relief teacher, every library teacher. It is never-ending. Not only that, you have to carefully pick your battles, and you have to be willing to stand down sometimes, for the greater good.

Buzz and Woody were so cute and lovable, sort of like little puppies, when they started school. And like puppies, sometimes they needed time outside to run around. But the teachers couldn't take Buzz and Woody outside when they needed to run, and it caused problems. Teachers don't have endless energy, neither are they given much money for aides or other support, but they have to teach all our kids. Teaching is a tough gig, and I will never understand how tough. Because – and here is the real kicker – the Australian education system cannot support every child. I wish I had a voice to change the entire system, but I don't. All I can do is try to tackle issues that I see at my kids' schools. But once a teacher stands up in front of that class, they have to be impartial. If they aren't, everyone knows: the kids know, the parents know – believe me, everyone knows. And it can make or break a child.

When I talk about being an advocate, sometimes it's trying to get more aide time or ed-support time, or freeing up my kids from the classes that 'matter the least' for catch-up times with the maths teacher. But sometimes it is fighting injustices, such as forcing all kids to give a two-minute talk in assembly. Come on, schools! Talks can be really cool iPad presentations, cartoons or TikTok clips. All kids shouldn't have to present in the same way. At school, I loved oral presentations. They came easily to me. I could wing half of it, I didn't get nervous and had a reasonable grasp of the English language, which, despite my father being Irish, was the language spoken at home. And I was neurotypical, to tick another box. I *volunteered* to give the talk when we had group assignments. Don't tell me it is character-building or it 'builds resilience' (the best line ever invented) to make all kids stand up in front of a class and talk. Do all workers at all work-places do it? I get that it is a fantastic life skill, but it also assumes we all have or need the same skills in life. Bollocks! We absolutely don't, and at best that attitude shames the kids who are not neu-rotypical, have a speech delay, a processing delay or are just shy. Why do they all have to do it at the same time, too? You turned ten so you can speak in public now?

Sometimes I wonder if my childhood, as the daughter of an outspoken father and a fiercely protective mother, growing up in a strange religion in the 1980s in very suburban Sydney and Melbourne made me a bit 'odd'. I was definitely not a typical kid. My parents didn't drink, attend barbecues or watch sport on the weekends but, as much as I hated being the only kid without a TV, it sure taught me you could be 'different' and still have friends. It taught me to stand up for what I believed in and perhaps gave me a little life lesson on being an advocate, although my parents would not have liked me adding the F word in front of it! Being different can be hard, but it should be embraced as we are all different. It's weird: once someone excels in their field, their differences are written about and welcomed – applauded, even – but in Year 3 at primary school, differences are quashed. Well, I say less quashing and more embracing!

I always think of the moment in *The Incredibles* where Frozone's wife says, 'Greater good? I am your wife! I'm the greatest good you are ever gonna get!' We are the greatest good our kids are ever going to get, and through all the tears and rage we feel, it is so bloody worth it.

Mandy says

Advocating has not come easy for me. I am a people-pleaser, and an expert at tricking people into thinking that I am coping. It took until the twins were seven for me to begin to find the truth-teller within. Around their seventh birthday, I realised that their little growing bodies were what they were. No amount of therapy, botox, casting, night splints, AFOs, surgery, stretching, walkers, wheelchairs, speech therapy, occupational therapy or physio appointments was going to change the fact that they both had brain injuries. Their peers were blossoming right alongside them and it was hard to watch those kids' bodies go from strength to strength, agile and free and fast and stable. I was so tired of the endless cycle of appointments, hospitals and therapists. And that's when I started to tell the truth.

My favourite story was when I was not coping with the amount of appointments between the girls from an allied health team. I was not answering or returning their 'no caller ID' phone calls. When they finally got onto me, I said, 'This is not family-centred. You can just write in the notes that the mother is being uncooperative and not answering phone calls. Put it back on me; save your own butt. You have done your job, I am doing mine.'

I felt so empowered that I actually laughed when I hung up the phone, although I'm sure that poor therapist on the other end has their own story to tell about that day.

I also had to learn to tell the truth in big professional hospitals like the Royal Children's Hospital, to very important surgeons and world-leading physicians and the best X-ray guy out there.

The twins had to have orthopaedic leg surgery when they were six. In the lead-up to the twins' operations I discussed with Professor Kerr Graham whether we would have the twins operated on the same day or not. 'Have you had any other twin families?' I asked, and he said 'Yes' and that they did it on the same day. I thought to myself, 'If that mummy can do it, then so can I.' The plan was that both girls would have the surgery and recover together; that way, no one had to watch the other one go through it first.

I remember explaining everything to Molly, who stared up at me with big, trusting eyes as she lay on a bed while strangers touched her body. The advocacy started again the moment Molly woke up after surgery, screaming with pain. I had no idea what was going on but it was only after I yelled 'Help her!' that pain relief was given.

It happened again when I spoke to the nurses, saying, 'When can we bathe her? Can you please help with feeding? She hates needles so how can we put medication in her IV without the absolute trauma?' It just went on and on. Miss Ten was only ten months old when the twins had their leg surgeries. How on earth could I advocate properly for two children when I was also breastfeeding a baby once a day? I felt like I was letting every single one of my daughters down.

Since moving Molly to a special education setting, my time as a mainstream advocate is over. The specialist school isn't perfect, but all the same, I cried with relief on the day that the teachers said to me, 'You must be so tired. We can help you.' Music to my exhausted ears. There is much to be argued against segregated schools, but I will leave that to people much smarter than me. All I know is that my daughter is not fighting anymore, and so neither am I.

The NDIS has demanded from me the most intensive, persistent advocacy work I have ever done. There is always a meeting, supporting letters, documents, tests, WISC (Wechsler Intelligence Scale for Children), speech reports, physio – are they all in order before we go and visit the LAC (what the hell is a LAC?) and then implementing the plan. *Shit! We haven't used the money, we better hurry up and use it or else they are going to cut it.* Going into plan reviews every year, trying to speak up and ask for what my children need, while a person across the desk looks at me trying to discern if what I am asking for is 'fair and reasonable'. Am I? What is fair and reasonable? Private swimming lessons? No? Even though we could never do them in a group?

I know that I will be an advocate for Molly until the day I die, but then again, as my mum says, 'You never stop caring for any of your children, Mandy.' Maybe I just need to reframe again and know that each day, week, month and year I am becoming more adept at advocacy. I know I have many, many years to come and what I will do is what I currently do: listen to the women who have gone before me.

18

Stigma

How are you feeling? Want to go from banging your head against that plasterboard wall to solid brick or concrete? Let's have a look at what 'stigma' really means:

Stigma: a mark of disgrace associated with a particular circumstance, quality, or person.

The word 'stigma' makes us weep. A mark of disgrace, what a shit thing to have to deal with! It goes hand in hand with judgement, really, doesn't it? There is no good stigma. It's the mouldy cherry on top of Shit Mountain. Many people face stigma, but when stigma slaps your kids down, that is a monumentally shit day in your parenting life. The thing with stigma is that it's like its own weird whirlpool. You didn't put yourself in there, so you can't get yourself out of it – and no one from *Bondi Rescue* is coming to save you. People are afraid that, if they get too close to the stigma whirlpool maybe they will get sucked in too, so they stay away.

Every time you sit quietly with your coffee while the head of the Parents and Friends Association mouths off about the 'special-needs kids' taking all the teachers' time', when you pretend not to hear when a parent constantly blames the little girl with ADHD for every single playground incident, slowly turning an entire class against her, when you don't disagree with less on-court time for the five-year-old with less developed gross motor skills – well, you are adding to the stigma, increasing its power.

We are probably all guilty of this. It's hard to stand up to dickheads. For some reason they feel no shame in mouthing off, and that gives them power to keep being a dick. And, truth be told, we don't want them to turn their power on us. Who wants to turn around mid-parent–teacher association meeting and call out the president? Informing her of her inaccuracies, and the fact that the teacher spends time with all the kids, and every child has a right to be in the classroom, not just hers? But if we don't, pea friends, the stigma grows and gets passed through the kinder and the school, and the playground, and the sports field. Then before you know it there are little shitty lumps of stigma everywhere. They get stuck on our shoes and we bring them home, traipse them down the hallway and that stigma spreads in our families too.

The insidious thing about stigma is that sometimes we don't even know we are stigmatising someone. It's an unconscious bias, sort of like when you don't examine your beliefs, prejudices and discriminatory thoughts. The good thing is that it's not too late to examine these biases and change them. Over the last few years, lots of us in society have had to have a good hard look at ourselves and that is a bloody good thing. How great is it that we have the freedom and ability to change how we think? That we can do research, and realise our previous beliefs were bullshit and not based on science but rather on playground gossip?

One of the worst things about stigma is that the more 'invisible' a disability is, you can bet that the more widespread the attendant stigma is. Mental illness, ADHD, additional learning needs – if it doesn't conform to people's (well, rectums') understanding of what a 'disability should look like', watch out for the stigma truck, backing in to dump all over you. This impulse to judge people before you understand them needs to stop.

We believe there will be a day when the education departments of Australia will have to apologise for the way children with ADHD have been treated in the school system. Little lives broken, parents so crushed watching their children excluded and judged. Students with no self-belief; it is beyond comprehension and we should all hang our heads in shame!

Can we fight stigma? Sure we can. Once we realise it is there, and even better, once we realise how damaging it is, then we can all change our approach. Sorry, schools, but a lot of this is up to you (although we can recommend two dynamic women called Mandy and Kate to come and chat with you if you would like some education on the topic). You need to have a de-stigmatisation. It is hard and exhausting for the parents to keep fighting; they need that energy to play with their kids, help them do homework and set screen-time limits! Oh and hey, peas – if you find yourself having to do a lot of this work yourself, why not give the school this book?

Kate says

If I could turn back time, what would I tell 2012 Kate about stigma? Firstly, I would say it doesn't matter if people know about the boys' meds or not, they will still judge them. It is going to hurt you and, more importantly, them, but you will eventually find a better school and the boys will recover. The choices you have made are good ones, I promise, but if you don't tell people what those choices are and why you made them (despite the fact that it's really none of their business), they will just gossip. Even once you do tell them, they will still gossip, but at least it won't be lies, and you might get to control the narrative. Also, even when you're right in the thick of the fog of diagnosis and choosing to medicate the boys, you will meet the best few friends, and they will stick with you. They will love the boys and the others don't matter!

This topic gets me right in the feels. I believe that children with ADHD, which really should be called executive functioning disorder (not that I think it is a disorder – it is just a difference), are some of the most stigmatised kids in Australian schools today. And sadly they are stigmatised by pretty much everyone – parents, teachers, principals, even the canteen staff! Approximately one in twenty people has ADHD[9]: all those hundreds of thousands of people and children living with a secret, or ashamed of how they were born, because uneducated people think their uneducated opinions are so valid that they share them around. Just so we are clear, here is what ADHD is:

> Attention Deficit Hyperactivity Disorder (ADHD) is a complex neuro-developmental disorder which affects a person's ability to exert age-appropriate self-control. It is characterised by persistent patterns of inattentive, impulsive, and sometimes hyperactive behaviour, and is frequently accompanied by emotional regulation challenges.
>
> People with ADHD have little control over these behaviours as they stem from underlying neurological differences. They arise due to an impaired ability to inhibit and regulate attention, behaviour and emotions; to reliably recall information in the moment; to plan and problem solve; to self-reflect and self-monitor; and to self-soothe.
>
> ADHD can cause significant functional disability throughout the lifespan and in all areas of life, and without appropriate intervention can lead to significantly unfavourable outcomes. However, with evidence-based treatment and support, people with ADHD can embrace their strengths and interests, learn to manage their challenges and live a full and rewarding life.[10]

This might be the first time you have seen ADHD defined in this way. Now think about all the things you have heard about ADHD over the years. Maybe you have seen one of the many ADHD memes floating around on the internet. This is the one I really dislike: 'ADHD? When I was a kid it was called your dad getting the belt out!' If you share shit like that on Facebook *you* should be stigmatised!

Did you know that children with ADHD (and let's assume they don't also have ASD, dyslexia, processing delays or something else) can take up to 30 per cent longer (or three to six years) to develop executive function?[11] They can't help it; they can't speed it up, but they are constantly punished, suspended or even expelled from school. And what happens to their self-esteem? Not only that, friends, but most children with ADHD only develop 75 to 80 per cent of the executive functioning capacity of their neurotypical peers.[12] While you are doing such a good job at learning all this (and thanks for sticking with me, by the way) did you know that your executive function enables you to control your emotions and thoughts – what you say and what you do? It can affect your time management skills, and really affect your social skills. Why do we just keep allowing society to treat ADHD as if it is made up? Or perhaps the result of bad parenting, or processed food? The discrimination children (and adults) with ADHD receive is mind blowing. ADHD does not qualify for the NDIS, nor does it qualify for an aide at school, even though it's not uncommon for kids with ADHD to have a few extra learning needs as well.

Whew. I find it hard to control my bubbling rage when I talk about the stigma surrounding ADHD. Maybe it's my Irish heritage, but I cannot stay silent about it. I want to yell it from a soapbox, but it's like talking to flat-earthers. And I always worry that ranting about it might cause more people to cast judgement on my kids.

I didn't understand much about ADHD until I got two bundles of energy of my own. But I think how Mandy felt at diagnosis time was how I felt when I realised my beautiful, amazing kids were going to be stigmatised for life. It is a heavy feeling, especially when it's all bullshit. Nothing has made me cry more than watching my kids be excluded, all because they took a tablet at school at lunchtime. The real kicker here is that my awesome Buzz and Woody were not naughty in class, but parents still judged. The only parties we got asked to were whole-class parties. These two little boys (cute as mud, mind you) saw everyone else go to parties and weekend playdates and even got excluded from social sports teams that parents ran on the weekends. And (this is subjective, I'll admit) the other kids were allowed to make mistakes or get away with misbehaving but mine were seen as trouble.

My heart bursts when I see these boys of mine, who nearly didn't get here, in their little school uniforms walking towards my car at the end of the day after having put up with cruel comments.

'What's actually wrong with you?'

'Why do you take medication, you love drugs don't you?'

'Did you know your BMI is so unhealthy?'

'No one goes to ed support as much as you!'

'Why are you so skinny?'

'You are so short, how can you be so short?'

Try sleeping at night as a mum when you are sending your kids off to deal with that every day. Try not being frustrated to the point of despair when people doubt the validity of ADHD, when people give you a completely uneducated opinion on medicating children. When you realise that your kids get stigmatised for not learning the same as other kids, yet the NDIS won't help them.

In the end, all we can do is cry together and then get on with it. There is something other parents have to do too: they need to judge less and teach kindness at home.

Mandy says

When we covered this topic on the podcast I wasn't sure what it meant for me and my girls. Having a disability like cerebral palsy immediately tells people about a serious brain injury. When you are telling people about it, you can see that people already have an idea of what it means. Then explaining that there are many ways that cerebral palsy shows up: hemiplegia (in our case), diplegia, quadriplegia, spasticity, ataxia, dystonia – all the words you have to learn and then be able to recite to people to accurately describe your beautiful children's bodies is really something. It will be interesting to hear from my daughters about how stigmatised they felt/feel about living with this diagnosis.

I think what crept up on me was the stigma surrounding *me* before I was diagnosed with PTSD. I was acutely aware that people were talking behind my back. 'What mental illness do you think she has? Depression, postnatal depression, anxiety? What's wrong with her?' It wasn't until I received my diagnosis, and sent an email to everyone explaining what it meant that I felt like I had stopped the speculation. People even told me that it made sense.

I then sensed stigma surrounding the choice for both my girls to have botox injections. In the late 2000s it was pretty standard for children with spasticity to receive botox injections into their spastic muscles to relieve the pain. My girls had botox so many times I have lost count. I trusted the experts and went along with the dream that botox would give my girls a few months of respite from the pain of spasticity. It was like a nugget of hope that would help their muscles, and, with the therapy afterwards, teach the brain to use parts of their arms and legs while the spasticity was 'out of the way'. There was also medication for Molly's saliva control, as she had trouble with it and I didn't want children teasing her. We medicated her for a couple of years until she grew a little older and was able to control it a bit more. I wanted the help so as to give her a chance to not be stigmatised. Don't we all, sing the peas.

The biggest stigma I have had to confront was about specialist schools. I had always been relieved that we hadn't sent Molly to one and it was a hard call to make. I didn't immediately warm to the decision and I had to confront why that was. Like lots of things in life, once I actually went and visited the school, I could see that it was going to be great for her. I had to let go of the feeling that I was letting her down, that I was letting down the families who fought so hard to mainstream their children. I was blatantly going against the activists who fight so hard for inclusion. I was worn out by inclusion and the lack thereof, and so I felt like I was turning my back on the people who were fighting and saying, 'I'm sorry I can't be on your team; I tried, and it nearly broke us both.' I have spoken to many women who have had similar feelings, the feelings of giving up on their children by sending them to specialist schools. Then, I meet the women and men who choose these settings from the beginning and have no such guilt and I think, 'Man, why didn't I work this out sooner?'

19

Anti-rectum comments

Do you remember the most heartwarming compliment you ever received? The time someone held your hands during a crisis and said the right words or, to paraphrase Ronan Keating, they said it best when they said nothing at all? When a teacher said something that changed the trajectory of your learning? The comments that stick with you for life? The good stuff. We will get to the chapter on the rectum comments, and we think it's mighty powerful, but what about the sunshine comments? We asked the peas: 'Tell us the comments that stopped you in your tracks for the right reason!' And once again, they delivered. All of these are from the *Too Peas* community. Read on, Macduff, read on! And damned be the rectum who first cries, 'Hold, enough!'

 'My seven-year-old was having a sensory meltdown and the security guard let him hold his M16 and put them at the front of the line.' *Um, yep, you read that right. The security guard let him hold a gun. We don't know the how or why either, but at least a seven-year-old had a much better experience that day, so yay!*

 'She will have a wonderful life.' (GP.) *So much strength and power in these six words. Never forget them, peafessionals. This mum didn't! And on her behalf, we thank you!*

'Now, you need to forget everything you have seen on the screen and just love your baby and let them guide you. I have seen babies with far worse brain damage go on to defy the odds and be able to do things that they shouldn't be able to do.' (Neurologist.) *Isn't this perfection? Just go love your baby and let them guide you. This is advice for every parent in our opinion, but in this case, well . . . you can see why the parents never forgot it.*

'I understand. Here's what we are going to do . . .' (Teacher.) *Rectum teachers, listen to this sentence. Firstly, 'I understand': thank you! And secondly, 'Here's what we are going to do!' Double thank you for using that magnificent field of knowledge you have and doing something for this child!*

'Far out, you are absolutely unstoppable and you are a tiger for him.' (Friend.) *You know it is nice to be occasionally acknowledged for being the advocate! Great friend here! You can take this sentence and use it yourself if you like!*

'I was at the *School of Rock* musical and the front of house manager noticed my child was wearing ear protection. He came up to us and explained that if he needed anything, or if the show was too loud he should look for someone in a similar uniform and they would take care of him.' *Oh, the kindness and understanding of strangers, it always does us in, it's the best!*

'A worker at a library told us where to park and a phone number to call when we came back so we didn't have to struggle with the babies and returning toys.' *Seems simple, but actually a game-changer: making people's lives easier brings equality!*

'My daughter has anorexia and while she was in hospital I went to Lululemon to buy a pair of leggings in the size up so she wouldn't notice she had put on a few kilos when she returned home. When the worker and store manager found out why we were buying a new pair they didn't charge us for them because of the circumstances.' *What can we say, but grab the tissues and celebrate all that is good in the world.*

 'My child does one-on-one swimming lessons that cross over with the "old folks" swimming time. One day one of the quieter older ladies said to me, "His eye contact is getting better and better. You know, it all works out okay in the end."' *We just thought this was beautiful!*

 'I don't know what to say. It is not as hopeless as it feels. It is going to be okay. You are going to have two beautiful twin children and be a rocking mum. Screw any stigma or fear. You will blossom and he will blossom.' (Sister after diagnosis.) *Sisters doing it for themselves – actually, sisters doing it for their sister! Incredible input there!*

 'Thank you for all that you do; you're amazing. How you know so much and keep fighting.' *Being thanked by someone else for the work you do for your child! Oh, that's big fat tears – and we will never forget it!*

 'When I was flying internationally with three pea babies, the airline wouldn't let me preboard, but a woman and eventually a crowd started yelling at them for me, "Let them on, let them on!"' *We can just hear it now! A mob of advocators! Woohoo.*

 'That's okay, we love him.' (Grandfather about grandson being diagnosed with autism.) *And you know what? It is okay; we all just need to be loved.*

'My daughter's friend has hearing aids so they put the prep class in a different room that was specially carpeted to reduce background noise and support his learning.' *A+ for that, teacher, and great job, school! We all deserve the same chance to learn.*

 'He's going to be brilliant. You know that, don't you?' (Teacher.) *This teacher probably never thought about that statement again, but this mum did!*

 'My determined pea shoot wanted to enter all her age races in the swim carnival, despite vision and hearing impairment, missing balance sense and low muscle tone. By halfway through the race, she was a length behind, but the schoolkids starting cheering for her. The sports teacher walked alongside her lane (they had put her in the lane closest to the side), at the ready in case she needed to be rescued. He waited at the halfway end, in case she wanted to get out. She just turned and completed the second lap. Kids cheered her to the end. It was like they were all with me in that moment, understanding and acknowledging how very hard she works! It felt so good.' *Inclusion and support! It's life-changing!*

 'My son wouldn't eat his lunch at kinder because the container had his sister's name on it. He was upset that his sister was missing her lunch and it "wasn't his lunch". The teacher asked him to close his eyes and when he opened them, she had removed his sandwich and placed it on a paper towel that said "Eli's lunch".' *Ah, magic right there in the classroom.*

 'After a thirteen-hour flight we were going through customs and my pea shoot was exhausted and hiding under the desk. The customs officer had to compare faces to passport photos and he came out of his cubicle and squatted under the bench. He calmingly told our screaming child that he just wanted to see his face for a second and spoke to him about his photo and his holiday.' *Wow! Just wow! No offence, customs officials, we know you have a super serious and hard job, but this is amazing; so often customs is the hardest part of the holiday!*

 'Thank you for sharing your beautiful, amazing brain with me – I feel so lucky!' (Psychologist after an assessment.) *Take a bow, psychologist, and the rest of you, take note.*

 'My paediatrician wrapped his arms around me and said, "You have got this, and I am right here beside you" on the first day I got the CP diagnosis.' *That is one awesome pea-fessional right there!*

 'He is a remarkable little boy.' (Pea-diatrician.) *Of course he is, but thank you for saying it, so often it doesn't get said.*

 'My daughter has a rare genetic condition called Kleefstra Syndrome (KS) and its awareness day is 17 September. My daughter's childcare took it upon themselves to celebrate this day, encouraging all the kids and staff to wear the KS colour of purple, had purple balloons, and posted info about the syndrome on their Facebook page. There was no mention of my daughter, they just noted it as a condition close to their heart. When I saw the photos they posted on their FB page of all the kids and staff dressed in purple, I just bawled that they went to all this effort to acknowledge my daughter.' *No grandstanding, just pitching in, and getting on with supporting!*

 'I was at the supermarket with my three under three and heading back to the carpark with my twins and newborn. All three of them were crying and out of nowhere a stranger came up and put $2 in the parking machine for me and said, "You've got enough to be juggling right now."' *Oh yes! This times a thousand!*

 'After seven weeks in NICU with no family support or guide-books I was overwhelmed at home with my tube-fed, medically complex, undiagnosed child. My friend put an organisation called Mums4Mums in touch and they came once a week and listened and helped look after my other child while I tube-fed my baby. I felt so supported by these two special ladies who volunteered each week.' *We have said it before and we will say it again: volunteers keep this country going!*

 'My daughter has anxiety and ended up in sick bay after a lockdown drill at school. Her teacher went to the $2 store while she was on a break and bought some small squeezy toys. She gave these to my daughter to discreetly put in her pocket and squeeze to help her feel better.' *Peachers going the extra mile, wow. Just know this: you rock!*

 'A staff member gave all three of my kids lollipops when my boy with ADHD toppled the trolley. Instead of judging, she asked if we were okay and if she could give them lollipops to help with the tears.' *Lollipops not judgement! That's a movement of its own, we think!*

 'A memory of an event that still brings tears to my eyes: a peashoot with Down syndrome at my child's school has noise sensitivity and wore headphones to assembly. She didn't like getting up for awards because people looked and clapped. One day her name was called and she stood up. All the kids in the school without prompting instantly dropped their heads to their laps and didn't make a sound until she had gone up, got her award and sat down again. She was beaming from ear to ear and her mum and I were in floods of tears.

The kids were so excited for her but knew what she needed to feel comfortable (the advantage of a small school).' *We think this is absolutely one of the most inclusive stories we have heard! Yay for kids who live with diversity and understand and respect it.*

'Every day my pea shoot's teacher brings him to our car for pickup and goes through all the positives of the day and all the things he was successful at.' *Oh yes! Virtual high fives to this peacher, talking about the positives AND bringing pea shoot to the car! Teacher of the year right there!*

'We went away on holidays and my brother-in-law joined us. My little four-year-old guy with ASD was having a ball in very short bursts, then in total sensory overload a lot of the time. So often I had him in our suite for room-service meals (spaghetti, sauce on the side) and quiet time. My hubby and brother-in-law stayed with the other kids and had a noisy, awesome time. One morning, my brother-in-law found us in the suite. He had come for one-on-one time with our little guy. He said he'd previously heard my hubby and me speaking about the pressure on our son, the preparation, the sensory strug-gles but never understood it because our son presented so well for the majority of family functions. He really had no idea how much effort went into every social situation we'd managed in the past. The holiday was a huge eye-opener for him. He thanked us for still joining family events, said we were amazing parents for being able to prepare our little guy so well, and that we were raising an awesome kid. Since that holiday he always checks on us during family functions to see how we're coping; if we leave the group he often joins us for quiet time and he always offers to get things for us or saves me dessert.' *Everything about this is divine, but to us, the most divine thing is someone saving you dessert because you always miss out. Who doesn't want the cake?*

'Whenever I visit my brother and I walk through the door he immediately says, "Do you need help? What can I do?"' *Is he single? 'Cause we are in love!*

 'I took my pea to the barber because he wanted his head shaved bald. He has quite substantial scarring on his head from having a tumour removed and the barber took his time and was ever so gentle. Once finished, the barber looked at me with tears in his eyes and said, "Is he going to be okay?" I said, "Yes, we are lucky." I went to pay but he refused and said, "Spend that money on milkshakes! That kid is one of the bravest I have ever seen and deserves a milkshake."' *Spend that money on milkshakes! There are the best people out there, and when you find them, you never forget them.*

 'A doctor said to me, "I wouldn't bother with the breastfeeding. This one will be using the bottle." When I repeated this to the lactation consultant she said, "Ignore him, that's just an opinion." She worked with me for the next three weeks until my son came home tube-free and fully breastfed.' *For starters, 'This one'? You're talking about a baby! And potent advice: it's just an opinion! We love that.*

 'It may seem such a little thing, but the orthoptist at my daughter's eye clinic when she was four months old (and we were still very much in the scared stage following her diagnosis at three weeks old) said, "I have two friends whose sister has that syndrome, and they are the most caring, responsible, lovely people and have a great relationship with their sister." It was like she knew one of my main concerns at that early diagnosis stage was for my neurotypical firstborn and the impact gaining a sister with a diagnosis would have on him. It was the first positive thing anyone had said to me when speaking about the syndrome she had been diagnosed with and just gave me hope and made my day. I still worry for my son, but always think of her comment and it gives me comfort.' *What a perfect thing to say.*

 'When my pea shoot was two weeks old he was still in hospital and they were trying to get his seizures under control. I was contacted by the newborn photographer I had booked. I had totally forgotten and I explained he was very sick and in hospital so I couldn't come. Instead, she decided to come to us. She took amazing photographs in hospital, never charged me and the next day a huge teddy bear and chocolates arrived for us on the ward, sent by her!' *Just all the feels, like all of them!*

 'My daughter has type 1 diabetes (T1D), diagnosed at seven. I have a very special group of friends that always cater ALL food to be T1D friendly so she never feels left out . . . that includes their birthday parties. We are very lucky.' *Lucky, yep, but this is also the way it should be!*

 'My daughter's Year 7 classmate plays murderball (wheelchair bas-ketball). And so does their teacher's dad, coincidentally. The other day their teacher (and her dad) arranged for their whole class to play a game of murderball together at school – wheelchairs, equipment and all. It was a big hit, as you might imagine!' *This is a peacher in action, and one with lived experience who changes lives daily.*

 'To the wonderful woman I met getting some medical imaging with my pea shoot. She was on maternity leave too and had her baby with her. She told me she had a Masters in Special Education and I told her of our diagnosis which I was just coming to terms with. So I asked her what was her top tip and make it a goodie. Straight away she said, "He will surprise and amaze you, don't underesti-mate him." Such great advice. I think of that conversation often.

He does amaze us daily, and I hope we meet this peacher again someday.' *Peachers, we love you!*

'I'd had a complicated pregnancy and spent the last month of it in a city hours from home so my son could have surgery when he was born. When we thought the surgeons had finally cleared us to go home, a nurse said, "Oh no, they won't let you go until he's regained his birth weight. And you'll need to spend a few nights in the family room on your own when it's available." I burst into tears. My husband was already out of leave and this might take another week. She was immediately apologetic and kind and secretly swung into action. An hour later she informed us that we were allowed to take our son for a walk outside the hospital; our first time leaving that building together and showing him the sky. It was so special. She didn't stop there; she went on a one-woman mission to get us discharged ASAP. She worked out all the boxes we'd need to tick and made plans for ticking them all, from gaining weight and losing his NGT [nasogastric tube] to having his first bath. Suddenly we had permission to take our son back to Ronald McDonald House for two nights rather than waiting for the family room to be available. She even phoned us personally to check how the plan was going and that was when we worked out it was all her doing. We were home three days later and it meant the world.' *People who go above and beyond are the true heroes! Sorry, Iron Man!*

'My guy had an amazing Year 3–4 teacher at a mainstream public school. Back then he was obsessed with *Thomas the Tank Engine*. That year his class created an expo for parents and students to answer the question "How can we design and curate our own museum?" Most of the kids created science experiments or other things like that BUT his wonderful teacher allowed him to bring in and exhibit his collection of Thomas trains and write (to the best of his ability at the time) everything he knew about the Isle of Sodor and Thomas trains. It was a really beautiful, completely "reformed rectum" way of using his interests to learn! He even had his exhibit featured in the school newsletter AND the parents who attended were also really kind and patient, asking him questions all about his exhibit. He was beaming! I wish he could have stayed in that class forever!' *We all get attached to peachers – they make our children and our whole families' lives brighter and can mean the difference between a family having a great or a horrible year.*

'I was feeling utterly helpless with absolutely no way to help my 23-year-old son who was in ICU on life support after multiple brain surgeries and months in hospital. A beautiful nurse who had pre-viously worked in paediatric ICU said, "I know he's a 23-year-old man but I also know he'll always be your boy and you've always done everything for him." She then asked me if I'd like to help her wash him. Terrified I'd knock his tubing out, with great tender-ness she gently guided me through giving him a shave, washing the yellow antiseptic funk off his body and finally giving him 'the *Romper Stomper*' head shave after repeated surgery had left him with big bald patches. After we finished, I just cried and hugged her. I'll NEVER EVER forget it.' *The profoundness of a nurse walking side by side.*

Kate says

There are three times in my life when people have said things that are seared into my memory (in a good way, not in an ankle-tattoo-of-an-ex-boyfriend's-name sort of way).

The first was right after Number One Daughter was born. I was lying there in my own blood and who knows what else; the umbilical cord had been wrapped around her little neck and her eyes were bloodshot. It had been fast and furious and we both were probably a little shocked. The nurse who helped me to the shower said to me, 'I have a surprise for you!' and when I got out, somewhat freshened up, I realised she had made me a pot of tea in a little teapot with a lovely teacup. She said, 'You birthed beautifully today, and deserve a beautiful cup of tea!' I don't even know if I had the words to thank her at the time but I will never forget it.

The next time someone rained sunshine down on me with their words was when I was walking down the driveway of my OB/GYN's office while pregnant with Buzz and Woody. His wife saw me and called me over to her car. Then she said, while patting my hand, 'You are never far from our thoughts; we know what you are going through.' It made me cry and feel seen. It was the perfect thing to say in a very not-perfect time!

Lastly, beautiful pea-diatrician Dr Shane, after one of our many consults, came out to the reception area where I was paying and said, 'Kate, I probably don't tell you this enough, but you are doing an amazing job. Your boys would not be who they are today without you. I just wanted to let you know.' I am crying writing this.

I think back on these seemingly insignificant times and comments often, because they were not insignificant at all. The power of kindness! It undoes me and does me right back up!

Mandy says

I have lost count of all the times that people have been kind to me, my daughters and my family. If there was a total amount of encouragement allowed in the universe, then I have probably been gifted a large proportion of it. How can one woman be so fortunate to have family, friends and professionals so fiercely on her side?

Let's start with the meal trains after having premature twins. This mostly consisted of people dropping off food at my house but they also mowed the lawn, sent me songs and sat by my side in the nursery. It was as if my friends and family had read a manual on how to support a family with twins in NICU. There was kindness in every single lasagne, lovingly placed in a sturdy sensible dish, to nourish us when we could not nourish ourselves.

I remember the nurse at the local centre when I went to her with my concerns about Molly at eight months. I was in shock and crying, demanding people to see what I could see. She grabbed me by the shoulders, looked me in the eye and said, 'Yes, I see what you are saying. We are going to need to investigate, and you will be okay, she is a loved baby, you are doing a wonderful job and let's get you help.' I knew my world was about to change forever, but she knew that what I needed in that moment was kindness, respect and a firm reassurance that I was being listened to.

When Milly and Molly had botox injections at Monash Hospital, there was a generous nurse, Fiona, who was always welcoming, despite being presented with two very tired and hungry toddlers who were not looking forward to general anaesthetic and injections. She greeted us kindly and we always had a laugh, usually at something the girls said. At one stage, when they were around three or four, they arrived for each appointment in princess costumes and hats (whatever it took to help them feel happy on those hard days!). She always saw in my heart how tired I was.

Another bright spot was our early intervention physio, Helen. She was an experienced physio who saw us multiple times a week and put up with a *lot*. Twins in physio together is really a sight to behold. She laughed, she was firm and I will never forget the day when she said to me about Molly, 'She has the best early intervention 24/7 with her twin sister Milly. She is a lucky little girl to have a twin to teach her, to talk to her, to sing, to push, to sit on her face in the sandpit, to pull her hair.' (I always put Molly in the pram on her left side so that she could use her right hand to reach out for leaves.) I think I cried that day, as I could see what she was saying, and I was so thankful to have both my girls and so grateful to Milly for being so ferocious and incredible in her twin sistering.

Our Year 4 teacher, Shai, who was very new to her career, was young and kind and loved Molly and was sitting in our student support group meeting as I was discussing moving her from mainstream school to a specialist school. She said, 'Well, the good news is, if it doesn't work out, then she can come back.' I just cried and cried, realising that indeed, she was right, and it was what I needed to hear.

Finally, when I accidentally stabbed my hand with a knife while getting the stone out of an avocado, Molly showed me so much kindness.

A kind word is never a wasted one. Turning back and giving someone a little hug or word of encouragement could change their life. Right now, we want to tell you – and you know we would be friends if we could hang out and we would *never* lie to our friends – well, we want to tell you that you are doing an awesome job, be it as a parent, friend, or just navigating today. We hope someone says something kind to you today, or that you can think back to those words that we never forget and draw on them when you need them. Or just reread this chapter!

20

Thanks, asshole!

We don't recommend looking up 'outer rectum' in the dictionary – or googling it, for that matter! You certainly won't find the *Too Peas* definition as the top search result. For sure it will make it in there soon, but how it started was not something the peas did. It came about after reformed rectum, now pea friend Kylie posed a question in the *Too Peas* Facebook group.

> What are those of us who are not #peas called? I remember outer sanctum was mentioned. Maybe it should be rectum instead of sanctum because we are the arseholes that say lots of stupid shit to #peas without thinking because of our ignorance?

Little did she (or we, for that matter) know what this comment would generate. We laughed at it, but man, did momentum grow – and quickly. People started to walk up to us and say, 'Hi, I'm Sue and I am a rectum!' We are not joking! We receive so many emails and messages that start with 'I am a rectum'. Needless to say, it has provided much laughter.

Here is the thing, though. There is a difference between our pea rectums who are part of our pea community – they are actually pea friends and we love them. A true rectum is ignorant – and has no desire to be less ignorant. Rectums, the lot of them!

We often say, 'We are all someone's rectum' meaning that we have all made hurtful comments (we hope unintentionally) to someone who is living with or experiencing something we don't understand. It happens! No one is perfect. But we here in the pea community try to counter that by living by the wise words of Oprah: 'Know better, do better'.

Maybe when you read this, if you are a rectum, you too can 'know better and do better'.

Here's the thing: of course it hurts when people say these things. It tears at the very soul of our motherhood, but we are here to tell you this: these people are ASSHOLES! The pain of what they said takes your breath away and it's almost impossible in that moment to think of something to say in return.

The following comments were made to peas and pea shoots. We've included them here, plus some helpful, pea-endorsed retorts to help you or your friend or family member next time they are confronted with an unpleasant rectum comment. Strap in, friends . . . we are going deep into the rectum!

 'Maybe if your child ate a more balanced diet he wouldn't be so autistic.' *Maybe if you were a little kinder you wouldn't say things without doing any research?*

 'If you remove preservatives from your boys' diets they won't have ADHD. Here is a book on it.' *Yeah, well, maybe if you removed ignorance from your brain you wouldn't hand me the book!*

 'She'll eat when she's hungry. She won't starve.' *Okay, as parents we know this is not true, but some of you rectums may need proof. So here you go: Someone with more time and way more qualifications has researched this and they say, 'Children will not eat, even if they are hungry, if eating is a negative experience (e.g. due to pain) or if*

they do not have the skills to successfully manage the food.[13] She may actually starve!

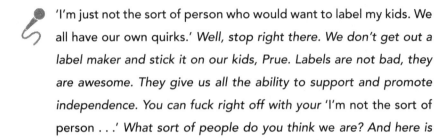

'I'm just not the sort of person who would want to label my kids. We all have our own quirks.' Well, stop right there. We don't get out a label maker and stick it on our kids, Prue. Labels are not bad, they are awesome. They give us all the ability to support and promote independence. You can fuck right off with your 'I'm not the sort of person . . .' What sort of people do you think we are? And here is the thing, whether you get the diagnosis or not, you still have the diagnosis!

'We're all a little bit on the autism spectrum, aren't we?' Um, no, or we would all understand it and never make a comment like that. And why do you want to minimise our experience by saying things like that?

'Oh, but you look so normal, do you really need that?' (Referring to various anxiety aids, cards and fidget toys.) Here is the thing: what the hell does 'normal' look like? Why do you think that the way people look makes them behave in a certain way? Once again, you don't have to comment if you don't understand it; why not google it later, and not make a dick of yourself and ruin someone's day?

'But that's not real autism though, is it? What now? What is 'fake autism'? And show me your medical degree again, or here's the door. Don't let it catch your heels on the way out!

'God, druggie alert.' (What someone said to a pea mum who has diabetes while she was giving herself an injection in a restaurant.) And also, 'Can't you do that in the toilets? I hate needles.' You're not the one getting the injection! Druggie alert? As if she was sitting *in a restaurant shooting up some heroin before the entrée? And as for 'Can't you do that in the toilet?' – why don't you go eat your lunch in the toilet? We hate eating near rude assholes!*

'What's wrong with that one's head?' *This was actually said to a mother of twins, while pointing at one of her precious babies! Um, we want to know what in the name of all things holy is wrong with your head? Why did those words come out of it?*

'I don't know why you bother with paying school fees; it's not as if he's going to get a job.' *Why not just spit on us and be done with it? These words are never leaving our hearts, you know, as much as we try. Where our children are happy and learning is none of anyone's business, and sorry we missed the memo where the only goal of school is getting the sort of work you consider a job!*

'What did you do wrong when you were pregnant?' *This needs to be never said again!*

'Well, you know vaccines caused that autism; I would never vacci-nate my child.' *Actually, Prue, no one can prove that vaccines cause autism. That was made up and there is no peer-reviewed research to prove that, but as you take YouTube as gospel truth it's probably not worth getting into it with you. You're welcome to apologise for saying to us that you think my child and his/her life is so terrible that you would rather your child caught polio than live like we do . . . who the hell do you think you are? We love our life, and we are so glad that you are no longer a part of it!*

'I think they're putting a lot of this on.' *They sure are! We haven't told anyone but they have won several Academy Awards. They are magnificent actors!*

'All kids do that.' *Really, all kids do that? Wow, could you come to the paediatrician with me and explain it to them?*

 'That's normal. My son did that and he's fine.' *Once again with the normal, Prue . . . what is your obsession with that word? Could you tell us once and for all what normal is? Also, this is an incredibly hurtful comment. We have just told you something that is going on in our life and you completely shut us down. We didn't say our child wasn't 'fine', we just said what is going on, and your son and his experience is not our experience!*

 'She's so pretty, it's just such a shame.' *Oh, a shame my child is attractive? Please explain?*

 'She just needs to try harder.' *No, actually you need to try harder: try to not be such a rectum, and try for one minute to appreciate how hard she tries!*

 'What's wrong with her?' *I beg your pardon? Once again, what is wrong with you?!*

 'It's better to have a screaming baby than one that dies from SIDS.' (Comment made by a postnatal nurse.) *What in the actual hell? My baby screaming is still upsetting to me. Please don't compare it to a parent who has gone through the hell of losing their baby, but don't diminish my feelings either!*

 'Kids on the spectrum don't mind if they have no friends.' *Okay, take that knife in your hand and plunge it into my heart. That is the most hurtful thing you can say to me as a parent, and guess what? My child does bloody care, but I don't need your address because you have enough friends and don't need a Christmas card from me!*

'I knew something was wrong, I just didn't want to tell you.' *You did, did you? Did you talk to other people about this too, or did you just 'know' and not tell me? Also it took a lot of medical peafessionals a lot of time to diagnose my child, so what did you actually know! Also, and here is the thing, maybe I knew too and trusted my gut not to talk to you!*

 'Can she do anything?' 'She can sit up.' 'Oh, there is something to her after all!' (Comment made by a doctor.) *Now this takes your breath away, and it may probably make you reach for tissues. What rectum doctor said that? No excuses! None!*

 'You'll want her to wear the sleep apnoea machine; it can help her development. She'll never be a rocket scientist but it helps!' (Comment made by doctor.) *How about this, lovely doctor: you are no rocket scientist yourself! And when exactly did we get so obsessed with high IQs and quality of life?*

 'I couldn't handle having a child with special needs.' *Well, we can't handle having people like you in our life, yet here we are!*

 'I know about a boy who had Down syndrome and he grew out of it, so your daughter might grow out of her [rare and undiagnosed] syndrome too.' *Did you? Because you can't grow out of a genetic chromosomal disorder, so either you are lying or you are really uneducated, which one is it? And why do you assume I want her to grow out of it?*

 'That is my worst nightmare.' (In response to an autism diagnosis.) *My worst nightmare is my child will have people like you with that mentality in his/her life, you massive rectum.*

'It's two years in a row now that your son has ruined the school Christmas play. What can we do about it?' *Well, for starters, you can leave the education system now, because it is the rectum teachers like you ruining it for everyone else. Also, my precious child has defied all the odds in just being here, he was born so early, and went through so much. He should be applauded for getting up on that stage! I am sorry – are we inclusive in words or actions at this school?*

 'You can always have another baby.' *I don't want another baby, I want this baby! And I want them to know they are loved and sup-ported, and that involves you supporting me, and not saying shitty things like that!*

 'There is nothing wrong with him; it's just the poor diet you feed him.' (Referring to a child with ADHD.) *So true, there is nothing wrong with him; he is perfect the way he is, but the only thing that helps him manage his executive function is therapy and medication. The chicken nuggets have nothing to do with it, but your comment – that hurt and it will hurt forever!*

 'He really is quite cute, he must only have it a little bit.' (Comment made by a doctor about a child with Down syndrome.) *Oh, for fuck's sake! Children with disabilities are cute! Why is everyone so bloody obsessed with appearance? And what you think is cute is not the same as what I think is cute. I mean, I gave birth to him, so I may have mum beer-goggles on but I know he is cute!*

 'Did you drink while you were pregnant? Or is it because you are so old?' (Following a rare chromosome diagnosis.) *Are you drunk now? Because surely a sober person would never, ever ask such a ridicu-lous question. Do you have any clue about how not to be offensive?*

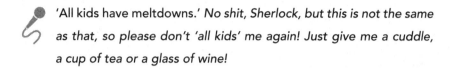 'All kids have meltdowns.' *No shit, Sherlock, but this is not the same as that, so please don't 'all kids' me again! Just give me a cuddle, a cup of tea or a glass of wine!*

'She'll catch up, she's just lazy.' (On delayed development.) *Lazy! Of course my child is lazy. I mean, aren't lots of toddlers so lazy? That's why there are so many books written on how to motivate them to get up and run around! GAH.*

'He doesn't look as bad as I expected.' (Comment made by psychologist.) *What the hell do you say to that? But you can bet that psychologist didn't get a repeat visit!*

'How old are you? You look too old to be behaving this way!' (To a six-year-old child.) *Listen, you can't tell me how to behave based on the year of my birth. It's about as accurate as those horoscopes you love, Prue, now please be quiet!*

'Why didn't you have the test done when you were pregnant so you could have terminated?' (Comment made by a medical professional.) *Perhaps the only response for this absolutely thoughtless rectum of a person is 'Fuck off! And don't come near my baby!' Remember what Dr Seuss said: 'A person's a person no matter how small!' This got Kate through her pregnancy.*

'Don't go looking for problems; you have enough to deal with.' (Comment made by paediatrician after being asked for support.) *Oh great, you think I'm making this stuff up? I know I have a lot to deal with, that's why I want support, and answers!*

'What a pity. Lucky you have two other children.' (Comment made by a random person pointing at a child in wheelchair.) *Um, what a pity you opened your mouth and said something so hurtful about my child, who, by the way, is an awesome human! I am lucky to have all three of them!*

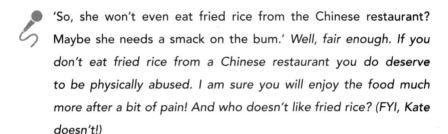

'So, she won't even eat fried rice from the Chinese restaurant? Maybe she needs a smack on the bum.' *Well, fair enough. If you don't eat fried rice from a Chinese restaurant you do deserve to be physically abused. I am sure you will enjoy the food much more after a bit of pain! And who doesn't like fried rice? (FYI, Kate doesn't!)*

'Is he dying?' *What on earth would you answer to that? NEVER, EVER ask a parent (or anyone, for that matter) that question!*

'You're not going to have any more children, are you?' (To someone who has three children, all with autism.) *I don't think when and if my partner and I have unprotected sex has anything to do with you!*

'Oh, so she's just a lazy little thing.' (Twin with cerebral palsy who wasn't walking at eighteen months.) *Okay, once again folks, babies and toddlers are not lazy. And don't minimise my concerns by spouting crap. She wants to move just like her twin. Part of me will never forgive you for saying that!*

'An ASD diagnosis will mean funding!' *Are you telling me to get the diagnosis to help my child or to get money for your program?!*

'Do you think it would have been better, you know, for her, if she hadn't survived?' *Do you think it would be better if you knew how to close your mouth? Because I do. This child is so precious to me; she nearly didn't make it and every day I look at her and am so glad she did make it!*

'He'll never love you, you'll just be his source of food.' (Comment made by paediatrician.) *Oh my gosh, what? Of course he will love me, and love me fiercely. The beautiful thing about love is, there is no right or wrong way to express it, so we will get to have something you may never experience!*

'I will tell you what is wrong with him – he's autistic, but that's okay because we will get funding.' (School principal.) *So lucky you are a doctor as well as a principal! And so lucky you know it's 'okay'!*

'I will need to warn my friends because they will be expecting a normal child.' (Comment made by mother.) *If your friends need warning that a child with additional needs is attending an event, you should maybe try and widen your friendship circle a little bit, pet!*

'I can understand that one child would have a disability, that's just bad luck. But two? What did you do for that to happen?' *Well, here is the thing, we don't actually have any control over lots of things in life: our children's gender, sexuality, disabilities, hair colour to name a few, but I can control who I chat to, and it won't be you after this!*

'Is there really any point in doing speech therapy if she can't hear properly?' (Comment made by medical professional.) *Every speech therapist reading this has just thrown the book across the room, and we with them will scream in unison, 'YES, THERE IS A POINT! A very pointy point!'*

'You don't need to visit your son every day; he doesn't even really know you're there or who you are. And the nurses take care of him.' (Referring to a baby in NICU.) *I do need to visit him every day, because it is like my heart is there with him, and as you know I can't survive without my heart. I want to watch his little chest rise and fall,*

I want to sing to him, and read to him; he should still be inside me. I miss him!

'You just love the drama and attention; you're wishing this to happen.' (When getting more assessments done.) *Ha, so true, would much rather be here getting assessments than having coffee with friends, going to work or having five minutes to myself! I love being in this office!*

'God only gives you what you can handle.' *Do you think God gave this epilepsy/cancer/learning disability to my child because He looked down from heaven and went, 'Well that's one tough mother, I'm going to give her family something unique!' I understand you think this is some sort of weird compliment, but actually it is hurtful and just stupid. No one copes better, or worse; you handle what you handle because you have to, and maybe because of comments like these, you learn to shower cry!*

'He has Down syndrome? At least he's a good-looking one. Don't worry; your next baby will be a beautiful normal one. Let's hope he doesn't have autism, as those children are horrid.' (Comment made by a GP.) *Yep, a doctor with an actual medical degree said that to a mother about her precious, beloved child, and what the fuck? Autistic children are horrid?! This doctor is more of a rectum than haemorrhoids are.*

'I knew you would have a miscarriage! You weren't sick enough.' *Why do people have to say things like this? The truth is that every pregnant woman is different; no one can predict miscarriage, but after a miscarriage we can predict that the person who had one needs a shit tonne of support, not platitudes like that!*

'But we have to give all the deserving children who don't have a disability a part in the school production before giving your child a part.' *All children are deserving, you rectum teacher! All children deserve a part in the play. Why don't you go look up the word, inclusive, for homework!*

 'I know he's sending you photos every week of the food he is cooking but I want you to know the aide is doing 90 per cent of the work. I am worried about the aide and how stressful it is for her to have to work with him. He's a danger to have in the Food Tech room with all the knives and stuff around because he is so wobbly on his feet. I have been a teacher for over twenty-five years so I know how difficult it is to teach students like him.' *Just so you have some background here, pea friend, this was a response to a mother who had been saying how much her son loved Food Tech and cooking. This cut won't heal! How have you been teaching for twenty-five years without learning any kindness at all?*

 'Are you going to keep her?' (After the birth of her child with a congenital disorder.) *Yes, please, I really want to, because you see, I love her. I mean who says that? It's a baby, a human being, a longed-for little girl! Bloody hell.*

 'Does she still have Down syndrome and cerebral palsy?' (Centrelink worker.) *We don't want to diss Centrelink workers – most of them are amazing – but we have heard a lot of stories like this. Maybe the powers that be at Centrelink need to do a little bit of educating if they don't want the peas to explode.*

 'Calm down. There's nothing wrong. You waited all your life for a sensitive man, here he is.' (Nurse.) *Pardon? This is my son, not a life partner; I already knew I would raise him to be sensitive!*

'You are lucky your twins are in NICU and you can go home and get a full night's sleep each night.' *No, I am not lucky. My babies are kilometres away from me, hooked up to machines. I can't sleep properly for lots of reasons, one being I am up expressing milk, another being that my heart is broken. I miss my babies; I am anxious; I am worried and grieving the pregnancy I didn't get to have.*

 'He's probably retarded, but he is a very good-looking boy.' (Department of Education psychologist.) *Again with the 'good-looking' comments! What is this about? And the R word, too! This person should not be in that job.*

 'See that's the difference between my daughter and your kids. She listens the first time.' *Wow, Prue, what a perfect little daughter you have. And yes, that is the difference, apart from the fact that my kids, whom I consider amazing, have some processing delays; they also have personalities, and sometimes they make their own choices. It's why parenting can be tricky. How boring your parenting must be!*

 'Your sister is such a good little mummy.' (About a sister who has neurotypical kids.) *Ouch. The truth is sometimes our family can inflict the worst emotional wounds; sometimes they are purposeful, sometimes said flippantly, but we are all 'good little mummies' and probably this mummy works twice as bloody hard!*

 'Autistic? But he can talk!' *Yes, he can. Sort of a shame that you can, though.*

 'Oh, but it's fine because she won't ever know what she's missing out on.' (Said during period of diagnosis.) *How do you know that? Also, I know! And I love her. Diagnosis time is a time for love and*

support – flowers, wine, food, coffee, a giant Dumbo-sized listening ear – not hurtful comments!

 Doctor: 'Is he intelligent?' Mother: 'Yes, he is physically impaired but he is intellectually on par with his peers.' Doctor: 'That's a shame. It would be better if he wasn't. Life is going to be very hard for him; it would be better if he didn't understand.' *Hard doesn't equal bad, Dr Rectum, but your words are cruel. My son has a magnificent mind, and so much to offer to our family, his friends and the world. Can you say that about yourself?*

We don't know if you need some time to pick your jaw back up off the floor, but we really hope no one will ever say anything that hurtful again. And hey, if you hear any of this crap, maybe you have a response now.

If that fails, maybe you can reply with the response that our lovely American pea Lana told us about when we interviewed her on the podcast. When someone said something rectum to her, she replied, '*Thanks, asshole!*' It feels quite good, to be honest!

21

The downside to resilience

When a child has characteristics that schools or childcare centres or sports teams or doctors find 'hard to manage' (even though there is research they could read to learn how to manage these awesome kids), caregivers are often told, 'Oh, they just need to build resilience.'

'Stop right there, asshole!' we want to scream as we try to remain outwardly calm, tilt our heads and nod along with this nonsense. Our children don't need to build resilience, *we* do for dealing with ignorant people like you all day. These kids have more resilience in their little toe than the debating captain or the head prefect will ever have! Walking into a classroom when you have dyslexia is a big deal and that kid is a hero. Everything that child does at school is harder than anything everyone else does!

Granted, there are some children who do need to work on building resilience (and there are amazing books and resources on it) but not our kids! And to be honest, rectum teachers use it as an excuse for getting away with all sorts of rectum behaviour. 'Well, not everyone gets to bat in cricket, it will build her resilience!' To which we say, 'Will it, though?' Because she already spent all morning building resilience during class time. And sitting on the bench sure as hell won't improve her batting skills.' Or this little gem: 'We choose the kids to be the school leaders based on many things, and characteristics the parents don't see. Anyway, missing out this one time will build resilience.' Um, no, we want to scream: all those kids for whom school comes easy don't need this; our kids need this. You are not building resilience . . . it sounds like bullying to us. It sounds a lot like resilience is just 'okaying' exclusion and pawning it off as a personal growth exercise.

Kate says

Let's think now about the children with ADHD and look at the survey the Parents for ADHD Advocacy Australia (PAAA) did. Ready?

- Parents perceived a lack of knowledge, skills and resources to support students with ADHD in schools. One in three (34 per cent) parents rated their school's strategies for supporting students with ADHD as poor/non-existent or inadequate.
- 30 per cent of parents had changed their child's school due to ADHD-related issues.
- Parents reported high rates of detentions, exclusions and suspensions among their children with ADHD resulting in reduced time in education and a negative impact on mental health.[14]

I won't mention again all the things that my children had to put up with at school because of their ADHD but, after all the shaming and exclusion, being told to build resilience is unhelpful, offensive and distressing. Imagine if your child was trying to gain control in this difficult situation, and then being punished for it. Can you imagine being punished and taken away from your friends when something upsets you so much you cry? And just being told to 'build resilience'?

What about the most resilient kids who come into school with AFOs on, who do more physio, OT, speech and hydrotherapy than most kids do after-school sport? Should they build resilience when they don't get chosen to be class captain? Explain again how that goes?

Don't all children deserve to be seen? When did school become a 'perfection' show? Or local footy? When did we miss that announcement that said the only thing that mattered was perfection? Winning at sports day? Having the best dance troupe in the suburb? Getting the best NAPLAN results? Getting the best HSC/VCE scores? When did all of this become more important than inclusion? When did this apparently build resilience? And for whom did it build resilience?

- Don't get picked for the cricket team = resilience
- Don't get invited to birthday parties = resilience
- Never get a speaking part in the play = resilience
- Name on the board = resilience
- Staying in at recess = resilience
- Lowest spelling group = resilience
- Teased for going to ed support = resilience
- Comes last in all the races = resilience
- Modified learning program with a big stamp on it that says modified = resilience
- Getting teased for taking medication at school = resilience
- Being 'skinny' at the swimming carnival = resilience
- Being 'overweight' at the swimming carnival = resilience
- Not going up reading levels on the big poster = resilience
- Being told to sit still when your disability requires you to move = resilience

- Taking longer to eat your lunch and missing play = resilience
- Missing out on eating certain foods due to allergy = resilience
- Missing out on chocolate frogs due to type 1 diabetes = resilience
- Spending school days at the hospital = resilience

No one recognises how hard these amazing kids train for life, but if they did, wow, imagine.

One of the reasons we started this podcast and wrote this book was so you, dear reader, could remember you are not alone. If you are reading this and feel triggered and sad as a parent or caregiver, we see you. Grab the tissues or have a shower cry, and remember we have your back. Next time someone says to you, 'Hey, Mrs Jones, it just builds resilience,' we give you permission to tell them that they are being ridiculous and to read them this chapter! You can even rip it out of the book! And you, super-human parent – we see your resilience, and your unique child is so lucky to have you!

Mandy says

Whenever I hear the word 'resilience' in relation to my twin daughters, this is what happens. My eyes wander, my heart starts thumping, I start to sweat, and the memories come seeping back of the time they were born at thirty-one weeks and they were in NICU fighting to live. That right there is resilience. Don't even get me started on the early interventions, the surgeries, the painful recoveries, the painful orthotics, the looking different, the people staring . . . I could go on and on.

How about other pea families whose children have spent weeks and months in hospital? These children have survived cancer and chemotherapy and epilepsy and seizures, diabetes and needles just to name a few. They are the poster children for resilience. They have been so incredibly frightened, been out of control, screamed 'nooooo' and been ignored. Never forget these children.

I know 'resilience' has significant meaning to many people; it's actually life-changing for them, and I applaud all the people doing work in this space. I truly mean this. But I am afraid it just doesn't sit with me. For me and my family, the word 'resilience' can be a big signal to shut up, to not ask, to not stand up for our children, to be silenced again, to put our children in situations every day that are simply not fair.

If you want to promote resilience, then look at our kids. Really take the time to look at them and where they have come in their little lives. You know the other people who don't need to build resilience? Parents, siblings, and other family members. Parents of premature babies, like Kate and me, very quickly had to build it. And as time went on and we received the diagnoses, our resilience grew. It grew again with every new therapist, specialist, doctor, nurse, surgeon, orthotist, wheelchair provider, adaptive bike mechanic, teacher, teacher's aide, principal, support worker, NDIS support coordinator, LAC and planner. We are for the most part polite, supportive and thankful, and when we are not that's not because we need to build our resilience, it's because we are exhausted.

Find a mum or dad with a child with a profound disability and see the resilience in their eyes. They love their children with a fierceness most of us will never know. When I am around my friends who fit this group of peas, I am in awe: I am listening, I am proud, I am humbled, I am grateful that they are my friends. I am ready to fight the resilience fight with them and stand right beside them and say, 'Don't you mess with my friend, she is resilient in her love for her child; her protection and her desire for them to be treated with respect and love and tenderness are second to none.'

Some peas are worn down by fighting for the recognition for their child. They tried, they did their best and eventually changed tack, sometimes to save their lives, save them from anxiety and stress and demand and to concentrate on the most important thing: loving their child. They, too, are resilient.

22

Laugh!

What does the dictionary say laughter is?

Laugh: To make the spontaneous sounds and movements of the face and body that are the instinctive expressions of lively amusement and sometimes also of derision.

Is there any better sound in the whole wide world than a baby or child's laugh? There really isn't and that's why there are about one trillion YouTube videos of them: because they make us so happy. I know there are many peas who have never heard their child laugh and I can imagine that must be a longing like no other, perhaps up there with hearing 'Mum' or 'Dad'.

We knew when we started the podcast that it needed light to go with the shade. Our favourite podcasts were the ones that made us laugh so hard we spat out food or cried. We introduced the 'Laugh, Cry, Make a Difference' section of the podcast pretty early on. We wanted people to have something to look forward to at the end of each episode, and something that we hoped would keep them listening.

Laugh, Cry, Make a Difference is also a form of self-care, but we wanted it to be a truthful account of what a day or a week might look like for us. Crying and laughing, yes, but also what had actually made a difference to our lives that week that got us to move on from the crying or the despair. Even in the hardest moments there is always something to laugh at.

When we saw the Cry, Laugh, Make a Difference hoodie, designed by Merch Pea Luke, it felt like we had really made it. We couldn't believe that our segment had made such an impact.

Mandy says

Laughing has always been my thing. I am quick to laugh and always have been. When I met Kate and she loved to laugh too, I knew I was onto a winner. Kate can tell a great story and often had our group of friends laughing at the ridiculousness of situations she was finding herself in with her five kids.

My grandma Mary loved to laugh as well. She loved to see the cheeky and the fun side of life and anyone who has listened to the podcast episode of my dad and his twin will hear it in them as well.

I spent a fair amount of time in the 1990s getting kicked out of the classroom – and church, for that matter – for laughing. At my friends, at myself, at nothing. You know the feeling; when you are not allowed to laugh everything is so much funnier. At school, if there was any subject I couldn't get the hang of right away, I just gave up and started to distract others. I was thrown out of the classroom, and then stood in the doorway making faces through the window. It's terrible to remember, but I loved being the class clown. I am obsessed with personality types; my Myers-Briggs personality is The Entertainer, and that is no surprise to me.

I love nothing more than running my sleep workshops and having the room laughing. I love to tell funny stories at every chance I can get and boy, have I had them since I became a mummy. I have a book that I have written all my daughters' funny sayings in and they love to read back over them. My girls are also funny and witty and I absolutely love that about their personalities.

Being light-hearted has helped me immensely. And having worked with children since I was sixteen makes for a workplace and career that is sprinkled with joy. Children are the ultimate stand-up comedians and if we allow ourselves to engage with that, the joy is right there, each and every day. This is one of the parts of having a daughter with an intellectual disability that I absolutely adore and gives us all life. Her ability to say funny things that make our whole family laugh is just incredible. As long as we aren't laughing at her – and she knows the difference and will tell us – she loves making us laugh. She has a great ability to read a room and knows when to throw the joke in, or repeat it. Laughter has helped my marriage, too. When it all felt too hard, a great joke or a funny one-liner has helped ease tension so many times.

The ability to laugh with the professionals and teachers in our lives has also been amazing. Man, do I love a teacher with a sense of humour. It can make all the difference in your year together. I imagine it can be a fine line as a teacher to know which days you can joke with a parent and which days you can't. I always appreciated the teachers who knew the difference.

I also got a good glimpse of that when I spent time with our pea-diatrician, Dr Shane. He first showed me his sense of humour in the special care nursery when the girls were eight days old. Darren and I always appreciated having a laugh with Shane when at that time nothing really felt that funny. He is a man who appreciates children and their humour and I have spent many a time in his office watching him work his magic. Molly's and my favourite Dr Shane joke was when he asked her what she wanted in her

NDIS plan. Molly said, 'I want a pool,' and Shane's response was, 'Well, if we buy a truck and put a pool on the back of the truck, then you can swim to appointments.' She has never forgotten that joke and when we drive past his rooms nearly every day on the way home from school she will say, 'Shane, he said a pool on a truck.'

Shane and the rest of the staff at the Royal Children's Hospital are used to children being awesome, they appreciate child development and some take the time to really listen to what the children are saying. There have been light moments when Dr Shane has taken the time to ask the girls how they are and has laughed at their funny responses to his questions. Being able to visit the meerkats or the fish tank on clinic days also helps lighten the mood at our beautiful hospital.

The team from the Starlight Foundation has also made the utmost difference to our time after surgeries. I will do anything to get them in our room or on the phone, or get the girls to visit the Starlight Room. These staff members are built for laughter, and they can improvise like I have never seen, which is both ridiculous and helpful. One memory I have is trying to get Molly to sit in the wheelchair for the first time after surgery and she was refusing. The Starlight person came into the room and then she crawled into the wheelchair for what seemed like about ten minutes in so many different ways that eventually Molly was brave enough to do so too. You don't need to go to drama school, people – get a job at the Starlight Foundation and you will have done enough improvisation to win you all an Oscar.

My favourite story that made us all laugh is when we were discussing a new medication for Molly with our orthopaedic surgeon. I was feeling nervous about side effects and he said to her, 'This medication might make you sleep at school and we are deciding if it's worth it.' Molly said, 'I want to sleep at school,' and we all roared with laughter. It was the most exquisite moment.

If all else fails, bloody laugh, please; it's the best way to live.

Kate says

When I think of laughter this quote always comes to mind: 'At the height of laughter, the universe is flung into a kaleidoscope of new possibilities.' (Jean Houston) Is there a better way to describe laughter? For me it's like watching a waterfall; you get mesmerised for a moment and everything else fades away. The true magic of laughter is that it is universal. We all speak different languages and dialects. Sometimes we speak the same language but our accents make communication hard. But you can be with someone who does not speak your language and still find the same thing outrageously funny.

Babies laugh before they speak. It is such a huge part of being human, and connecting with humans. Have you ever been on a train or in a cafe and heard people really laugh and been drawn to the conversation? Nothing can stop me quite like hearing laughter, and seeing people with tears streaming down their cheeks and trying not to wee their pants. Is that not the best feeling ever? Better than sex times a million, if you ask me.

Each April, Melbourne hosts one of the biggest comedy festivals in the world. We flock to big crowded theatres and small hidey-hole venues; we see famous comedians and people trying out the stage for the first time. No matter the venue or the show, laughter unites us. It's the closest thing to a miracle I have ever experienced. And the feeling, the physical response to being with a group of people and all laughing – wow. It's a natural high. Laughing and humour compel me like a magnet. My friends are so funny; it is the balm to my sometimes-weary soul. I don't know who said 'laughter is the best medicine' (I mean, if you have ever had thrush I think you will say Canesten is the best medicine, but they were pretty close).

If you listen to our podcast, you will know that laughter is a very big part of *Too Peas*. We are the first to admit we are not seasoned comedians, but we certainly make each other laugh. Mandy introduced me to the funniest podcasts and after we saw *The Book of Mormon* my stomach hurt for three or four days – and you better believe it wasn't because I was doing ab crunches at intermission. We have laughed (and cried) through our entire friendship. We see humour and we gravitate towards it.

And apart from Mandy, my other main source of comedy is my kids. If anyone ever asks me, 'What is the best part about having kids?' my answer will always be, 'For the laughs.' True, there's also unconditional love and all that, but the laughter is magic. Each day, it is unexpected like a jack-in-the-box. It changes your mood and just makes everything worthwhile: you get that happy high.

One time, Buzz said to me, 'Mum, do you know why you don't look like Jabba the Hutt?'

I mean, to me it is pretty obvious, but I played along and said, 'No, why don't I look like Jabba the Hutt?'

The answer makes me laugh to this day: 'Because you have elbows and a neck!'

I mean, come on. That's comedy gold, right there in my kitchen!

Newbies to *Too Peas* are often puzzled that the podcast contains so much laughter. I suppose they assume that parenting kids with additional needs and disabilities is an always-serious topic. But I have never laughed so much since having my boys, and Mandy's stories ... oh my word! Laughter constantly rings out in our home; it is the thing I am most proud of. But once again there is someone who can articulate this much better than me so I will leave you with this quote from John Cleese, who said, 'Laughter connects you with people. It is almost impossible to maintain any kind of distance or any sense of social hierarchy when you're just howling with laughter. Laughter is a force for democracy.'

In conclusion

Kate says

My very favourite part about writing an essay at school was when I could say 'in conclusion' and just recap the topics or arguments, but it's harder to do that in a book. Also, if you have listened to the podcast you will know Mandy and I struggle to stop talking, so stopping writing is no different! The starting was easy; it was coming out of me, like, well, gastro. But ending? Not so easy. And what am I concluding? *The Invisible Life of Us*, sure, but as for everything I have talked about in the book – my parenting journey, my friendship with Mandy, the podcast? Absolutely not.

So, dear reader, in conclusion I want to say thank you for making the time to read all of this, for buying or borrowing this book and making space in your life for it! *The Invisible Life of Us* has been such a joy to write – sure, it made me cry sometimes, but life is boring without tears. Mostly it made me grateful for the chance to tell the story of neurodiverse families, the opportunity to unload all my frustrations and joys and get paid to do it! The chance to do a group assignment in my forties with an ace friend, and the chance to tell all of you – rectums, peas, chickpeas, therapeas, the lot of you – how much you have brought to my life. How your listening to the podcast has changed my life and given me courage and hope. I love you all! Peas are the best bloody vegetable there is!

Mandy says

Writing this book is the biggest thing I have achieved – apart from keeping three daughters alive. I am a simple woman. I have a diploma that I got in 1996. I have never written anything like this. I knew that I had stories to tell, but had zero confidence in writing. That's why I started the podcast, because I knew I could talk.

We wrote this book in the midst of the second lockdown in Melbourne in 2020. I had children sitting next to me, the dog at my feet, and wrote in between cooking, hiding in my bedroom, and sending filtered Snapchat messages to Kate. This was not conducive to concentration, but, looking back, it was exactly the chaos I live and breathe and I hope the authenticity of this time shows through in my writing. Diverse mothering in a pandemic is not for the faint-hearted.

I am so grateful for the opportunity and for our community who will read it. I hope that the honesty we have both shared further enhances the feelings of women around the world that they are not alone. My story is my story and yours is different, but if anything I have written resonates with you and you feel seen, I will be so proud.

The time's up, world; this book is a part of the ongoing work in the disability community, one which we know we sit to the side of, to bring about change and respect, and show the power of two mothers' love for their children.

Never in our wildest dreams did we believe we would be writing this book. When we sat in the driveway in our cars, so many years ago, telling each other our truths, we could never have envisioned this moment.

We hope that you have laughed, and felt challenged and moved to think about how this world treats our disabled children and those also with additional needs, and their families.

You won't see greater love for children anywhere else. The pea tribe is extraordinary and we are so proud to be a part of it. We know that some readers might disagree with some of this book. This is the risk we take and we believe it's worth it because, if the podcast listeners have taught us anything, it's that our and their stories matter.

We were middle-aged, mediocre women, who fiercely loved their families and wanted to start a revolution of inclusion for parents and particularly mothers on the road less travelled. We see you, we *are* you, and for some of you we have walked ahead of you and paved a tiny path forwards for you. Keep going, peas. I am proud to know you.

Notes

1   Cherry, K., 'The Health Consequences of Loneliness: Causes and Health Consequences of Feeling Lonely', Very Well Mind, 23 March 2020, verywellmind.com/loneliness-causes-effects-and-treatments-2795749, accessed 15 April 2021.
2   'Women', BeyondBlue, n.d., beyondblue.org.au/who-does-it-affect/women, accessed 15 April 2021.
3   Australian Bureau of Statistics, 'Religion in Australia', *Census of Population and Housing: Reflecting Australia – Stories from the Census, 2016*, cat. no. 2071.0, 28 June 2017, abs.gov.au/ausstats/abs@.nsf/Lookup/by%20Subject/2071.0~2016~Main%20Features~Religion%20Data%20Summary~70, accessed 15 April 2021.
4   'Disability Statistics', Australian Network on Disability, n.d., and.org.au/pages/disability-statistics.html, accessed 15 April 2021.
5   Taken from: 'Your Child's Health and Development, Birth to 6 years', Victorian Department of Education, education.vic.gov.au/Documents/childhood/parents/health/chlchart6years.pdf, accessed 15 April 2021.
6   'Food allergy', Australasian Society of Clinical Immunology and Allergy, allergy.org.au/patients/food-allergy/food-allergy, accessed 15 April 2021.
7   'Being the parent of a NICU/special care baby', Life's Little Treasures Foundation, lifeslittletreasures.org.au/information/information-for-families/survival-guide-to-nicu-and-special-care/being-the-parent-of-a-nicuspecial-care-baby, accessed 15 April 2021.
8   'About Every Australian Counts: The grassroots campaign for the National Disability Insurance Scheme', Every Australian Counts, everyaustraliancounts.com.au/about/, accessed 15 April 2021.

9   'What is ADHD?', ADHD Australia, Fact sheet version 1.4, ADHD
     Australia, Sydney, 2019, adhdaustralia.org.au/wp-content/uploads/
     2019/09/What-is-ADHD-201909-v1.4-web.pdf, accessed 15 April
     2021.

10 Ibid.

11 'The role of executive functions: what are they defined as and how do
     they help us in our everyday?', ADHD Australia, n.d., adhdaustralia.
     org.au/about-adhd/the-role-of-executive-functioning-in-adhd,
     adhdaustralia.org.au/about-adhd/the-role-of-executive-functioning-
     in-adhd, accessed 15 April 2021.

12 Ibid.

13 Mason, S. J., Harris, G., Blissett, J., 'Tube feeding in infancy: implications
     for the development of normal eating and drinking skills', *Dysphagia*,
     vol. 20, no. 1, 2005, pp. 46–61.

14 Parents for ADHD Advocacy Australia, *Parent and carer experiences
     of ADHD in Australian schools: Critical gaps*, PAAA, n.p., 2019,
     parentsforadhdadvocacy.com.au/wp-content/uploads/2019/06/
     UNBL15971M_ADHD_Report_A7_C2_FA3_Interactive.pdf,
     accessed 15 April 2021.

Bibliograpea

'About Every Australian Counts: the grassroots campaign for the National Disability Insurance Scheme', Every Australian Counts, n.d., https://everyaustraliancounts.com.au/about/

ADHD Australia, 'What is ADHD?', Fact sheet version 1.4, ADHD Australia, Sydney, 2019.

Australian Bureau of Statistics, 'Religion in Australia', *Census of Population and Housing: Reflecting Australia – Stories from the Census, 2016*, cat. no. 2071.0, 28 June 2017, abs.gov.au/ausstats/abs@.nsf/Lookup/by%20Subject/2071.0~2016~Main%20Features~Religion%20Data%20Summary~70

'Being the parent of a NICU/special care baby', Life's Little Treasures Foundation, n.d., https://lifeslittletreasures.org.au/information/information-for-families/survival-guide-to-nicu-and-special-care/being-the-parent-of-a-nicuspecial-care-baby/

Cherry, Kendra, 'The health consequences of loneliness: causes and health consequences of feeling lonely', verywellmind, 23 March 2020, verywellmind.com/loneliness-causes-effects-and-treatments-2795749

Dimmitt, Melanie, *Special: Antidotes to the obsessions that come with a child's disability*, Ventura Press, Sydney, 2019.

'Disability Statistics', Australian Network on Disability, n.d., and.org.au/pages/disability-statistics.html

Evans, Rachel Held, *Searching for Sunday: Loving, leaving, and finding the church*, Nelson Books, Nashville, TN, 2015.

'Food allergy', Australasian Society of Clinical Immunology and Allergy, May 2019, allergy.org.au/patients/food-allergy/food-allergy

Mason, S. J., Harris, G., Blissett, J., 'Tube feeding in infancy: implications for the development of normal eating and drinking skills', *Dysphagia*, vol. 20, no. 1, 2005, pp. 46–61.

Parents for ADHD Advocacy Australia, *Parent and carer experiences of ADHD in Australian schools: Critical gaps*, PAAA, n.p., 2019.

Sheridan, Mary D., *From Birth to Five Years: Children's developmental progress*, 3rd edn, ACER, Melbourne, 1988.

'The role of executive functions: what are they defined as and how do they help us in our everyday?', ADHD Australia, n.d., adhdaustralia. org.au/about-adhd/the-role-of-executive-functioning-in-adhd

'Therapy', Wikipedia, 16 March 2021.

'What is ADHD?' ADHD is attention deficit hyperactivity disorder', ADHD Australia, n.d., adhdaustralia.org.au/about-adhd/what-is-attention-deficit-hyperactivity-disorder-adhd

'Women', Beyond Blue, n.d., beyondblue.org.au/who-does-it-affect/women

Yancey, Philip, *What's So Amazing about Grace?* Zondervan, Grand Rapids, MI, 2003.

Acknowledgements

Where do we start? Well, with the pea tribe, of course. You believed in us, listened to us, and bought our book. You changed our lives and we love you all. We made this for you.

Sound Engineer – you started this journey with us and we are forever grateful for your time and skill in making us sound awesome. You have put up with a lot.

Adam, for writing and producing the best podcast music. We love our pea song.

Andy and Andrea, for building and maintaining our website. Thank you for being on our team.

Akke, for doing our show notes when we were floundering, and Annelise, for taking over so beautifully.

Pea friend Loraine, for being our roadie, our sales staff, our bookkeeper, our driver and listening to every podcast and telling us, 'That episode was great!'

Matthew Hardy – so glad we decided to have coffee with you. It turned out okay, didn't it? (Oh, and go Saints!)

Dr Shane – you named the podcast and have laughed and cried with us. Thank you!

Sophie, Genevieve and everyone at Penguin Random House – your patience is remarkable. Thanks for believing in two women whose previous writing ability was mostly writing lunch orders.

Annabel Crabb and Leigh Sales (and all the Chatter peas), thanks for casually mentioning us on *Chat 10 Looks 3*. You changed everything for us!

Mia Freedman, for your support and encouragement.

Jordan and the team at ACAST! Best podcast support team ever.

Luke and Carly, our merch peas. How glad we are to have you in our lives.

Kellie, our designer. Thank you for creating our logo; we loved it immediately. Thank you also for designing our booklet.

Finally, to the really special person that we have missed in these thank yous. You know who you are. We are mediocre authors, so we are sure we have missed someone.

Kate says

Thank you to Dr John Regan and Dr Andrew Edwards. Without you, Buzz and Woody would not be here. John, thanks for insisting on a second opinion, and Andrew, thank you for being that second opinion.

To the teachers who went the extra mile – you know who you are. You changed Buzz and Woody's lives!

To Rachael – you don't listen to the podcast, but you do love and support me. Being my friend for thirty-eight years probably hasn't been easy. I love you.

To Carly, Briohny and Christie – who knew, all those years ago on the AMBA forum, that life would be so much harder without each other?

To Kate, Katy, Clare, Marita, Melissa and Loraine – you know why!

Darren (boyfriend) and Melissa – you have always loved me, and it means more than you will know.

Tammy and Jenny, what a friendship we have. Did you ever scroll back to our first Messenger message, Jen?

To 'the work boys' – I love you all ... but yes, I have a favourite and it's Kieran.

To my father, Patrick Kenneth Mulholland. You inspired me. I will love you and miss you until I take my last breath. Thanks for showing me a love like that exists.

Mum, I love you. I hope you still love me after how honest this book was (but actually I know you will because you love your kids unconditionally). Thank you!

My family – what a great family we are. Mulhollands are such fun people! 'Teaghlach' is everything. Shannon, you are my favourite too.

Amy, my Snapchat cousin, I love you.

David – your support of the podcast and all the changes it has brought into our lives is unwavering, and I am forever grateful. Thanks for the love. (But, please, could you sneeze quieter?)

And, lastly, thank you to Mandy. I think I gave you several paragraphs in the book, so you know how I feel. I doubt anyone else has ever written a book via Snapchat! You are remarkable; there is no one like you. Thanks for being my friend. I love you!

Mandy says

To Mum and Dad (Margaret and Graham) for your unfailing love and support in so many ways – too many to name! The girls love Grandma and Grandpa, and know that you love them too. I am the woman I am today because of you both. I love you, and sorry for swearing, Mum.

To Annelise, for enduring life as my little sister, for loving my girls as your own, and for making me laugh. We are kindred spirits.

To Adam (and Lauren), for enduring life as my little brother. You are way better than a cat.

To Margaret and John and all the Hoses, for so many ways you have stepped in and loved our family. For every thoughtful gift, hospital visit and the love you have for the girls. They love you, Nana and Popa. Thank you.

To my book club friends – every single one of you, past and present. You have stood by me, listened to me, made food for me, laughed and cried and probably despaired at me. Let's hurry back to Mount Martha and rest. True friends are always together in spirit.

The gang – my oldest friends. Thank you for loving the old, the changing and the new Mandy.

My mother's group – we met in 2005 and you went through so much alongside me at that time. Thank you to all of you for those precious and challenging (for me) years.

My school friends, from all the schools – the women who have seen me running to school or to school bus stops with wet hair and PJs. Thank you for wiping away my tears of tiredness and laughter.

To my neighbour, Lindie, who moved into our street and changed our lives. Thank you for reading the book and taking the time to give me feedback. I am so grateful for you.

To all my friends at Vocal Vibes, for giving me back my harmony.

To all my friends who are peas. I have gathered you around me for soft places to fall. You held me up when I was too tired to stand, you listened, and you sent lasagnes and doughnuts. The best part about this life is meeting you all.

To all the therapeas who have ever worked with my family. There are a lot of you. Thank you for putting all your effort into my daughters. You have been patient, kind and helpful, and the fruit of your work shines out through my daughters today.

To all the teachers, aides and education support workers (Flossy, our favourite!) – thank you for being peachers, for trying your best and showing us all kindness. I know it can't be an easy job and I thank you for all the ways you have supported my family.

To Professor Kerr Graham, Mela and all the team at the Gait Laboratory at the Royal Children's Hospital in Melbourne – your skills have changed my daughters' lives. How can I ever thank you enough?

To Felicity and Ange, my support coordinators, for helping me make the most out of our NDIS. I need you!

To Darren, for loving our daughters as fiercely as you do, for giving them every opportunity to shine at sport, attending every appointment and surgery, juggling your career and study to provide for us all, and booking holidays when I don't. I love and thank you. The licorice bullets are on me.

To Kate – we did it; we finished the book. I am in awe of you for getting it started and having a vision when I didn't know where to begin. Thank you for being the best podcast co-host and book co-author I could ever dream of. We took our loneliness and made a change in the world. I am so proud of us. I love you too.